LET THE CHIPS FALL WHERE THEY MAY

The Story of Legendary Harlan Community Football Coach, Curt Bladt

Dr. Nate Booth

HARRISON ACORN PRESS, LLC
LAS VEGAS

Harrison Acorn Press
1930 Village Center Circle
#3-747
Las Vegas, NV 89134
800-917-0008
www.harrisonacornpress.com

ISBN 13: 978-0-9649500-4-7
ISBN 10: 0-9649500-4-9

LCCN 2006936804

Cover designed by Leah Speaker for Moxie Photo & Design—*www.moxiephotoanddesign.com*

Interior design and typeset by Renata Anderson for Typing Pro.

Edited by About Books, Inc.—*www.About-Books.com*

Newspaper articles and photos used with permission of the Harlan Newspapers and the *Omaha World-Herald*.

Excerpts from the book, *Bernie Saggau & the Iowa Boys,* reprinted with permission from the Iowa High School Athletic Association.

Photos used with permission of Noble Photography and Logeland Studios, Harlan, Iowa.

Dedication

This book, a story of high school football
in a small area of Iowa, focuses on one man,
Coach Curt Bladt. In reality, the story is repeated
thousands of times in varying forms in tiny towns and
large cities from California to Connecticut. This book is
dedicated to high school football, the kids who play it,
the parents and communities who support it,
and the people who coach it.

Acknowledgments

Thank you to Curt and Jill Bladt for sharing their lives with me so I can share their story with you.

I can see why my boyhood neighbor, Ruthanne Grimsley, was the 2004 Citizen of the Year for Shelby County. She has spent countless hours being my contact person in Harlan. Ruthanne knows everybody and knows how to do almost everything.

The ladies at the Harlan Library (Jill Pannkuk, Elaine Sprague, Jan Phifer, Linda Burger, Teresa Russman, and Pat Engemann) helped me do a week's worth of research rummaging through old newspapers. Sandy Bauer at the Exira public library helped me corral many of the old photos you'll see in the book.

Let the Chips Fall Where They May wouldn't have been possible if it weren't for vintage *Harlan Tribunes* and *News-Advertisers*. If you want to spend an interesting afternoon sometime, rummage through the old newspapers in the library. Steve Mores, Alan Mores, Bob Bjoin, Mike Oeffner, and Maggie Hatcher at the Harlan Newspapers graciously let me use all the articles and photos I requested.

Thanks also to Jim Noble and Mark Jacobs at Noble Photography/Jacobs Photographic and Laura Rose at Logeland Studio, who took the team photos you will find in Section Three.

Thank you to former Iowa High School Athletic Association (IHSAA) Executive Director, Bernie Saggau, for writing the foreword to the book. Thanks also to IHSAA executive director, Rick Wulkow, and Information Director, Bud Legg, for their assistance.

KNOD's Ron "TOUCHDOWN, HARLAN COMMUNITY CYCLONES!" Novotny, HMU's Doug Hammer, FMCTC's Tom Conry, and Krogman & Associates' Tom Krogman graciously provided audio and video for the DVD. Matt Schmitz did a wonderful job of editing the DVD. Thank you!

To the fifty people I interviewed for the book, thank you for your time. You will see their names throughout the book.

I think you'll agree that Leah Spieker of Moxie Photo & Design did a wonderful job designing the cover as did Renata Anderson of Typing Pro on the interior of the book.

Deb Ellis, Debi Flora, Allan Burns, and Kate Deubert at About Books, Inc., were a pleasure to work with on the book's editing and proofreading.

I'm sure the wonderful people at Concerned Inc. will do a fantastic job distributing the book.

I'd also like to thank the Harlan Community Athletic Booster Club for marketing the book and DVD. Pam and Brian Gubbels have been my contact couple from the beginning.

Finally, I'd like to thank you, the reader, for buying the book. In one way or another, I'm sure most of you have been supporters of the various activities at the Harlan Community Schools. You will be glad to know a healthy portion of the book profits go to the Booster Club. Thanks in advance for keeping the saga of Curt Bladt alive and well. We need more stories like his floating around.

Contents

Foreword

There is more to Curt Bladt than meets the eye. The story that Nate Booth tells on the following pages is one any sports fan will appreciate. It offers a glimpse of a gentle giant of a man who is so much more than a winning coach on Friday nights.

In my forty years with the Iowa High School Athletic Association, both as an assistant to the late Lyle T. Quinn and subsequently thirty-eight years as the Executive Director, it was my pleasure to work with and observe tens of thousands of coaches. Curt Bladt was one. He shatters the stereotype of the tough and mean football coach that Hollywood might portray. To the contrary, he possesses the qualities that make a difference in the lives of kids.

All coaches try to teach desire, determination, courage, and teamwork. But one quality that sometimes is missing is a deep caring for the important people in their lives—kids, family, and friends. As an example, a few years ago Curt and I spoke at a memorial service for former Harlan athletic director, Harold "Swede" Johnson. While speaking of Swede, Curt's voice and emotions were evident. The feelings of respect and admiration for his former mentor exemplified that deep caring quality that some coaches have a difficult time showing. The moment emphasized that Coach Bladt's body size is small compared to the size of his heart—and that he cares deeply for kids, friends, and family.

Curt waited patiently—ten years to be exact—to become the head football coach at Harlan Community High School, a group of western Iowa communities that could easily lay claim to being the football capital of Iowa. He was an assistant coach for those ten seasons before ascending to the position he has defined with excellence and character—two qualities his players must cherish.

Now a winner of the National High School Football Coach of the Year Award, Curt never misses the opportunity to praise the effort and dedication of his players and staff (many of whom have been with him for more than twenty-five years) and the support of the administration and community. As accomplished as Curt is, his unselfishness is pervasive. Fame has never turned his head or enlarged his cap size.

Curt learned some valuable lessons as an all-state football player at Exira for Iowa Hall of Fame coach Denny Frerichs. One was the commitment to excellence; another was the importance of solid line play. And yet another was that if you were going to play for Coach Frerichs, you needed to sing for the school's vocal music teacher, Mrs. Frerichs. It is a little-known fact about Curt that, if given the opportunity, he proudly recalls being a member of one of Exira's first vocal groups to earn an "I" rating at the state contest.

Guess which vocalist is Curt?

Curt shows remarkable balance in his life through his willingness to share players with the other highly successful sports and activities at Harlan Community High School and through his teaching as a popular health and science instructor.

With just twenty-eight years of head coaching experience, Curt reached the 301 win level faster than any coach in Iowa history. His teams have won ten state titles—the most by any Iowa coach. He has led twenty-five of his twenty-eight teams to the playoffs. His seventy-four playoff victories are the most in Iowa.

But as I have suggested above, and as the famous sportswriter, Grantland Rice, once wrote, "There are other things more important than winning championships." Curt's players emerge from Harlan's program with a unique sense of responsibility and a pride in community and self—in spite of the bizarre red- and gold-dyed hair they sport in games at the Dome during the playoffs.

They end each practice and break each huddle with a convincing chorus of "next play!" It is a philosophy they all can apply not just to football, but to life. It is a philosophy that says, "What you just did may have been good. It may have been not so good. But it is what you do next that is most important."

Curt had a chance to implement the "next play" philosophy in his own life when, after the Cyclone's state championship in 2004, he was diagnosed with Miller-Fisher Syndrome. In a moment of personal crisis, Curt proved to be every bit the competitor he expects his players to be. The people of Harlan Community rallied behind their coach. Just as he helped so many athletes and students improve, they helped him return to health.

Since returning from the hospital, Curt has gone on to win another state championship. As a grateful individual, he has networked and encouraged others who have conditions similar to the one he conquered. Curt Bladt has modeled the characteristics he expects from his students and players. It is an important life lesson he has learned and earned through a life well lived.

—Bernie Saggau
Boone, Iowa

Preface

Sometimes, life is like a roller coaster ride. In November 2004, Coach Curt Bladt, the invincible pillar of strength, was at the top of a hill as he won his ninth Iowa Class 3A football championship. Now, though, about one month after the victory, he was lying flat on his back in a bed at the University of Nebraska Medical Center. He couldn't open his eyelids; his face was sagging; he had difficulty breathing and severe headaches; and he couldn't walk. To make matters worse, the doctors didn't know what the problem was.

As he was lying there, Curt had a chance to examine his past—the 288 wins as the Harlan Community Cyclones' head coach, the nine state championships, the thousands of kids he positively influenced on the field and in the classroom as a biology teacher, the time he spent with his wife, Jill, three sons, and new grandbabies. He also had a chance to ponder his future. Would he be there to see his kids and grandkids grow up? Teach and coach again? Even walk again? Being the man he was, Curt decided that he had to follow the advice he'd given hundreds of boys before more than three hundred football games. He had to give it his best shot and *Let the Chips Fall Where They May.*

It's a well-known and true axiom that playing high school football teaches boys how to live their lives well. What isn't so widely realized is that, in return, life teaches people how to coach and play football well. As he lay in that bed, at a big dip in the roller coaster ride, life was teaching Curt yet another lesson—one that would mold the man to mentor boys even more magnificently.

Curt Bladt coaches football well. He lives life well. This is his story.

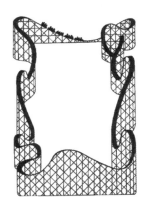

Introduction

Friday nights in the fall have always been special in Harlan, Iowa. I know they were for me. I grew up six blocks north of historic Merrill Field, the home of the beloved Harlan Community Cyclones football team. The Merrill Field lights that illuminated the sky at 6:30 p.m. drew me to them like a moth to a flame. Maybe it was in my blood. My grandfather, Nate, played for Harlan and coached their first undefeated team in 1906. My dad, Bob, played for the Cyclones in the early 1930s. Later in his life, he kept the records for all Harlan games played. I wore a Cyclone uniform in the early 1960s, as did my brother, Sandy, six years later. My son, Chris, played freshman football for the Cyclones in 1980.

At any rate, I had a burning desire to head south on Tenth Street to Merrill Field to watch and someday emulate my high school heroes—Harlan halfbacks Skip Louis, Gary Larsen, and Gary Jorgensen. I wore a football jersey with Skip's #27 on it to the first day of kindergarten at Laurel School. My favorite number is 27 to this day.

Like high school football in so many towns across America, Harlan Cyclone football is a chance for teenage boys to shine briefly under those lights. Even more importantly, it's a chance for them to learn the vital lessons they will need to shine in their future lives.

This book examines one football program's history and one coach's life. In order to understand Curt Bladt The Person, I believe it's important to understand The Preparation that molded his character. Section 1 examines Curt's boyhood, high school, and college years.

In addition to The Preparation, it's vital that you know The Place where The Person achieved success. Thus, in Section 2, you will have a brief history lesson on Shelby County, Harlan football, and Merrill Field. You will also learn how The Cyclone Way serves as the foundation for all of Harlan Community School District's activities. Finally, you will discover the Six Building Blocks of Cyclone Football Success.

After you understand The Preparation and The Place, in Section 3, you will meet The Players who made it happen. One year at a time, from Curt's first year as an assistant in 1968 through the state championship year of 2005, you will get to know the hundreds of players who proudly wore the Cyclone uniform.

In Section 4, after The Preparation, The Place, and The Players have been discussed, you will discover The Person Curt Bladt really is.

Throughout the book, I've sprinkled a few of Curt's favorite quotations and comments posted on the CoachBladt.com website created by Ruthanne Grimsley. To date, there have been 900,000 hits and 250,000 unique visitors!

Those website numbers generated by players, friends, community members, officials, opposing coaches, and complete strangers reveal the depth and breadth of people's admiration for Curt Bladt the man and the football coach. Great men and football coaches aren't born. They're made. There is always the story before the story—The Preparation.

Section: 1
The Preparation

Long-term success on the gridiron or in life is like a well-built house, and every sturdy house needs a solid foundation. In this section, you will hop in a time machine for a journey back to Curt's boyhood years, to visit the places and meet the people who helped lay the bricks and spread the mortar that created Curt's sturdy foundation.

In Chapter 1, you will take a voyage back in time to Exira, Iowa, and get a glimpse of Curt's boyhood memories. In Chapter 2, you travel from Exira to Sioux City, as Young Mr. Bladt goes to college at Morningside College, plays a higher level of football, and meets his future wife.

The time machine door is open, and the electromagnetronic transponder is fired up. It's time to step through the portal and be whisked off to Exira, Iowa, in 1944.

Chapter: 1
Exira Boyhood Memories

The town of Exira, Iowa, has been kind to the Harlan Community Cyclone football team. The two coaches with the highest winning percentages—Terry Eagan (1967–1973) and Curt Bladt—both hail from this small southwest Iowa burg.

Curtis Melvin Bladt popped into this world on October 14, 1944. Curt says that at birth his mom wanted to name him "Quits" because of the size of his head. Dr. Payne (aptly named) delivered Curt at the Exira Hospital, which also happened to be Dr. Payne's house.

Curt's parents' names were Ruby and Melvin. He grew up an only child on a farm located two miles north and two miles west of Exira. The house never had an indoor bathroom, so Curt learned the fancy footwork he would need for football as he scurried to and from the outhouse on cold winter days.

The farm's separate bathhouse was equally impressive. It had three areas: a storage area for the corncobs the family used to start the fire in the stove, which was used for cooking and heating; a laundry area, where Ruby washed the family's clothes; and a bathhouse complete with galvanized tub for bathing. Hot water for the tub was provided by a kerosene stove and a large copper pot.

Curt remembers, "The bathhouse and lack of indoor plumbing really impressed my future wife, Jill, when I brought her to the farm to meet the parents. When Jill used the outhouse at night, I had to stand guard by the door. The sounds the coyotes, owls, and other assorted critters made weren't exactly comforting to the big-city (Sioux City) girl."

Ruby had this to say about Jill's food consumption habits: "She eats like a bird."

When Jill saw a calf one day, she exclaimed, "Oh, look, a baby cow!"

Ruby smiled and responded, "Oh, my."

As strange as it seems to those who know him, many of Curt's earliest memories were about food. One of Ruby's chores was to make liver once a week. One of Mel's chores was to make Curt eat it. Curt now says, "This is how I learned to love ketchup and mustard."

As you can tell, Mel Bladt had the personality of legendary Green Bay Packer football coach Vince Lombardi. Curt learned quickly that it was mandatory to clean up his plate. Curt doesn't eat liver now, but he does frequently clean up his plate.

Mel worked the farm until Curt was in junior high. Then Mel started working for the Rock Is-

The Bladt family farmstead

land Railroad, but the family remained on the farm. Ruby was always a full-time liver-fixer and homemaker.

Young Curt and his dog

Off to Grade School

To Curt, it seemed like he was the only red-headed kid in school. Even though he was teased frequently and heard the Redheaded Milkman Story hundreds of times, it never got him down. It just toughened him up and prepared him for life. So did the farm chores. "I've cut enough weeds and chased enough cows, pigs, chicken, and guinea fowl to last a lifetime," Curt laments.

For grades one through five, Curt went to a country school—Hamlin #8. There were three rooms in the school—the classroom, the cloak room, and the cave, where the only teacher, Mrs. Hyke, would take the kids when storms were brewing outside.

Da Bears, Friday Night Fights, and Toy's Tavern

When Curt was in fifth grade, the Bladt family got their first TV—a fourteen-inch black-and-white Zenith. On Sunday afternoons, father and son watched Mel's beloved Chicago Bears. The duo could identify with the Bears' ultra-tough linemen: Bill George, Doug Atkin, George Connor, and Joe Fortunato. Little wonder the Bears were called The Monsters of the Midway.

They also watched the *Friday Night Fights* together. One Friday evening, when Curt was a sophomore, he defiantly announced to his dad, "We're not watching the fights. I'm turning the channel."

As Curt recalls, a scuffle ensued that only had two hits. "My dad hit me, and I hit the floor."

Mel preferred to view the incident as "a short instructional phase on how to defend oneself." After Curt scraped himself off the floor, Mel told him, "Son, keep your hands up." The pair proceeded to sit down and watch the rest of the fights. Lesson learned. Case closed.

Saturday evening was the highlight of the week. The whole family got dressed up and went into town. The main street in Exira was a beehive of activity in those days. Curt used his ten-cent allowance to buy a comic book and an ice cream cone at Killion's Drug Store. Mom did the shopping for the week while Dad played four point pitch with the guys at Toy's Tavern. As the evening wound down, Curt's mom would send him into the bar to tell Mel it was time to leave. After the customary, "Just one more hand," they all would pile into the car and head home.

High School Hero

After playing junior high football, Curt moved onto high school, where he was exposed to three influential coaches. The first was Curt's freshman coach, Howard Justice, who went on to lead the Atlantic Trojans. In addition to having one of the greatest coach's names ever, Howard was a total disciplinarian. Before the first game in early September, he would hold practice three times a day—in the morning, afternoon, and evening.

Coach Justice had a list of rules concerning smoking, drinking, and, of course, girls. At an early practice, he would read the list to the team and then look each player in the eye and ask if he could trust the boy to follow the rules. Each player was required to maintain eye contact and answer him out loud.

As a sophomore, Curt played defense on the varsity squad. The head coach, Don McCauley, was another tough guy. Are you noticing a tough guy trend in Curt's life so far? One day Curt was helping his coach line the 220-yard dirt running track at Legion Field. Curt was holding the string when the machine Don was using blew lime into the coach's face. Refusing to go to the hospital, Don had Curt drive him home, where he washed out his own eyes. Curt said, "Coach's eyes were beet red!"

When Curt was a senior, his coach was Dennis Frerichs, who went on to coach at Urbandale High School. By this time, Curt was playing on the offensive and defensive lines. Coach Frerichs also liked to mix it up with the boys. "He would don the pads, scrimmage with us, and end up seeing the chiropractor for a month." Sixteen years later, Coach Curt Bladt defeated his old coach 23 to 22 in a playoff game in Urbandale.

1962 Exira football team
Curt is in the third row, second from the left, standing next to Coach Frerichs

In his senior year, Curt was all-conference and honorable mention all-state. He also excelled in track—sometimes with only one good leg. The day of the district track meet in Villisca, Curt rolled his ankle sliding into home in a softball game. That night he qualified for the state meet by standing at the front of the shotput ring and just heaving the hunk of iron. He qualified for the state meet in the discus, too. He did this in spite of some fun-loving teammates hiding his discus under the wheel of a Volkswagen. Curt lifted up the Volkswagen by himself, retrieved the platter, and limped off to a third-place finish. Curt wasn't just about blocking and tackling in high school. He was also the senior class president.

President Bladt and his cabinet

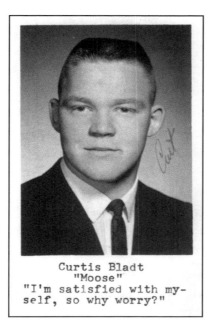

Curtis Bladt
"Moose"
"I'm satisfied with my-
self, so why worry?"

The last time Curt
wore a suit and tie

Despite all his experiences with liver and guinea fowl, his personal Friday Night Fight, and a dimpled discus, Curtis Melvin Bladt graduated from Exira High School in 1963 and moved on to the next stage of his life with not a worry in the world.

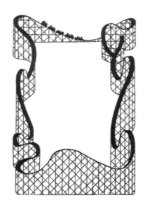

Chapter: 2
Morningside College Years

After making the decision to attend Morningside College on a football scholarship, Curt, along with his parents, toured the campus in the spring of 1963. Their guide was none other than former Harlan football player Lee Moran. Lee remembers, "Curt was a little rough around the edges. In addition to wearing a pair of farm-friendly, plier-pant jeans, Curt had a distinctive appearance with a super-sized head on his 190-pound body." This was an older version of the head that had caused Ruby some discomfort eighteen years earlier.

All the Food You Can Eat

A thief was once asked why he made the decision to rob only banks. He replied, "Because that's where the money is."

Using similar logic, Curt chose to join many of his football buddies who worked for their meals at Bishop's Cafeteria because "That's where the food is." As an added bonus, Bishop's never served liver.

By carrying trays every weekday noon for an hour, Curt earned his all-you-can-eat lunch and dinner for that day. By working three hours on Sunday, he earned his weekend meals. From this experience, Curt learned a valuable lesson: "There is no such thing as a free lunch at Bishop's—or in life."

A Morningside teammate and ex-Harlan player also worked at Bishop's—Max (Toad) Brodersen. Bishop's had a customer who came in every day and demanded that the line workers give him a fresh cup of coffee. This guy was such a pain that Curt, Max, and the other workers hurried him through the line. One day Max handed the man a cup of coffee as the guy asked his usual question, "Is that coffee hot?"

Feeling especially daring that day, Max stuck his finger in the coffee and proclaimed, "You bet your ass it's hot!"

Believe it or not, that didn't go over particularly well with Mrs. Creek, the Marine Drill Sergeant–like supervisor. She immediately doled out her usual punishment for screw-ups—banishment to the kitchen to wash dishes. At least back there, Max could help himself to unlimited shrimp and strawberries from the cooler.

An Intercepted Wink

In addition to serving (and consuming) a truckload of super-sweet Chocolate Ambrosia Pies, Curt met his sweetheart and future wife, Jill, at Bishop's during his sophomore year. "She was winking at another guy, and I thought it was me," Curt recalls. "Jill told her friends she would never go out with an ornery redhead because she had to put up with one in grade school. I guess my persistence overcame her common sense."

Jill remembers it this way. "Curt was friendly and funny. We worked together and had a good time together. Besides, he was just so cute!"

Curt's freshman year

Curt and His Harlan Buddies

His head coach at Morningside College was Dewey Halford. Dewey's favorite saying was, "It's not the size of the dog in the fight, but the size of the fight in the dog." The saying was particularly appropriate for Curt. At 198 pounds, Curt wasn't

Morningside College 1964 Football Squad
Curt is #70. Harlan players are Randy Conrad #37,
Ken Hoogensen #83, Lee Moran #81, and Max Brodersen #51

the biggest dog in the fight. He did, however, possess the fighting spirit necessary to be successful. As he did in high school, Curt played on the defensive line as a sophomore. As a junior and senior, he played both defense and offense.

In the early 1960s, Morningside was a magnet for football players from Harlan High School. Curt played with Graham Gould, Lee Moran, Max Brodersen, Chuck Stanley, Randy Conrad, and Kenny Hoogensen.

A Wedding, Arnolds Park, and Iowa Beef Processors

Curt and Jill tied the knot on May 27, 1967, in Sioux City, immediately after Curt's graduation from college. They spent their honeymoon at Lake Okoboji in a little cabin by Arnolds Park. Curt recalls, "Among other things, we rode the Wild Mouse and the old wooden roller coaster. We stayed Saturday and Sunday night and drove back to Sioux City on Monday—just in time for me to go work at Iowa Beef Processors in South Sioux City, Nebraska."

The honeymoon was definitely over.

Ruby, Jill, Curt, and Mel on the Big Day

With his tongue firmly planted in his cheek, Curt points out that, "We've been happily married for 29 years—and 29 years out of 39 years is a pretty good average. Jill is extremely tolerant. She has to be, living with me."

Their first summer together wasn't exactly a scene from the movie *Breakfast at Tiffany's*. At 6 a.m., Curt drove Jill to work. Then he took a short nap. From 8 a.m. to noon, he attended summer school classes. Then he took another nap. Curt picked up Jill from work at 3 p.m. and took a third nap. From 7 p.m. to 4 a.m., he worked at the packing plant. To end the day (or maybe it was to start the day), Curt took a final nap before taking Jill to work in the morning.

An Important Last-Minute Decision

In August, the couple traveled from Sioux City to St. Louis for a job interview at a high school. On the way, they saw an ad in the *Des Moines Register* for a science teacher opening at Harlan Community Schools. With school consolidation, the size of the high school had doubled overnight, and seventeen new teachers were desperately needed. On a Sunday, Curt and Jill stopped to talk with the high school principal, Merle Deskin. He offered Curt a contract that day for $5,000 a year. Curt and Jill thought about it for a few minutes and accepted.

They moved into the Hoyt-Tague apartments, which are still located just west of the old library building in Harlan, with a total of $20 between them. The $65-a-month rent check came out of Curt's $408-a-month paycheck.

Curt remembers getting his first check, putting it in the Harlan National Bank, and going to buy some food at the IGA grocery store that used to be next to Norgaard's Drug Store. He didn't have his personalized checks yet, so the clerk offered him a counter check—a pink one for Harlan National Bank or a white one for Shelby County State Bank.

Then she told him, "There's a new teacher in town who looks just like you." With the red hair and super-sized body frame, she thought he was former Cyclone player Al Burchett.

Curt courteously replied, "I *am* that new teacher."

Up the Down Staircase

It's ironic that the most successful high school football coach in Iowa history learned of the Harlan teaching position at the last minute and almost didn't coach football at all. The year was 1967. The Vietnam War was heating up, and Curt's primary goals were to "get a job and get a deferment."

Curt was actually drafted. He received a notice from a woman by the name of Verda Watts. (Funny, the names we remember, isn't it?) She told Curt to report to Camp Dodge in Des Moines immediately. Her last words were "Pack lightly."

At the physical, the doctor determined that Curt's knees were shot. He received a deferment.

During the 1967–1968 school year, Curt taught sophomore biology and assisted Dave Trotter with the Cyclone wrestling team, which had won the state title the season before. It was the first year of the school consolidation, so the high school building was bursting at the seams with kids. The decision was made to make one set of stairways the "up" stairway and the other set the "down" stairway. Curt was standing at the top of the "down" stairway one day. His bum knee locked up, and Curt fell head over heels down the steps. Surprisingly, nobody jumped in front of the runaway train to stop the descent. Curt reached the landing, got up, dusted himself off, acted like it didn't hurt, and proclaimed, "I meant to do that."

Another Important Decision

It wasn't until the following summer that Terry Eagen asked Curt to join his staff. In typical Bladtonian style, Curt answered, "Yeah, I guess so."

He guessed right.

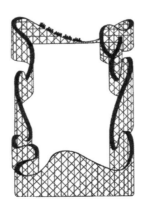

Do you think Curt Bladt would be as successful a coach as he is today if he had accepted a position in St. Louis, or stayed in Exira, or coached in Audubon or Atlantic? In other words, after The Preparation, does The Place where The Person ends up make a difference in his or her level of success?

Who knows for certain? But one thing is for sure. In 1967, the Harlan Community School District that Curt entered was in a state of flux and was a breeding ground for football excellence.

In this section, you will examine The Place. Chapter 3 is a very short course on Shelby County history. Chapter 4 retells the fascinating story of Harlan High School football. Chapter 5 traces the evolution of Merrill Field. Chapter 6 reveals The Cyclone Way, and Chapter 7 examines the Six Building Blocks of Cyclone Football Success.

Even if you didn't like your history class in high school, I know you will enjoy the five chapters in this section. Read on. The past welcomes you.

Chapter: 3
Shelby County History

Much of the information in this chapter was taken from the book, *Past and Present History of Shelby County Iowa* by Edward S. White, copyright 1915, published by B.F. Bowen & Company Inc., Indianapolis, Indiana. Special thanks to Opal Bertsch and John Kinkennon of the Shelby County Historical Society for providing additional information and photos.

Shelby County is comfortably situated in southwestern Iowa. The county was initially inhabited by the Pottawattamie and Omaha Indian tribes. The earliest European settlers were members of the Church of Jesus Christ of Latter Day Saints. In the late 1840s, they came from Navoo, Illinois, and settled in the groves of the county. Galland's Grove near Manteno Park in the northwest part of the county was the first.

In 1855, the Danish began settling in the eastern and southern parts of the county. In 1870, the Germans began to settle the western parts of the county and built the towns of Defiance, Westphalia, Earling, Panama, and Portsmouth. These towns were originally called The Colonies. In 1875, out of the 6,654 people living in Shelby County, 2,072 were born in Iowa, 2,737 were born elsewhere in the United States, and 855 were foreign-born.

Harlan History

The town of Harlan was settled in 1858 and incorporated in 1879. It was named after James Harlan, a U.S. Senator from eastern Iowa who was elected in 1855.

In 1859, the first term of school in Harlan was taught by L.W. Woodruff in a log house that stood on the northeast corner of 7th and Court. Another schoolhouse was erected in 1859 on the present site of the Methodist Church. The 20 x 24 foot structure served as a schoolhouse and a public hall for church and political gatherings and county fairs.

In 1871, as Harlan's population increased, a new two-story, wood-frame school building was constructed.

A new three-story brick school building was built in 1881 for a cost of $18,000. It stood on Baldwin Street between 7th Street and 8th Street.

In 1915, the Harlan Independent School District had thirteen teachers, 621 students, and an annual budget of $20,100. That same year a $90,000 bond issue was passed to build a new high school. Harlan High School opened its doors on September 25, 1916. The building welcomed its last high school students in the spring of

Central School—Constructed in 1881

1971 and its last middle school students in the spring of 1998, when the new middle school was constructed. The building stood in the same location as the school built in 1881. It was torn down in 2000 to make room for the new Therkildsen Activity Center.

Harlan High School: 1916–2000

The current Harlan Community High School was built for $2,250,000 and opened its doors on September 13, 1971.

Harlan High School: 1971–Present

School Consolidation

In Chapter 6, The Cyclone Way, you will revisit the school consolidation process, which occurred in 1967. The parochial high schools that served the towns of Earling, Defiance, Westphalia, Panama, and Portsmouth closed down, and their students came to Harlan as part of the newly formed Harlan Community School District.

The five parochial school buildings are shown below. Only the Earling, Panama, and Westphalia buildings are standing today.

Defiance   *Earling*

Panama   *Portsmouth*

Westphalia

Beautiful Rolling Hills and Tough Kids

So what does this brief Shelby County history have to do with Harlan Community football? In Chapter 7, you will discover the Six Building Blocks of Cyclone Football Success. One building block is Tough Kids—kids who grow up in German and Danish families in the small towns and on the farms of the beautiful rolling hills of Shelby County, Iowa—kids who add a new chapter to the history book of Harlan Community High School Football each year.

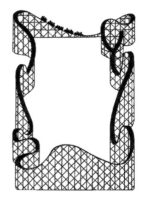

Chapter: 4
Harlan Community High School
Football History

It all began quietly enough. The following brief announcement appeared in the *Harlan Tribune* on September 30, 1896:

Foot Ball Match

The first matched game of foot ball under association rules will come off between our High School and the Denison Normal College team Saturday afternoon at the fairgrounds at 2:30. Admission 20 cents, school children 15. Turn out a big crowd for the encouragement of the boys.

Unlike most of the games since then, the first one didn't turn out favorably, as the article in the October 6, 1896, edition of *The Tribune* relates:

The Denison Normal school foot ball team defeated our boys Saturday afternoon by a close score of 10 to 0. The local eleven was greatly overmatched in weight and experience but made the visitors earn every foot of ground. For a first game it was a great exhibition on the part of the home team, and all they have to do to become winners is to keep at it. The game was witnessed by a large crowd and was contested in a very friendly manner.

The words "all they have to do is keep at it" proved to be prophetic. After the initial defeat, the team compiled a record of nine wins, five losses, and three ties over the next five years under the leadership of coach and high school principal, Ed White.

The first football game played in Harlan wasn't in 1896, however. As early as 1873, players would get together on fall weekends on the courthouse square lawn to play a game called association football—a combination of rugby and football.

The 1898 Harlan football team
*Front row (left to right): James Byers, Vern Pieffer, Nate Booth, Gus Wick,
unknown player. Middle row (left to right): Will Baughn, Ben Wyland, Tom
Burcham, Leslie Anthony, Henry (last name unknown). Back row (left to right):
Will Kollbeck (manager), Emmet Tilten, Clarence Luecke, Ed White (coach)*

The First Undefeated Team

The following appeared in the September 19, 1906, edition of the *Harlan
Tribune:*

FOOTBALL GAME SATURDAY
Opening Game to Be with Audubon
Changes in the Rules Will Add Interest
Next Saturday the opening game of the football season will be played on the
home grounds with the high school eleven from Audubon. Last year our boys
went to Audubon for a game and although only ten minute halves were played
owing to the rain, our fellows were well treated. Let us return the compliment
when the visitors make their appearance.

Many changes were made in the rules last year by the conference committee of the big colleges. Teams are compelled to gain ten yards to make the distance, and the formations allowed force the adoption of open play tactics, consequently there will be demand for kickers, and men fast on foot for forward plays. End runs may be looked for, or attempts at them, by both sides, and for that reason special pains should be taken to keep the field clear.

The Harlan team has been practicing faithfully when the weather would permit and will be in fair condition. Deputy clerk Booth has the boys in charge as coach and has been putting them through some lively stunts. More than half the team will be made up of new men. From last year's team there is Bagley, center; Wirth, left end; Arrasmith, left tackle; Crosier, right half; and Robinson at full. Who will take the other positions has not been fully decided, and the whole line-up is in doubt, but the team may be counted on to make a good showing. The general admission will be 25 cents; school children 15 cents. The game will be played on the Bieletzky grounds on east Market street.

The 1906 season went well, as you can tell from this article in the December 5, 1906, edition of the *Harlan Tribune:*

THANKSGIVING FOOTBALL
Harlan High Goes Into Championship Class by Winning Last Game
The loyalty of the Harlan people toward their school football eleven was properly shown Thanksgiving day, when a large crowd turned out to cheer the boys in their deciding game with Creighton in spite of the weather. The curtain raiser was a match between then Harlan second team and Avoca's first team, which the former won 23 to 5. Then following was the list of Harlan players.

Those who played on the Harlan team were: re, Charley Wicks; rt, Hoisington, Parmley; rg, Bisgard; c, Swift; lg, Dacken, Plummer; lt, Parker; le, Ed Byers; rh, Bryan; lb, Potter; qb, Don Byers; fb, Burcham. Harlan High won against Creighton Academy by a score of 22 to 0. Touch downs were made by Campbell, Crosier, Robinson and Bagley. It was a kicking game in which Booth showed to advantage over Mugan. The work of the Harlan line and ends was excellent.

The following dispatch sent by the visitors to the *Omaha World-Herald* pays a high compliment to the home team:

Harlan, Ia., Nov. 29—Harlan high school gained undisputed title of champions of the two states of Iowa and Nebraska by defeating the third team of

Creighton university, which heretofore had a clean record of no defeats for the entire season.

The game was characterized by Harlan's wonderful interference and Creighton's tackling. Both teams played fine ball, the Creighton team, however, being handicapped by the slippery field. The game was free from rough play and few penalties were inflicted. The Creighton team is unanimous in the statement that they were never accorded better treatment from any aggregation than Harlan.

A Firsthand Account of the 1906 Season

One of the players on the 1906 team reviewed the season. His summary appeared in the November 13, 1961, edition of the *Harlan New-Advertiser:*

THE FOOTBALL SEASON OF 1906
by Otis Robinson

At the beginning of the season we felt pretty good, and the outlook was very favorable with Crosiar as our captain and about 20 young husky fellows to pick from, but we has a big drawback, as the schedule had been neglected, which, however, was soon remedied by the hard work of Ferguson.

A subscription paper was passed among the business men who donated sixty-five dollars toward a coach. Mr. N.P. Booth was chosen as our coach who put in lots of hard work and patience on us.

After practicing a couple of weeks Audubon was brought over here, September 22, but on account of lack of practice we did not play together and the final score was 11 to 4 in our favor.

The next week was put in with hard practice, as out next game was with Shelby. After driving down there and when the game was called we felt rather tired, but we went into the game with the old Harlan grit and came out winners 9 to 6.

The next game was October 6, with Atlantic at Harlan. They came up here with an expectation of holding us down to an even score, but in twenty minutes halves were beaten 38 to 0.

Just as the team got to working well and together, Bagley and Crosier, working from one to three days out of the week, were forced to give up practice, to the regret of the team. This left us very down hearted, losing two of our best players, but we called a meeting and Otis Robinson was elected captain.

Having lost a week's practice we went to work the next Monday night with almost a new line-up. After a hard week's practice we started to Omaha the next Saturday morning. We felt pretty well but were somewhat afraid of losing the game, but after reaching Omaha and enjoying a good dinner we felt better. At 2:30 we boarded the street car for the football grounds. After both teams warmed up the game was called, which consisted mostly of punting. Booth making a punt of sixty-five yards, and a few long end runs were made it brought us with in a few yards of their goal, then we played ball and forced them back for a touchdown. The game ended 6 to 0 in our favor.

November 2, Missouri Valley came over here but it was only a good practice game; the game ending 28 to 6.

November 10, Shelby gave us another hard game by playing two ineligible players, but Harlan played ball all the time and we came out 11 to 0 winners.

Having an open date the next Saturday, a challenge from the town team was accepted. Some of the high school team laid out, and the town team outweighing us twenty pounds to a man, we were compelled to take a defeat of 19 to 0.

The next Saturday was an open date, and consequently there was no practice.

We were put through a double quick practice Monday and Tuesday night in order to meet Creighton, Thanksgiving. It was a cold day but a fair crowd came out to witness the game. At three the whistle blew and the words, "Play ball" were heard from the referee. They received the ball and punted to us, we soon went for a touch down by our long end runs and line smashes. The blocking and formation of the H.H.S. was as good as any team of the past has ever shown. The game ended 22 to 0 in our favor.

The High School foot ball Team received congratulations from every team we played with on the treatment they were given.

Season notes: The Omaha team mentioned above went on to become Omaha Central High School. The game with the adults on the town team was an exhibition and didn't count as an official loss.

You've Come a Long Way, Cyclones!

As you discovered from the accounts above, it's not just the spelling of the word "football" that has changed since 1906. Here are more examples of the changes from "Sideline Shots," the column written by sports editor Dick Gilbert, in the November 23, 1961, issue of the *Harlan Tribune*. Dick went on to become the publisher of the *Des Moines Register*.

1. Harlan football players were evicted from their dressing room according to Roy Smith of Harlan. Smith was a right tackle on the 1906 Harlan team— the last H.H.S. outfit to go unbeaten, untied in high school play until this year.

The '06 squad had to pay rent on a dressing room located above the present Briley's store on the north side of the Harlan square, Smith relates.

One night after the boys had walked back from a hard practice at the football field—then located at the fairgrounds—they found their clothes and positions blocking the stairway.

The unsympathetic landlord had pitched their belongings down the stairs in a sneak eviction raid. The boys were behind in their rent.

2. In those days, the team traveled to games by horse and buggy. Smith recalled a 3-buggy caravan to Shelby. "When we got there," he said, "Shelby was short a man so their superintendent who also coached played for them. Harlan won, however, 11-0. For longer trips, like the Harlan-Creighton game, the boys took the train.

3. Audubon had a potent drop-kicker then, Roy said. The player scored most of Audubon's points by drop-kicking the ball over the goal posts—a maneuver that counted two points.

An excellent review of Harlan High School football appeared in a 1978 edition of the Harlan Newspapers:

HCHS HAS PROUD FOOTBALL HERITAGE

Many changes have taken place since the first Harlan teams played in 1896, such as filmed games, statistics on the entire year, and buses taken to and from the game. Electric scoreboards and lighted fields have been added, which have helped to make football in Harlan and across the nation one of the most popular sports.

Harlan was not an official football team until 1900, when it was sanctioned by the ISHSAA (Iowa State High School Athletic Association), which then only had 90 schools involved; at present more than 500 schools are participating.

With only 50 schools participating in the early years, games were often hard to find. So Harlan teams went across the state line frequently to play Nebraska schools such as Lincoln, Omaha Central, North and South, and Community. The caliber of team opponents included not only high school but college and pro teams. Early Harlan teams battled Denison, Omaha, and Woodbine Community Colleges and even the Drake University freshmen.

Harlan teams not only played college teams but also played before college games. In 1904 they played in Lincoln before the Nebraska game and were defeated. That same year they played before an Iowa State game and tied Ames.

More than 55 different teams have been Harlan opponents since 1896. Teams such as Adair, Boone, Exira, and Walnut were early foes.

Weather

In traveling to Adair in 1916 the team was hit by torrential rains. The game was not called off, and Harlan and Adair played in three inches of mud. In 1943 Cyclones fans found the Denison field covered with six inches to a foot of snow. The game was played, and Harlan won 33-0.

Illness due to the weather took the 1918 team out of action, as influenza hit the coaches and players, and three games were cancelled. The players competing for Harlan and other teams were sometimes a "questionable lot," as some of the players were out of school or had been hired to play. The two World Wars caused havoc on eligibility requirements, as many players were protested as being too old. Occasionally, the coaches and even male cheerleaders would don a uniform to play as other team members were injured or kicked out of the games.

Transportation

No tape decks or radios accompanied teams as they do now. In 1904 when the team went to Woodbine with a "wagonette and four horses," it took an entire day to make the first leg of the trip and the night was spent in Panama. The team arrived the next day and won 13-0.

Travel by train was first mentioned in 1916, when they rode to Adair.

Conferences

For the football team, the beginning of conference action was in a complete muddle until 1938, when they joined the Midwest Conference. In the *Harpoon* there were mentions of the Coon Valley Conference and Tri-Valley Conference but with no regularity. For 33 years Harlan participated in the Midwest Conference— 12 conference titles were won. In 1971 Harlan joined the Hawkeye Eight Conference, where they have won the conference title four times.

Coaching

Available coaches and money were early difficulties faced by the Harlan teams. One reason for the lack of teams during the 1911–1914 seasons was that there was no one who would coach the team. Team members usually went to local businesses for money to pay for the coaches' salaries. Harlan has had 27 different coaches over its history.

The Coaching Carousel

Here is an updated list of Harlan's coaches and their records.

Year	Coach	Won	Lost	Tie	Games	%
1896–1900	Ed White	9	6	3	18	60%
1901–1903	C. Nicoulin	14	7	2	23	67%
1904–1906	Nate Booth	21	5	1	27	81%
1907	Fred Williams	4	4	3	11	50%
1908	H.W. Campbell	1	4	1	6	20%
1909	Robert Jenson	3	1	2	6	75%
1910	Glenn Howard	0	2	0	2	0%
1911–1913	no team					
1914	Parmley	1	6	0	7	14%
1915	Withrow	4	3	0	7	57%
1916	J.G. Schmidt	2	3	1	6	40%
1917	no coach	2	5	1	8	29%
1918	Allbright & Byers	1	2	0	3	33%
1919	Forrest Baker	3	3	1	7	50%
1920–1929	T.K. Lloyd	38	32	9	79	54%
1930–1933	Verlem McBride	21	17	0	38	55%
1934–1937	Paul Brechler	23	12	6	41	66%
1938–1940	Lowell Crippen	11	15	3	29	42%
1941–1942	Gene Hertz	13	5	0	18	72%
1943	Willis Wolcott	6	1	1	8	86%
1944–1945	F.N. Mason	9	6	2	17	60%
1946–1947	Gordon Matson	11	6	1	18	65%
1948–1949	Russell Null	6	8	4	18	43%
1950–1962	Harold Johnson	72	37	7	116	66%
1963–1966	Robert Simpson	13	21	2	36	38%
1967–1973	Terry Eagen	56	9	1	66	86%
1974–1977	Ken Papp	25	11	0	36	69%
1978–2005	Curt Bladt	301	31	0	331	91%
1896–2005		**671**	**261**	**51**	**982**	**72%**
1950–2005		**467**	**108**	**10**	**585**	**80%**
1967–2005		**382**	**50**	**1**	**433**	**88%**

Iowa Hall of Pride

Among the other fantastic and interactive displays at the Iowa Hall of Pride in Des Moines is one on Harlan Community High School football. See Appendix B for more information on the Iowa Hall of Pride.

Merrill Field Magic

This book isn't meant to be a comprehensive history of Harlan Cyclone football. That will come later. In Chapter 8, we will resume the saga with Harlan's next undefeated team of 1961.

Harlan Community High School has a long and tradition-rich football history. A 72% winning percentage is truly remarkable. Since 1936, many of those victories have taken place under the lights of one of Iowa's most historic sports venues—Merrill Field.

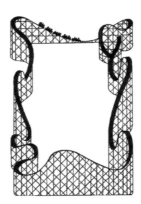

Before the 2005 quarterfinal playoff game between his Waukee Warriors and the Harlan Community Cyclones, coach Scott Carlson discussed playing at historic Merrill Field and "waking its ghosts."

Maybe there are ghosts at Merrill Field. Many a visiting team has experienced their vexing power; and many a Cyclone team has taken advantage of their friendly presence to gain an advantage on its opponents. If you don't believe me, give Scott Carlson a call.

The First Forty Years

Merrill Field's seventy-year history has sure seen its share of big games and Cyclone victories. The following article by Alan Mores (then a high school student) in the February 3, 1975, edition of the *Harlan News-Advertiser* is an excellent way to discover the history of Merrill Field's first forty years:

DEDICATED IN 1936
HOW MERRILL FIELD CAME INTO BEING

One of Harlan's most familiar sports arenas bears the name of an early Shelby County settler, Joseph W. Merrill. Merrill Athletic Field was partially made possible by the generosity of Merrill and his wife, Lilly, both of whom are now dead.

Merrill was born not far from the city of Rome, Italy in 1869 and died in Harlan in 1919 at the age of 52. At the age of 10 he and his father came to America and traveled throughout the U.S. as tourists.

Tragedy struck in 1878 when Merrill's father died—leaving him alone without money in a strange land with no money or relatives. One year later he came to Harlan with a friend and became acquainted with Mrs. Henry Childers with whom he lived until his marriage to Lillie Kees in 1895. They had one child who died in infancy.

Upon completion of courses in the Harlan schools, Mr. Merrill went into business with Joseph Beh. The partnership later resulted in one of Harlan's leading businesses, the Beh-Merrill Mercantile Association.

After retiring, Merrill returned to his acreage, site of the present football field, and raised fruits and vegetables. After his death in 1919, Mrs. Merrill built a home at 8th and Baldwin and let the cherry and apple orchard remain without care.

Mrs. Merrill died on June 4, 1940, following an illness.

HISTORY

When the Harlan school system sought land for an athletic field, Mrs. Merrill sold the land to them on very liberal terms so it could be put to use at once.

According to the *Harlan Tribune*, Aug. 27, 1930, the land was purchased in the spring of 1930 and games would hence be played at the new field rather than at the fairgrounds.

A donation of $4,950.00 was made the week of June 4, 1936 by Mr. Merrill to the Harlan school to be used in the improvement of the new field. The permanent arch was constructed in 1936 at the northeast entrance to the Merrill Athletic Field along with other improvements to give Harlan one of the most up to date fields in the state.

The arch at the northeast entrance consists of two large brick pillars flanked by two small pillars which support the gates to the entrance.

Work done by the Works Progress Administration (WPA) included a quarter mile track built around the football field, bleachers which would accommodate over 600 people and two bronze plaques placed on the main entrances to the field. The plaques read, "Joseph W. Merrill Memorial Athletic Field."

Old entrance to Merrill Field; ticket booth is on the left

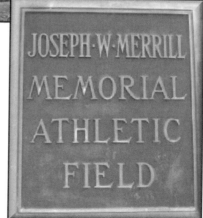

Bronze plaque on main entrance

DEDICATED IN 1936

The first "official" dedication was to have taken place on September 18, 1936, but rain forced the game to be played in Avoca. The second "official" dedication took place October 9, 1936 when Harlan entertained Missouri Valley. The following is an excerpt from the *Harlan News-Advertiser* of October 8, 1936.

"The dedication of Joseph Merrill athletic field will take place Friday evening at the above named field. Harlan High School will engage the Missouri Valley prepsters, in what is to be expected to be one of the best football games of the entire home schedule. This will be the annual Dad's Day game, a large crowd is anticipated to witness both features of the evening's entertainment."

"Between halves, the dedication of the field will take place…there will be the presentation of the field to the high school, with Rev. Arthur Eastman representing Mrs. Merrill, being the speaker. Mrs. Charles Paulk, president of the school board, will accept the field on behalf of the Harlan Schools and will read a poem written by Principal Ray Finn."

The first game ended in a dead heat according to the papers with a record crowd on hand to witness the dedication. Since 1936 HCHS has won nearly 70 per cent of their games on the field.

FIELD IMPROVEMENTS

Many great teams followed and many improvements to the field as well.

In 1951 with the help of the Jr. Chamber of Commerce a scoreboard was purchased and in 1973 a new board was purchased by the school system. In 1968, the press box was added with the help of athletic director Harold "Swede" Johnson and several school youths.

The track repairs included a new cinder running surface and runways for the long jump and pole vault were added. Seating was increased to upwards of 3,500 and new lights were added as well to improve nighttime viewing.

The first lights for the field were the results of donations by Harlan businessmen back in the thirties. As need for more lighting grew, additions were added such as the new mercury vapor lights.

Many memorable moments were played out on both the track and field as Harlan Community athletes competed in state playoffs, conference championships and heated rivalries.

A major thanks can be attributed to an Italian immigrant and his wife, Lillie, for the land upon which these events took place…and which we enjoy and use today.

Merrill Field, 1945

The Next Thirty Years

In an era when many high schools are abandoning their old football fields and building new ones close to their school buildings, Harlan Community High School continually updates historic Merrill Field. A new scoreboard was installed in 1995. A new all-weather track replacing the old cinder one was constructed in 1996. In 2004, a modern press box was added.

The new Merrill Field press box was added in 2004

The back of the new Merrill Field press box

Merrill Field of Dreams and scoreboard

Merrill Field Mojo

In the beginning of this chapter, Coach Scott Carlson talked about the tradition of Merrill Field and waking its ghosts. Scott was right about the ghosts' power. In a game between the #1 rated Cyclones and the #2 Warriors, his team lost 48 to 17 before a crowd of 5,000 people—the largest athletic event gathering in Harlan's history. The Merrill Field mojo had struck again.

It's interesting that, before 1936, Merrill Field was an orchard where young trees grew into mature ones, which produced a bountiful harvest of fruit. In Section 3, you will meet the Cyclone players who grew into young men while dancing under the Merrill Field lights, and who produced a bountiful harvest of victories. Merrill Field's apples have given way to its apparitions. These ghosts bid you farewell but look forward to your presence on Friday nights each fall when evidence of The Cyclone Way will again appear before your very eyes.

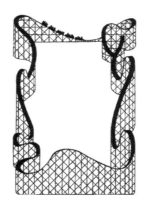

Chapter: 6
The Cyclone Way

"Joined as one, we get the job done."
—Superintendent Orville Frazier, 1967

A smart guy that Orville Frazier. His brief but brilliantly constructed statement was the genesis of The Cyclone Way. Almost forty years later, the statement is still its core.

A Tough Decision

In 1966, the Iowa legislature passed a law requiring all areas of the state to be part of a public school district. Previously, most of western Shelby County was an independent school district with schools in the five predominantly Catholic towns of Earling, Defiance, Westphalia, Panama, and Portsmouth.

In the spring of 1967, the parishes running the schools had a decision to make. They could continue operating their parochial high schools,

Orville Frazier

pay property taxes to support the new public school district, and send their children to the high schools of their choice. Or they could discontinue the operations of their three parochial high schools and send their children to the public high school in Harlan. They choose the latter.

A statement in the November 17, 1967, edition of the *Harlan News-Advertiser* from Msgr. Michael Schwarte, pastor of St. Mary's parish in Portsmouth, explained their decision:

> The decision to discontinue the parochial high schools of Shelby County was dictated by the fact that the State law forced us to relinquish our independent school district thereby imposing on us a high tax to support a second school system in addition to the one we were already financing. This factor, coupled with the ever increasing cost of school operation to maintain the standard we

37

demand for our schools, constituted a financial burden which brought about the decision to terminate the operation of our secondary parochial schools at this time.

From 550 to 920 Students in One Day

When the doors of Harlan Community High School opened in September of 1967, 473 new students walked through them. The number of high school students almost doubled—from 500 to 920. In one day, Harlan Community High School moved from being the 68th largest high school in Iowa to being the 21st. The area of the district increased to 280 square miles. Seventeen new teachers also walked through the door that day. Two of them were Terry Eagen and Curt Bladt.

Culture—The Invisible Framework

A school's culture is the invisible framework that supports and gives justification to the actions of students, teachers, and community. The individual pieces of that framework are values. Values are deep-seated beliefs about the world and how it operates. They are the emotional rules that govern people's attitudes and behavior. Values are also the guidelines people use to make decisions. Walt Disney's brother, Roy, summed it up best when he said, "When values are clear, decisions are easy."

Maintaining a culture and instilling values aren't easy. Organizations have to work at it consistently. One reason Southwest Airlines has been so successful over its thirty-five year history is because of the culture Southwest has created and maintained. Former CEO Herb Kelleher says, "Culture is the most precious thing a company (school district) has, so you must work harder at it than anything else." The Walt Disney Company agrees. Every new employee, whether a senior vice president or a person sweeping the sidewalks at Disneyland, must take a two-day Disney Traditions training program. Through a history lesson on the origins of the Disney tradition, and stories of people who have exemplified its values, each person learns what it means to represent The Walt Disney Company. When finished, their actions are purposeful and their decision-making process is clear.

The Cyclone Way Culture

Dan Leinen (Agricultural Education Teacher, FFA sponsor, and coach) picked up on the cultural "air" when he first arrived in Harlan. Dan says, "I got to Harlan and found…a caring administration, a truly

Dan Leinen

friendly and caring staff, motivated students, concerned community members, and an 'air' that existed that just told me, 'This is the place to be.'"

Harlan Community's new superintendent, Bill Decker, agrees with Dan. He was
part of an Iowa Department of Education
evaluation team that visited Harlan Community Schools in November of 2003. Here's how
he describes what he observed: "I came away
thinking, 'Boy, when that superintendent job
opens up, I want to have it.' Harlan had just
come off winning the state football championship, so the place was really humming. Being an ex-basketball coach, I dropped in on
one of Mitch Osborn's practices. It was a cut
above of anything I'd seen. I knew they were

Bill Decker

going to win a state championship, too! But The Cyclone Way culture isn't just in athletics. It's in all parts of the District."

Three Values That Support the Culture

The Mission Statement of Harlan Community Schools is:

The Harlan Community School District
will prepare lifelong learners and productive citizens.

There are three values that support the mission statement and are the back-bone of The Cyclone Way culture. They are The Expectation of Excellence, Coop-eration, and Hard Work.

1. **The Expectation of Excellence**—Harlan Community School District (HCSD) students are expected to excel in academic and extracurricular activities. This book focuses on football excellence. That same dedication to excellence has led to over 80% of Harlan Community High School's students pursuing postsecondary education after graduation—75% go to four-year academic institutions. The high school dropout rate is a measly 1.5%.

How about this for an academic/athletic excellence combination? The top eight runners on the 2005 state champion girls cross country team had a 3.7 GPA!

Excellence in any group is not achieved by lofty pronouncements from people in leadership positions. Excellence is achieved by expecting it, creating a culture that supports it, hiring and retaining people who embrace it, and setting goals that lead to the actions that strengthen it.

Here are two of the ten goals adopted by the Board of Education on July 24, 2006:

a. Hire the best teaching staff available regardless of salary schedule placement while considering both experienced and inexperienced applicants. Keep pay for staff in the upper echelon of comparably sized schools such as those in the Hawkeye Ten Athletic Conference.

b. Keep lower elementary (K-2) classroom numbers at twenty or less and continue to value pre-kindergarten programs.

Sally Claussen, who is entering her forty-sixth year as a language arts teacher, notes that for twenty-five years Harlan Community students have been able to take college credit courses while in high school. Harlan was one of the first schools in the state to do this.

Sally Claussen

And it's not just the HCHS guys who are displaying excellence in sports. During the 2005–2006 school year, the girls had their best year ever when they won the state cross country title, qualified for the state volleyball tournament, reached the semifinals of the state basketball tournament, and finished second in the state track and field meet and in the state softball tournament.

CoachBladt.com website posting
Name: Dan Jacobi
City, State: Cedar Rapids, IA
Date: 12/16/2004

Dear Coach,
Even though it's been 18 years since I graduated from HCHS I still keep track of what's going on back home with my alma mater. My wife gets humorously irritated whenever I open the paper every Saturday morning in the fall to see how "Perfectville" (her description of Harlan, not mine) did the night before. The tradition of excellence continues and gets stronger as the years pass.

You, along with all the other teachers I had at HCHS, embody what makes Harlan Community such a special place to call home. I am in my first year teaching high school band at Xavier High School in Cedar Rapids, and while I couldn't ask for a better first year experience, I'm sure that anyone who's ever been through the Harlan system as a student and gone on to teach elsewhere can say one thing…"There is no place like Harlan!"

The people of Iowa are aware of The Cyclone Way. The following Resolution passed both houses of the Iowa General Assembly in March of 2004:

SENATE RESOLUTION NO. 143
BY BOETTGER

A Resolution honoring Harlan Community Schools for
   their achievements in academics, music, vocational
   training, and sports.

   WHEREAS, Harlan Community Schools have recently excelled in
numerous curricular and extracurricular activities, and have
been recognized for significant achievements, especially in
the area of academic performance; and
   WHEREAS, last year Harlan Community High School seniors
averaged a score of 23.5 on ACT tests, exceeding both national
and state averages, as has occurred for many years; and
   WHEREAS, the Annual Report on Iowa Student Achievement and
Accountability prepared by the Department of Education for
2004 lists Harlan Community Schools as scoring among the top 5
percent of Iowa's fourth and eighth grade students in the
areas of math and reading; and
   WHEREAS, the Harlan Community School Marching Band has
received 22 consecutive number-one ratings at marching band
contests; and
   WHEREAS, Harlan Community School Jazz Bands have never
placed lower than fourth in state jazz contests over 30 years,
including two first-place finishes; and
   WHEREAS, Harlan Community Schools have recently qualified
four teams for the national Destination Imagination Contest in
Knoxville, Tennessee; and
   WHEREAS, the Harlan Community Future Farmers of America
(FFA) is the largest chapter in the state and this year is
being recognized by the state FFA as the Outstanding FFA
Chapter in Iowa; and
   WHEREAS, the Harlan Community High School Boys' Basketball
Team won the 2004 Class 3A State Championship with a 27-0
record; and
   WHEREAS, seventh, eighth, and ninth grade, and reserve
teams were all undefeated this basketball season; and
   WHEREAS, the Boys' Football Team won the 2003 Class 3A
State Championship with a 13-0 record, thus placing first or
second for 17 years out of the last 30 years; and
   WHEREAS, the Boys' Track Team won the 2003 Class 3A State
Championship; and
   WHEREAS, the Boys' Baseball Team won the 2003 Class 3A
State Championship with a 29-7 record; and
   WHEREAS, the boys' baseball, football, and basketball teams
recorded 57 consecutive wins through their respective seasons;
and
   WHEREAS, the students of Harlan Community School have
demonstrated the kind of character and competitive spirit
valued by their schools, their community, and the State of
Iowa, NOW THEREFORE,
   BE IT RESOLVED BY THE SENATE, That the Senate congratulates
the students, parents, teachers, and administrators of the
Harlan Community Schools for their many achievements and
thanks them for the honor and recognition they have brought to
their school and to the State of Iowa; and

   BE IT FURTHER RESOLVED, That, upon adoption, an official
copy of this Resolution be prepared for presentation to the
Superintendent of the Harlan Community Schools for sharing
with the entire Harlan community.

JEFFREY M. LAMBERTI
President of the Senate

   I hereby certify that this Resolution is known as
Senate Resolution 143, Eightieth General Assembly.

MICHAEL E. MARSHALL
Secretary of the Senate

2. **Cooperation**—By itself, The Expectation of Excellence is not enough. People have to work closely with others to create the excellence across boundaries. Unlike many schools, there is tremendous cooperation between the coaches of the different sports, departments, and individual teachers at HCHS. Kids are never pressured by coaches to play just one sport or do just one activity. On the contrary, they're encouraged to do many extracurricular activities.

Lee Nelson, the highly regarded past director of the award-winning Cyclone Marching Band, says, "In some schools there are strained relationships between teachers in music department and athletic department because they're vying for the kids' time and the school's resources. I always got along great with all the coaches. I called Curt 'Dr. Off-Tackle' and he called me 'Noted Dr. of Notes.' Curt appreciated what we did to make fall Friday evenings special in Harlan. Despite some real long trips and some real bad weather, our pep band has never missed a playoff game—home or away."

Lee Nelson

CoachBladt.com website posting
Name: Aaron Adams
City, State: Omaha, NE
Date: 01/23/2005

Coach,
First, I would like to say it is sad about what is happening to you, but I am happy to hear you are fighting this successfully. Before this happened, did you know that you have had such a heavy influence on THOUSANDS (maybe TENS OF THOUSANDS) of lives?! Although I decided it was more important my last couple of years in high school to work instead of play football, I will always remember my stint with you.

You have truly been an inspiration to many throughout the world, including myself. As my success in real estate and other ventures throughout the country continues, I often attribute this success to the foundation that was built in Harlan. You see, you began a "culture" of winning attitudes that has spread everywhere. It seems that nearly every child growing up in Harlan has dreams of being THE BEST at what he or she does because this is what we have seen from day one in the school system. Even though this attitude is carried out among MANY teachers, coaches, parents, students, and alumni of Harlan, it all started with YOU. Because of what YOU started, I wake up every morning wanting to be THE BEST.

I find it amusing that business partners of mine from as far away as New York, Miami, San Diego, and Seattle inquire how the Harlan Cyclone football program is doing. This is because I speak with tremendous enthusiasm about growing up in the winning tradition that is the Harlan Cyclones. In a round about way, I thank you for your part in the successes I have had and will continue to have in my own life. You are a TRUE LEADER whose personality has been contagious to thousands of people. I am sure you will get back to your normal self soon, and I wish you the best of luck!

3. **Hard Work**—By themselves, The Expectation of Excellence and Cooperation aren't enough. It takes a lot of hard work by all the people involved to manifest the excellence. Whether it's the football coaches staying up most of the night after a game watching film or a pep band traveling to Webster City to perform when there's an inch of ice on the ground (never good for effective clarinet playing), the administrators, teachers, support staff, and students of Harlan Community Schools work hard. Fortunately, the results they create reinforce their efforts and are deeply appreciated by the members of the community.

"Leaders aren't born, they're made.
And they are made just like anything else, through hard work.
And that's the price we have to pay to achieve a goal, any goal."
—Vince Lombardi

Perpetuating the Cyclone Way

Middle School principal Duane Magee has undertaken a project in which he is leading a team of veteran teachers to expose newly hired teachers to The Cyclone Way at an orientation session.

Duane enlisted several current and former teachers and administrators who had been around the block a few times to help him crystallize what The Cyclone Way truly is and then present an orientation session similar to the Disney Traditions training program mentioned earlier. The people are Curt Bladt, Bob Broomfield, Dan Leinen, Sally Claussen, Lee Nelson, Steve Lawson, and Doug Renkly. Below are Steve's, Doug's, and Bob's views on The Cyclone Way.

Duane Magee

Steve Lawson
Harlan Community Middle School Band Teacher,
High School Jazz Director
1970–2002

The Cyclone Way of doing things is based on always adjusting, pushing for higher goals, cooperating with other staff and making decisions based on what is best for kids. I learned early on that teaching in Harlan is not an 8-to-4 job. Harlan kids have a large appetite for going places and doing things. Maybe that is because we are a small town not real close to any larger city. I think the only 40-hour week I ever put in was the time we were snowed in for three days. I put thousands of miles on school buses driving to jazz and band events, and I always felt the kids would follow me anywhere.

Harlan seems to be a long way from everywhere. The fact that Harlan is a fairly big school in a small town always makes it the best show in town, resulting in great community support. Teachers that thirst for excellence find their way to our doors, and once caught in the WAY, they stay. I've always felt that we had the most experienced, creative, cooperative staff of any school around. Many times I heard other band directors

Steve Lawson

complaining about various problems they were dealing with. I was always happy to return home to Harlan and The Cyclone Way. The Cyclone Way is to ask for help when working out your small problems before they become big problems, to always be guided by what's best for the kids, to get parents involved, and to always keep the communication doors open.

Doug Renkly
Art Teacher, Cross Country and Girls' Track Coach
1996–Present

During the 2005 Cross Country season, there was much talk of elevating our game and doing the impossible. The phrase, "YOU HAVE MORE!" seemed fitting as we entered the post-season and pre-

pared to make a run at a state championship. As we got closer to race day, the phrase seemed to be less about athletic effort and more about everything we do! As Cyclones, we expect more from ourselves. We celebrate those who have set the standard academically and athletically, yet pursue that excellence unafraid of failure. We are regular people with a common goal.

Doug Renkly

We want the best for ourselves and those around us. The pursuit of excellence is not measured in the win/loss column at Harlan. It's measured in the effort each person gives on their individual journey to holistic self improvement. "YOU HAVE MORE!" is a reminder that our journey is never over. There is always more!

The cross country team demonstrates their motto: "You have more!"

Duane's strategy of collecting stories from veteran teachers and having the vets emotionally communicate their stories to the new people in the district is brilliant. Stories are so powerful. They are the primary way empowering cultures are explained and maintained. Southwest Airlines and Disney are constantly collecting and communicating a treasure chest of real-life stories of people who exemplify their cultures. HCSD is doing the same.

Henry David Thoreau said, "The greatest values are the farthest from being appreciated. We easily come to doubt if they exist. We soon forget them. They are the highest reality." Duane and his team are committed making sure the values that comprise The Cyclone Way are always the highest reality.

Bob Broomfield is the man who Bill Decker replaced. He got to see HCSD's events from the eye of The Cyclone Culture. Ever the poet, here are Bob's reflections on his six years at the helm:

Bob Broomfield
Superintendent
2000–2006

AN ODE TO HARLAN COMMUNITY SCHOOLS
The motto is *"United As One, We Get The Job Done"…* Words that say a lot.
So much can be accomplished when no individual credit is sought.
Passion for the task and wanting it done right is evident each and every time.
The right folks are on the bus, so their efforts have results that are prime.

High expectation is what so many will report when asked how it can be.
But there are so many less successful who have listed such goals for all to see.
There are many things that go into passing the high accomplishments test.
Having the thought in place that it takes many things seems best.

A vast majority of parents that not only understand, but take care,
to support their children, realize their abilities, and in conflicts be fair.
A board that sets the policies and allows district staff to do their work.
A community that supports one and all and in their contributions do not shirk.

Yes, simplistic it does seem, but that seems to cover all you really need,
because the combination allows kids to work hard and then succeed.
Hopefully, when new folks arrive upon the scene, it is possible to be shown
why all of us are so proud to be called a Harlan Community School Cyclone!

Bob Broomfield

Soft, Fuzzy, and Vitally Important

Culture and values are soft, fuzzy concepts that are often overshadowed by the hard, day-to-day realities of running a school district or coaching a football team. It's ironic that the soft things are the hardest to do, and the hard things are the easiest to do. Another soft, fuzzy concept is tradition. As you will soon discover, tradition is the first Building Block of Cyclone Football Success.

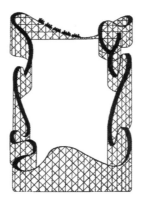

I n the thirty-four years of the Iowa football playoff system, the Harlan Cyclones have placed first or second an amazing nineteen times. After the fifth game of the 2006 season, the Cyclone football team had won forty-four consecutive games. The odds of that happening by chance are 1 in 17,592,186,000,000.

Seventeen and a half trillion to one is definitely not an accident. It's due to six *simple* factors—the Six Building Blocks of Cyclone Football Success. They are:

1. Tradition
2. Coaching Consistency
3. Community and Parental Support
4. Coaching Cooperation
5. Tough Kids
6. Confidence

Did you notice I said the Six Building Blocks are simple? They really are. There's nothing too complicated about any of them. But just because they're *simple* doesn't mean they're *easy* to do. If they were, many more schools would have football programs like the Harlan Community Cyclones. Constructing the Six Building Blocks takes thousands of the right people, taking thousands of right actions, in the right culture that reinforces the right values.

Building Block #1: Tradition

Webster's Dictionary defines the word tradition as "the handing down of information, beliefs, and customs by word of mouth or by example from one generation to another without written instruction."

There is no Cyclone Football owner's manual that the coaches give their players or that parents give their children at birth. Kids slowly, but surely, absorb the tradition from the stories they hear, the players they come to know, and the games they attend.

The Cyclone tradition creates two important outcomes:

Outcome #1—Desire: Boys grow up wanting to play football for the Cyclones. They begin attending the games at a very young age and are coached by the current Cyclone players in their 5th and 6th grade flag football league. Denison's head football coach, Dave Wiebers, says, "Kids love to play for Curt. They grow up, have families, and come back to Harlan so their kids can play for Curt."

CoachBladt.com website posting
Name: Tony, Kathi, & Cameron Beach
City, State: Harlan
Date: 12/16/2004

Hey Curt & Jill,
Glad to hear that things are looking a little brighter in the hospital room. We know you're in good hands! Every time we drive past the football field, which is quite often since we live so close, Cameron says "football." He might only be three years old, but he is already looking forward to being part of Cyclone tradition. Thanks for all the time and energy you invest in so many young people!

You're an inspiration,
Tony, Kathi, and Cameron Beach

In hundreds of front and back yards throughout the Harlan Community School District, future Cyclones are honing their skills and rehearsing their state championship celebrations. One example is the Booth/Magee and Louis/Deren front yard. For over fifty years, it has been a miniature Merrill Field.

Linda Deren explains the importance of the tradition in the following email she sent me:

Future Cyclones practicing in the Magee/Deren front yard

When the Magees purchased the house from your parents' estate, I made them promise that they would continue to allow kids of all ages to play in their front yard. (I may have even included that in the contract.) Of course, they agreed, and the tradition lives on! I cannot tell you how many games and state championships have been played there.

After they won their state championship 49-7, I remember asking my son, Brody, "How did you win by so much?"

His reply was simple, "Do you know how many times we practiced for this in our front yard?"

Outcome #2—High Expectations: Once the boys slip on the pads, there are very high expectations for them to play the game to the best of their abilities and uphold the Cyclone tradition. Former Superintendent Bob Broomfield says, "The people in the Harlan Community School District have high expectations for its students, and we usually deliver. The parents' support is fantastic. We have a lot of very educated people move away, and then come back to Harlan to raise and educate their kids."

In the book, *Bernie Saggau and the Iowa Boys,* Chuck Offenburger says the following about the Cyclone football tradition. The book was published in 2005 before Harlan's third consecutive state title. I have updated his figures to 2006 in brackets.

It's almost hard to believe there could be a football program more successful than Emmetsburg's, but as fans of the game in Iowa know, there is one—Harlan's.

Curt Bladt, 60 years old in the spring of 2005, has coached the Cyclones to nine [ten] state championships, including the most recent two [three]—in 2003 and 2004 [and 2005]. In his twenty-seven [twenty-eight] years as head coach, the team's worst record was 7-2, they've never lost a season opener, they've never lost two games in a row, and they've never lost a first-round game in 24 [25] appearances in the state playoffs. The Cyclones record under Bladt: 288-31-0 [301-31-0].

How has Bladt built such a successful program in Harlan?

"Well, first of all, I didn't start it," he told me in 2004.

Harold "Swede" Johnson won five conference championships with his teams from 1950 to 1962, the second to the last of which was undefeated. He then stepped aside as head football coach, but served a total of 33 years as athletic director. In a 1967 school consolidation, Harlan took in most of the students from Catholic high schools that closed in nearby Panama, Portsmouth, Earling, Defiance, and Westphalia, and that nearly doubled the size of the Harlan High study body.

Johnson hired Terry Eagen, a native of Exira, as head football coach, and Eagen's teams won 85 percent of their games, including the state championship in the first year the playoffs were held in 1972. Eagen left in 1973 for Marshalltown, but in his Harlan years, he persuaded his bosses to hire another Exira native, Curt Bladt, who had just graduated from Morningside College in Sioux City. He was hired to teach biology and be an assistant wrestling coach. In 1968, Eagen also asked him to be the line coach in football. Ken Papp succeeded Eagen as head coach in the 1974 season, and then Bladt took over in 1978.

"So, I didn't start the program," Bladt said. "I just took the reins and tried to keep it going."

And, oh, has he ever!

"A lot people use the word 'mystique' about the success we've had," he said. "But there's no mystique at all. We just get our kids to play hard. They invest a lot in our football program, and when you've invested a lot and have a winning program, it's hard to give it up."

Curt had more to say about the Cyclone tradition in an article titled, "An In-Depth Look at How Three High School Coaches Built Dominating Programs" by Terry Jacoby in *American Football Monthly*.

"The winning here goes back to 1972 when I was an assistant here," Bladt said. "The first year Iowa held state playoffs was in 1972, and we were the champs in 3A that year." If that was the start, then the 1980s was the boom. The Cyclones won titles in 1982, 1983, and 1984 and made six consecutive trips to the state finals starting in 1981.

When you have tradition on your side, you simultaneously have a bullseye on your back. People want to knock you off your pedestal and take your place. This fact was driven home to Curt when he was walking through an opposing team's locker room one day. On the wall was a sign with the team's three top goals:

#1 Beat Harlan.

#2 Beat Harlan.

#3 Beat Harlan.

Curt summed up the Cyclone Tradition best when he said, "Tradition is really a mind-set of the players. It's like the sturdy foundation of a house. Once the foundation is in place, the house you build on it can be different each year."

Building Block #2: Coaching Consistency

In the *American Football Monthly* article mentioned earlier, Curt had this to say about the consistency of his coaching staff:

"We have had basically the same coaching staff for the past twenty-five years," Bladt said. "Ken Carstens (defensive coordinator), Bill Hosack (secondary), Russ Gallinger (offensive backfield), and Al Simdorn have been around for a long time with me. Everybody has their own piece of the pie."

And the results have been some sweet seasons of success. Each coach has a role. Each coach knows his responsibilities. Curt lets his coaches do their own thing and stays out of their way. As high school principal Kent Klinkefus says, "If you want to be a leader, you've got to give leadership away. Curt Bladt has learned that lesson well."

The Cyclone football coaching team has been amazingly consistent over the years. Before Mark Kohorst replaced Russ Gallinger as offensive coordinator for the 2005 season, Curt and four assistant coaches had been together for a total of over 125 years! This is unheard of in high school football. Curt says, "We don't have to spend a lot of time writing down what we're going to do. We know each other and the system so well, we just go do it."

All of the coaches played football for small town high school teams and most of them grew up on the farm. In addition, the assistant coaches aren't looking to move on and be a head coach somewhere else. This says a lot about head coach Curt Bladt and the Cyclone football program.

Harlan Community Coaching Staff
Ken (Buck) Carstens—Varsity Defensive Coordinator

Ken Carstens has been on the staff for thirty-seven years. He has also been known to be slightly vocal at times. Curt agrees when he says, "In the halftime locker room, Carstens keeps yelling until he runs out of air. When that happens, we know we're ready to go back on the field for the second half."

In addition to being a person who isn't afraid to speak his mind, Ken uses his mind when he speaks. Curt remembers two games that illustrate the fact:

Ken Carstens

1. "We were in a playoff game against Webster City. We're in overtime, and it's snowing real bad. They had the ball inside our two yard line. If Webster City scores, they win the game. Buck called a defense that plugged all the holes on the inside, but basically left the outside open. One of our players, Tim Boettger, asked Carstens, 'What happens if they run wide?' Buck calmly answered, 'We lose.' They ran inside. We won."

A Harlan fan was standing on the Webster City side of the field watching the game. A Webster City fan standing beside him was constantly saying, "That's my son," as his boy successfully carried the ball during the overtime period mentioned above. When his son was stopped a quarter-inch short of the goal line on the game-winning defensive play, the Harlan fan asked the man, "Was that your son?"

2. "In the early 1990s, we played West Delaware in the state finals. They had a great quarterback and excellent receivers. Buck's game plan was to give them the deep passing routes and take away the short routes. This is the exact opposite of what 'the book' says you're 'supposed' to do. He also saw on the game film that the quarterback would look left before he threw a short pass to the right and vice versa. Turns out, Buck was right as usual. We didn't give up any long passes that day; and we intercepted two short passes and ran them back for touchdowns."

Bill Hosack—Varsity Defensive Secondary

Bill has been on the Cyclone staff for twenty-nine seasons. Curt tells a story of a game at Lewis Central where defensive coordinator Ken Carstens couldn't be at the game because of illness, so Bill took over his job. In a tight contest, LC was driving the ball late in the game and had a fourth down and less than a yard. Bill called a flare defense that leaves the middle of the line short-handed and puts more defenders on the outside. Curt told Bill, "If they run inside, they're going for fifty yards."

Bill Hosack

Bill replied, "They're going to pitch the ball."

He was correct. Lewis Central did, lost three yards, and had to punt.

Al Simdorn

Al Simdorn—Assistant Varsity and JV Coach

Al has coached football in Harlan for twenty-six years. During practices, he is responsible for duplicating the next opponent's defense for the varsity offense to run plays against.

At a team potluck dinner before a playoff game, Coach Carstens made a short speech and commented that, "It sure would be nice if someone made us cream puffs for us to eat on the trip." Sure enough, someone did. On the way to the game, Al and Ken were sitting next to each other on the bus. Al was about ready to take a bite out of his, unleashed an uncontrollable sneeze, and blew the powdered sugar all over Ken's face. Curt said he never laughed so hard in his life.

Mark Kohorst—Varsity Offensive Coordinator

In 2006, Mark entered his second year as the Cyclones' offensive coordinator. Before that, he had been the offensive coordinator for the freshman team, so he knew the offense. In his first state championship game, Harlan had a second down play on West Delaware's three yard line. This is typically a running down. Mark sent in a pass play. Curt looked at him and asked, "What?"

Mark Kohorst

Mark replied, "It'll work. They won't be looking for it."

To which Supreme Grand Master Bladt said, "It better."

It did. Six more points for the Cyclones.

Kelly Juhl and Tom Murtaugh—Assistant Coach and Film Guy

Kelly assists Al Simdorn with reproducing the next opponent's offense and defense. Tom Murtaugh shoots the video of the Cyclones' games.

Kelly Juhl

Seventh Grade Coaches—Russ Gallinger and Brent Tucker

After being offensive coordinator for twenty-eight seasons, Russ took a year off in 2005. In 2006, he's back at it, coaching the seventh graders. Mitch Osborn's son, Zach, is a quarterback on the squad and is reportedly lobbying Russ to run a west coast passing offense. Russ is a former varsity head football coach at Union Star, Missouri. He is assisted by Brent Tucker.

Russ Gallinger   *Brent Tucker*

Eighth Grade Coaches—Steve Daeges and Travis Kurth

Steve is the Cyclones' head baseball coach and was formerly a head varsity football coach in Ashland, Nebraska. He is assisted by Travis Kurth.

Steve Daeges   *Travis Kurth*

Ninth Grade Coaches—John Murtaugh and Dan Leinen

John is Harlan's head wrestling coach and was formerly head varsity football coach at Red Oak, Iowa, and Wayne, Nebraska. Did you notice that the Cyclones' seventh, eighth, and ninth grade head coaches were former varsity head coaches at other schools? This tells you about the quality of people Harlan Community Schools attract. John is assisted by Dan Leinen.

John Murtaugh

Activities Director Mitch Osborn

In addition to being the Harlan Community High School's activities director, Mitch is the head varsity basketball coach. Mitch oversees and provides resources for all of HCHS's extracurricular activities. Curt says this about Mitch, "He takes care of everyone just the way he would want to be treated. If you need something, it will be there."

Mitch Osborn

Media Magician—Barb Nelson

Barb is the media center director at HCHS. She and her team are responsible for making VHS and DVD copies of the game films for the coaches. As Curt says, "They make copies for the coaches and the players who want them. They do this out of the goodness of their hearts; and their hearts are good."

Barb Nelson

The Glue

There are no shrinking violets on the football coaching staff. Curt sums up their relationship this way, "Sure we fight sometimes. There are days when it's like a marriage gone sour. But when all is said and done, everyone realizes what we need to accomplish for our outcomes to be reached."

Ron Novotny, the long-time voice of the Cyclones on KNOD radio, agrees. He says, "They will argue and fight, but Curt is the glue that holds the whole thing together."

Honoring a Champion Coaching Staff

From an article by Bob Bjoin, managing editor, in the September 9, 2000, edition of the *Harlan Tribune:*

> You can call him Santa Claus. Or judge, at Shelby County Fair's apple pie morning. Remember the time he helped sandbag during the flood, filling sandbags and placing them in a line along Highway 44 with dozens of others?
>
> These are the things some of us remember. But for nearly everyone in the Harlan Community, the site of this red-haired, burly, sometimes imposing guy roaming the sidelines at Merrill Field is what we love to see and never want to forget…
>
> What would football be like in the Harlan Community without Curt and the talented coaching staff of Ken Carstens, Russ Gallinger, Bill Hosack, and Al Simdorn?
>
> As a group their feats have never been mastered by another team of coaches in the state. They, as a group or individually, have led or been a part of 14 HCHS football teams that have appeared in the Class 3A state football championship game—winning the championship in eight of those years. They've taught discipline, respect, hard work, teamwork, and dedication.
>
> Behind it all is the man who stands on the sidelines each Friday night watching the fruits of the coaching staff's labors and the heart and character of the teenagers who are proud enough to call themselves Cyclone football players forever.
>
> Never selfish, Curt is always quick to point to others for the community's football success, especially the coaching staff. In fact when he learned of this recognition event, he wanted to make sure that coaches Hosack, Gallinger, Carstens, and Simdorn will also be recognized. It already had been decided the community would honor Curt and the coaching staff. But for many, they associate Bladt with what has become the tradition of Cyclone Football.

"He's instilled a lot of that Cyclone tradition," said HCS Activities Director Mitch Osborn, one of the organizers of next weekend's event. "He's the glue that holds everything together."

Ask anyone about the Harlan Community School District and one of the first things that comes to mind is the football program. That's the main reason behind next Friday's event, said HCHS Principal Kent Klinkefus.

"People identify with the Harlan Community," said Klinkefus. "That's the big thing about Curt and that football program, as well as many of our other programs. They've given us identity in that people from all over the State of Iowa, as well as neighboring states, associate Harlan Community with excellence. And Curt has certainly been a big part of that. When you give a community that type of tag, it's something you'd better hang onto."

Klinkefus has seen first-hand the impact that a teacher and mentor can have on a student. His son, Rob, now a teacher at St. Mary's High School in Storm Lake and a coach himself, was part of the football tradition. Kent says he knows the importance these outstanding instructors have on a student's life.

"We feel like there are people on our staff who have, over the years, made a tremendous impact on students and the community, not to mention the success they've had in a program," Klinkefus said. "When you combine all of that, the number of people that they've touched, and the fact that our community has taken a great deal of pride in that program and the success that it has had...I think it's deserving of some recognition. When you look at the record books and what Curt Bladt has been associated with here in Harlan, it speaks for itself."

John Murtaugh is currently a social studies teacher in Wayne, Neb., and is also the head wrestling and head football coach. He credits Curt and the entire coaching staff for much of his decision to continue in education and coaching.

"I think I can speak for our entire class that it was a great experience playing under Coach Bladt and the other coaches," said Murtaugh, a 1979 graduate who played middle linebacker for the 10-1 Cyclones. "We all have great respect for them. They were the reason, through their actions, that I continued on into education."

Murtaugh says he takes much of what he learned here to the classroom and playing field in Wayne. There are "so many things that I've tried to instill in the program here—discipline, commitment, dedication, and Curt had exceptional motivational techniques."

Michael Burger plans to come next week if he can. Arguably one of the most recognized football players to wear a Cyclone uniform, he's a 1994 graduate who played tight end, safety, and in the backfield for the Cyclones who won the state championship that year. He went on to play fullback at the University of Iowa.

Currently teaching seventh-grade math at Mission Middle School in Bellevue, Neb., Burger also is offensive coordinator for the Bellevue East High School football team. He, like Murtaugh, takes much of what he learned here to his classroom and to the football field. When he went off to college, Bladt kept in close contact.

"My sophomore year in high school he stuck me in at tight end, and from then on it grew into not only a player-coach relationship, but a great friendship," said Burger. "(Curt) kept in contact with me in college, throughout the ups and downs. It was nice to always have a backbone like that."

Burger said after his years at Harlan Community, he knew he wanted to work with children and be their mentor as the HCHS coaching staff had been to him.

"I thought, how could I make a big difference in kids' lives, and education was

Michael Burger

where I had to go," Burger said. "Coaching just naturally came along. That's how much input (the HCHS coaches) had."

Burger said he'll never forget winning a state championship.

"After we won state, (Curt) just looked at me and I could see it in his eyes. We shook hands and hugged. It was a great moment, something I'll never forget."

Bryan Schwartz is a senior linebacker and co-captain on this year's Harlan Community Cyclone football team. He says he and his teammates know all about Cyclone tradition, and the coaches that have made it happen. He loves being a Cyclone.

"Ever since we were little, my friends and I every Friday night knew what was going to happen—we were going to the football game," Schwartz said. "Then we'd go home and play in the yard, and pretend we were playing for Harlan and playing the other teams. Some kids talk about wanting to grow up and being an NFL player, but when you're in Harlan, you want to play for Harlan. You looked up to those guys."

Schwartz said the chemistry of the coaching staff is a huge factor in the success of the team. He says the players have nothing but respect for the coaches.

"It's great that these guys can be together for as long as they have," Schwartz said. "They work so well together. It's a real advantage, and they know their stuff. They have a great pool of knowledge. We'll always be ready for a game."

The players look to Coach Bladt as a mentor.

"Mr. Bladt always stresses school and academics," said Schwartz. "If we go out as a group, he reminds us of our 'pleases' and 'thank you's.' He's just like a father figure to everyone on the team."

Friday Night Tape-Viewing Sessions

After each game, including the ones played on the road, the entire coaching staff looks at the video of the game and the game played that night by the following week's opponent. "I can never get to sleep the night of a game," Curt explains. "I'm up until 3, 4, 5 a.m. anyway. I might as well be watching tape."

The all-nighter takes place in the Bladts' basement—complete with chili, sandwiches, and/or nachos prepared by…you guessed it—Curt's wife, Jill.

> *"I've had smarter people around me all my life,*
> *but I haven't run into one yet that can outwork me.*
> *And if they can't outwork you,*
> *then smarts aren't going to do them much good.*
> *That's just the way it is.*
> *And if you believe that and live by that,*
> *you'd be surprised at how much fun you can have.'*
> **—Woody Hayes**

Consistency of Plays

The coaching staff is also consistent with their offensive and defensive formations and plays. Many high school football programs go through offensive and defensive schemes faster than Toad Brodersen used to go through twelve packs of Twinkies. Harlan may change which part of the offensive play collection gets emphasized—as shown by the 2003 team, which had Joel Osborn throwing the ball all over the place; the 2004 team, which featured the power running of Kevin Kruse; and the 2005 team, which played option football.

In addition, many of the plays run by the seventh grade are the same ones run by the varsity. This has a profound impact on the younger kids as they sit in the stands watching their heroes.

Building Block #3: Community and Parental Support

As Curt has repeatedly said, "One person doesn't do this. With as many play-off games as we have, with all the overnight stays and distance traveled, the parents spend a lot and time and money supporting their kids. And people in the community anonymously and happily contribute money so we can have better transportation, better food, and better hotels."

Game Night

In his book, *Bernie Saggau and the Iowa Boys,* Chuck Offenburger writes, "One other thing has helped 'sell' Harlan football in the Bladt era. Home games have become a wonderful spectacle, a total showcase of the high school and community experience. The Harlan High band is as good as the football team—they even march and play the opposing school's fight song in their pre-game performance—and a color guard from the local American Legion post unfurls a huge American flag before the National Anthem is played. Crowds of 3,000 or more are not unusual. The home fans rarely leave unhappy. 'It's a real show,' Bladt said, 'a big show, a whole lot of fun for people.'"

Harlan Community High School Band

Harlan Community Athletic Booster Club

The Harlan Community Athletic Booster Club was started in the early 1990s by a group of individuals who saw the need to supplement the school's athletic program budget. The Booster Club has grown in both members and dollars provided to the school over the years. In 2006, the Booster Club had 262 members—its highest number ever—and gave $57,000 to the school.

The Booster Club earns money at its concession stand at the home football games, track meets, and soccer matches. Additional fundraisers are an annual golf tournament, membership drive, and junior high basketball tournament.

The club has been able to help with three major projects in 2005–2006: the resurfacing of the all-weather track at Merrill Field, new scoreboards, and dugouts at J.J. Jensen softball/baseball complex. Because of its success, the Harlan Community Athletic Booster Club serves as a model for many other schools seeking to start their own clubs.

Long-Time Cyclone Boosters

Ruth and Roy Baron have been attending Cyclone games since 1930. They attended Harlan's first state championship game in 1972 in Iowa City with my parents, Mary Lou and Bob Booth.

Here's what Ruth has to say about Curt:

> "One year Coach Bladt held a class for women to help us understand football. He taught us about the game. We also saw the enthusiasm he had for the football. He said he would go home and re-run plays that excited him.
>
> Coach Bladt has instilled in his players the work ethic it takes to play as a team. Our players look forward to making the trip to the Dome. Coach Bladt deserves all the awards that he has received. Coach Bladt, thank you for your years in Harlan. You have done us proud."

Curt remembers a time when he was to show the previous week's game film at the Harlan Country Club. The weather was horrible, so only two people showed up—Ruth and Roy Baron. The daring duo proceeded to sit down with Curt and watch the film as the storm howled outside.

Building Block #4: Coaching Cooperation

It's not just the football coaches at Harlan who cooperate. It's all the coaches. They encourage the kids to play more than one sport and take part in various school activities.

The Cyclone Slam

The epitome of Cyclone coaching cooperation occurred in the years 2003–2004. The Harlan boys won the 3A track and field championship in the spring of 2003, the baseball title in the summer of 2003, the football championship in the fall of 2003, and the basketball title in the spring of 2004. This was the first time in Iowa history that a school held the most recent titles in those four sports.

The baseball, football, and basketball teams won a total of fifty-seven games in a row! The odds of that happening by chance are 1 in 144,115,188,000,000,000! In case your checkbook balance has never gotten that high, that big number is over 144 quadrillion.

State Title Town

Harlan has won eleven state football titles—more than any Iowa school in any class. And as the television infomercial announcer would say, "Wait, there's more!" The Cyclone girls have won state championships in the following sports:

- golf in 1993 and 1995 under coach Dave Lansing
- cross country in 2005 under coach Doug Renkly

In addition to the eleven football titles, the Cyclone boys have won state championships in the following sports:

- basketball in 2004 and 2006 under coach Mitch Osborn
- wrestling in 1967 under coach Dave Trotter
- baseball in 1996 and 2003 under coach Steve Daeges
- track and field in 1954 and 2003 under coaches Swede Johnson and Ken Carstens

A New Multi-Sport Winning Streak

In the 2005–2006 school year, the Harlan Community's boys and girls won three state championships, were runners-up in two sports, and made it to the state tournaments in three sports. As a result, HCHS won its first mid-school division all-around prep athletic program award.

As of September 25, 2006, Harlan's football, basketball, and baseball teams haven't lost to a Hawkeye Ten Conference opponent in over a year of regular and post-season games. The football team is 8 and 0. The basketball team is 20 and 0, and the baseball team is 23 and 0—making a total of 51 games in a row!

Building Block # 5: Tough Kids

In many ways, the Cyclone players are reflections of their coaches—tough kids who grew up on farms or in small towns.

In each high school grade, 20–25 boys (about one out of three) are on the football team. Curt says, "We get a lot of kids out, but we haven't had many Division I football players. We have a lot of Division II players though. We just have a lot of very good football players."

Here are the Cyclones who have earned Division I football scholarships:

- Steve Jacobsen, a 1968 graduate—Iowa State
- Todd Nelson, a 1971 graduate—Iowa State
- Alan Patton, a 1984 graduate—Iowa State
- Mike O'Brien, a 1985 graduate—Iowa State
- Michael Burger, a 1994 graduate—Iowa

Steve Jacobsen went on to play for the San Francisco 49ers. In addition, only 1984 graduate Todd Koos has been inducted into the Iowa High School Football Hall of Fame. His induction took place on November 17, 2006, at the UNI Dome.

The fact that so few players have moved on to Division I football or are in the Hall of Fame is a strong sign that:

1.   the Cyclone teams are extremely well coached;
2.   the players maximize their talents;
3.   Harlan always has a lot of tough kids who love to play football.

> *"Football isn't a contact sport.*
> *It's a collision sport.*
> *Dancing is a contact sport."*
> **—Duffy Daugherty**

CoachBladt.com website posting
Name: Brody Deren
City, State: San Diego, CA
Date: 12/19/2004

Coach-
There is only a handful of men in a boy's life that can have a lasting impact on them in their journey to manhood. It must be warming to know that you have been one of those men to so many, Coach. Lessons learned on that practice field in Harlan, Iowa have made men out of boys who now are spread out throughout the world…some doctors, some lawyers, some pilots, some coaches aspiring to be as successful as their mentor.

It's easy to see by reading this board that so many others have been as influenced by you as I have in my life. You are a remarkably tough individual, but as compassionate as Mother Teresa. That's why you see all these people writing on this board…you are so respected because they know how much you genuinely care about your students and players. I know you will fight through this setback like you've fought through every other challenge you've faced.

I remember you saying you never know what you're made of until you face a little adversity. I've always taken that to heart…

Anyway Coach, I am praying for you and wishing you well. Hello to all of the Bladt family!

Forever a Cyclone,
Brody

Maybe there haven't been many Harlan Community High School Cyclones who have gone on to play Division I football. But many of them have gone on to do something much more important—teach and coach thousands of other kids.

CoachBladt.com website posting
Name: David Schmitz class '84, Josh, and Justin
City, State: Urbandale, Iowa
Date: 12/15/2004

Bo Schembechler, Michigan coach, was asked one time what kind of team he would have that year. He said, "Ask me that question in 15 years." Confused, the guy asked, "Why?" Bo stated, "I will know what kind of fathers my players have become, what kind of lives they are leading, and what kind of people they have become."

It's apparent by all the outpouring of emails from former players and comments from everyone that you have had some great teams, and you have had tremendous impact on the lives of many others. You have taught me when I was there that, when a team outgrows individual performance and learns team confidence, excellence becomes a reality.

Coaching at DM Lincoln and WDM Valley and now with my own son's teams, I have tried to preach this. You and the coaching staff have been an incredible force in the development of strong character. Coaches like you hold an incredible amount of power over the lives of your players, and you have exercised it so wisely. Victory in the larger sense arises out of deep seated respect for the coaches, teammates, opponents and, most of all, themselves.

Building Block #6: Confidence

The Cyclones don't think they might win. They don't hope to win. They know they will win. They have contagious confidence, and it begins with the coaches.

Football official Tom Fuller tells this great story about the 2003 3A Championship game. "Harlan scored the first 17 points of the game against Mt. Vernon. The game looked like it was going to be a runaway. Then Mt. Vernon comes back and scores the next 28 points in a row. Harlan scores a touchdown, and Mt. Vernon answers with a TD of its own with about five minutes left in the game. Before the kickoff, Curt gets his team together, looks them in the eye and says, 'We're going to get this kickoff and score. Then we're going to stop them, get the ball, and score again!'"

Harlan did get the ball and scored on an 80-yard touchdown pass from Joel Osborn to Greg Applegate. The Cyclones did stop Mt. Vernon and forced a quick punt. Then lightning stuck twice as Osborn and Applegate connected on a 67-yard bomb, and Harlan won the game 38 to 35.

> *"Confidence is contagious.*
> *So is lack of confidence."*
> **—Vince Lombardi**

Referee Randy York notices that the Harlan players aren't cocky, just confident. When his officiating crew meets with both teams at midfield before the game, there is no trash-talking or stare-downs. Nonverbally, Harlan communicates to the opposing players that, "We have a good team, and in a couple of minutes we're going to show you why."

CoachBladt.com website posting
Name: Brent Jensen
City, State: Scottsdale, AZ
Date: 01/04/2005

Sitting in (then Assistant) Coach Bladt's freshman science class in 1972, he had some thoughts about the upcoming game against Cherokee in the first-ever Iowa H.S. football playoffs. He grinned, and said, "They're bigger than we are, faster than we are, and probably smarter than we are…but we're gonna win!"

Keep beating the odds Coach!

The Cyclone confidence level was in full force in a playoff game with Denison at the Monarch's home field. The Cyclones needed a field goal to win the game in overtime. Harlan's field goal kicker, Billy Cundiff, walked past Curt during a time-out just before he was going to attempt the game-winning boot. He slapped Curt on the back and said, "Don't worry, coach. This one's in." It was, too. Harlan won the game 10-7.

Billy and Steve Jacobsen were the only Harlan graduates to play in the NFL. While playing for the Dallas Cowboys against the New York Giants, Billy tied the all-time NFL record for field goals in a single game with seven.

Dave Wiebers, Denison's head coach, says that Harlan's confidence coming into games affects some opponents. "Harlan knows they're not going to get beat. After a while, some teams start to believe it too."

"Before you can win,
you have to believe you are worthy."
—Mike Ditka

In the next section, you will meet all the players who have been coached by Curt Bladt. As you view their photos and read their names, think about how all the attributes gained wearing a Cyclone uniform have positively affected their own lives and the lives of the people they've touched. Like a stone landing in smooth water and producing ripples, each of the Cyclone players has made the entire pond a better place to be.

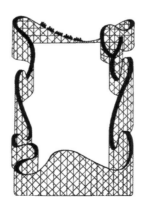

I n 1896, Ed White, Harlan's first football coach, described what it took to be a Harlan football player:

"The boy should have a sturdy body, will and also be of good physical health. The game is not to be played for the weak at heart, for other activities could be found for them."

Mr. White would be proud of the players you will meet in this section. They are representative of the 83,000 Iowa high school boys who compete in ten sports and the 60,000 high school girls who compete in nine sports each year. An amazing 65% of Iowa high school boys participate in three or more school activities. Four out of five Iowa boys play at least one sport.

This section of the book is divided into five chapters—the 1960s, the 1970s, the 1980s, the 1990s, and the 2000s. Starting with Coach Bladt's first year as an assistant in 1968 and proceeding all the way through the 2005 football season, you will read Curt's memories of the year, see the games scores, and meet the players who have contributed to Coach Bladt's 91% winning percentage. The action photos and their captions and the team photos were taken from the Harlan Community High School yearbook, the *Harpoon*. The photos vary greatly in quality.

As an added bonus, in the 1960s chapter, you will revisit Harlan's second undefeated team—the 1961 squad coached by Harold "Swede" Johnson.

At the end of each chapter, you will meet a Player from the Decade. These players are not meant to be the best of the decade. They're included to tell you what it was like playing for Coach Bladt and how the lessons they learned back then have enhanced their lives right now.

The Decade in Review

The 1960s started with a bang as the 1960 Cyclones won the Midwest Conference only to lose their bid for an undefeated season with a loss to Atlantic in the second to the last game of the year. The 1961 team again won the conference and this time defeated Atlantic 44-14 to cap a perfect year.

In 1963, Swede Johnson hung up his whistle and turned the program over to Bob Simpson, who coached through the 1966 season.

Swede Johnson   *Bob Simpson*

In 1967, three important events occurred:

1. With school consolidation, the number of high school students almost doubled.
2. Terry Eagen became the Cyclone's 25th head coach. During his seven-year tenure, Harlan Community's record was 56 wins, 9 losses, and 1 tie—a healthy winning percentage of 86%.
3. Curt and Jill Bladt moved to town.

Chapter: 8
The 1960s

As you discovered in Chapter 4, Harlan's first undefeated team was in 1906. Fifty-five years went by before another Cyclone crew would duplicate that feat. Even though Audubon was selected by the league's coaches to win the Midwest Conference in 1961, the expectations were high for Harlan High School.

The following article from the August 29, 1961, edition of the *Harlan News-Advertiser* previewed the team:

Weight Big Deficit as Cyclones Ready for '61 Grid Season
Ten Vets Back; Backfield Shows Much Potential

Weight will be the biggest deficit on the Cyclone football ledger this season according to head coach Harold "Swede" Johnson. Other things written in red will be lack of depth and inexperience for the returning Harlan crew.

"We're green, real green," Johnson says, "but the possibilities are definitely there. It's just way too early to tell just what we'll do this season, but we'll have a respectable ball club."

Ten lettermen returned for drill from last year's Midwest conference championship crew. Harlan posted a 7-1-1 overall mark in last year's action with a 6-0-1 conference record.

Included on the list of returning vets are seniors Dennis Stamp, Tom Paulson, Steve Allen, Gary Klindt, Randy Conrad, Ken Hoogensen, and Lynn Caldwell. Junior letter winners are Al Burchett, Glenn Petersen, and Bryce Hansen.

The weight deficit is evident when you consider that Al Burchett, last year a tackle, is the only one in the roster that weighs close to 200 pounds.

Harlan's speed looks good to Johnson at this early date—"Better than last year's," he said. In the Cyclone backfield, hopes rest with Conrad, Bryce Hansen, Judd Freeman, a transfer from Ames, Keith Svendsen, a senior transfer from Irwin, and Lynn Caldwell.

Johnson said he plans to do a little shuffling with Ken Hoogensen, moving the 170-pound senior from halfback to a guard slot—at least until the line picks up a little more experience.

Svendsen, who called the plays for the Irwin Hawkeyes last season, has made a good showing to date with the Midwest Conference squad. "Svendsen may be an asset in the passing department," Johnson said.

The Cyclones will run their offense mostly from the wing-T, a formation that has clicked for them in the past. Harlan coaches intend to do a little work with the belly series offense also.

Harlan got a good turn-out from the freshman class, with 20 reporting so far. All told, Johnson said the Cyclones will probably have 50–55 candidates as the season starts.

1961 Team

Front row (left to right): R. James; D. Sorensen; D. Conrad; T. Boeck; R. Bramer; R. Rickers; S. Neilsen; J. Klindt; B. McCoy; T. Hansen, Manager; S. Jacobsen, Mascot. **Second row:** H. Johnson, Head Coach; G. Johannsen; R. Burchett; K. Svendsen; D. Stamp; B. Hansen; P. Hansen; T. Paulsen; A. Burchett; S. Allen; B. Hoogensen; D. Calvert, Asst. Coach. **Third row:** N. Booth; G. Pedersen; S. Mores; J. Myrtue; R. Conrad; C. Thummel; K. Hoogensen; G. Klindt; J. Freeman; B. Baurle

The following article from the November 23, 1961 *Harlan Tribune* recapped the undefeated season of 1961:

Harlan Passing Gains Highest of State Teams

The Harlan Cyclones, as they rolled to their first undefeated football season since 1906 and their fourth Midwest conference championship in five years, led Iowa high school Class I football teams in yardage gained by passing.

The Cyclones, quarterbacked by a transfer from Irwin, netted 1,111 yards via the aerial route in 49 completions. Keith Svendsen, 170-pound senior, launched 42 of these passes during the 9-game circuit.

Svendsen, listed by head coach Harold "Swede" Johnson as "perhaps the best thrower we've ever had here" attempted 81 throws for a healthy 51.8 percentage. His tosses accounted for 983 yards and 13 touchdowns.

Chief receivers this season were Ken Hoogensen (caught 21 for 534 yards) Dennis Stamp (14 for 242), and Tom Paulsen (7 for 194).

1961 Scores (9-0)

Harlan 27	Red Oak 6
Harlan 13	Audubon 12
Harlan 7	Carroll 0
Harlan 46	Sac City 24
Harlan 24	Jefferson 0
Harlan 27	Ida Grove 6
Harlan 31	Lake City 20
Harlan 44	Atlantic 14
Harlan 18	Denison 6

*1961 Coaches—Swede Johnson, Gene Gettys,
and Ted Williams*

The 1968 and 1969 Seasons

Chapter 2 ended with Head Coach Terry Eagen asking Curt to join his staff for the 1968 season. Curt said "Yes" to Terry, and the gridiron gods nodded "Yes" to Curt.

As there were no football programs in their previous high schools, it took a while for the players from the parochial schools to learn to play football. In an article by the *World-Herald's* Stan Bowker that appeared in the September 11, 1967, edition of the *Harlan News-Advertiser*, Terry Eagen had this explanation:

> We would be pretty weak if a kid who had never played football before was first-team material right away. But these new kids are going through a learning process and we feel there are several who will be helpful to our program.
>
> We have been especially happy with the attitude of these new kids. Most of them realize that, having not played football before, they are at a big disadvantage. But they are giving their all and we can't ask anything more.

The title of Stan Bowker's article was "Consolidation Makes the Rich Get Richer." In the article he raised the question, "Have the Cyclones outgrown the Midwest Conference?" The rich did get richer, and the Cyclones did outgrow the Midwest Conference.

1968

Curt's Comments

"In our 6-0 loss at Denison's old field, our spotter had to climb to the top of their very small press box. The trip was so treacherous he didn't even come down at halftime. We had a sure touchdown going that would have tied the game, but our player who caught a pass tripped and fell on his own."

1968 Scores (6-3)

Harlan 14	Atlantic 41
Harlan 34	Audubon 26
Harlan 41	Carroll 7
Harlan 0	Denison 6
Harlan 14	Jefferson 20
Harlan 14	Lake City 12
Harlan 32	Perry 0
Harlan 26	Red Oak 0
Harlan 26	Sac City 13

Roger Boeck receives a pass from quarterback Phil Larsen

1968 Team

Front row (left to right): Coach Gettys, S. Klitgaard, D. Leschen, R. Jensen, D. McDermott, R. Rasmussen, B. Rust, B. Larsen, J. Ohlinger, G. Block, M. Findlay, C. Petersen, Coach Trotter. **Second row:** Coach Bladt, R. Bruck, P. Larsen, R. Boeck, R. Doran, J. Miles, B. Arkfelt, T. Heileson, V. Petersen, G. Lansman, T. Nelson, R. Pash, Coach Eagen. **Third row:** W. Sorensen, R. Tallman, T. Ouren, V. Nelsen, M. Gearhart, D. Jans, J. Chipman, D. Goede, T. Plumb, G. Nelson, S. Adams, R. Hansen. **Fourth row:** J. Nelsen, G. Findlay, R. Richards, M. Donlin, J. Massey, L. Stessman, K. Kaufman, M. Markham, R. Sondergaard, R. Krakau, C. Conrad, T. Oppold. **Back row:** F. Norgaard, C. Findlay, S. Parr, J. Schechinger, B. Weiss, T. Morris, A. Jensen, D. Jacobs, R. Musich, T. Gettys. **Not pictured:** B. Wingert, B. Schmitz, P. Stracke.

1969

Curt's Comments

"We tried an experiment to have the varsity assistant coaches scout the next week's opponent. I went to Perry to scout them. On the same night, we lost to Red Oak. They had a big, tough nose tackle who consistently beat our offensive line guys. I wasn't there to help us figure out how to stop him. Our scouting experiment lasted exactly one week."

1969 Scores (7-3)

Harlan 28	Atlantic 34
Harlan 35	Audubon 8
Harlan 21	Carroll 6
Harlan 35	Denison 28
Harlan 19	Jefferson 25
Harlan 21	Lake City 7
Harlan 33	Perry 14
Harlan 15	Red Oak 21
Harlan 48	Sac City 16
Harlan 25	Shenandoah 20

Don Goede splits the uprights for one of his
twenty PATs made during the season

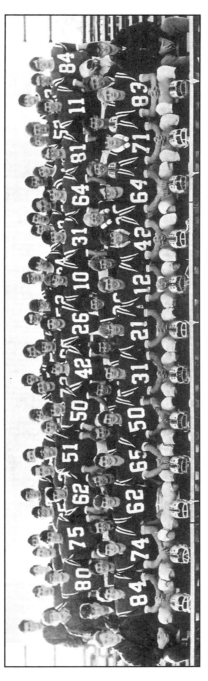

1969 Team

Front row (left to right): Coach Bladt, Tom Gettys, Vern Helson, Don Goede, Joe Lauterbach, Tom Ouren, Randy Pash, Steve Klitgaard, Phil Larsen, Todd Nelson, Dan Leuchen, Don Jans, Gary Lansman, Head Coach Terry Eagen. **Second row:** Coach Gettys, Mike Gearhart, Bob Rust, Keith Kaufman, Cole Findlay, John Olinger, Bruce Guyett, Greg Findlay, Steve Adams, Craig Petersen, Dan Jacobs, Mark Findlay, Coach O'Riley. **Third row:** Sandy Booth, Mark Petersen, Terry Morris, Erwin Erickson, Jim Chipman, Craig Martin, Gary Coats, Randy Richards, Roger Jacobsen, Larry Petersen, Ron McCord, Jeff Branstetter, Rick Tallman, Dan Arkfeld. **Fourth row:** Bill Sorensen, Bob Norgaard, Todd Plumb, Richard Olinger, Wade Jensen, Tim Hodapp, Bob Bogler, Ron Haas, Steve Daeges, Dwayne Hemminger, Mark Markham, Larry Rowan, Jim Kruse, Mike Sorensen, Greg Roecker. **Back row:** Jeff Nelson, Bob Swapiszeski, Rick Adams, Ken Rosman, Jim Weiss, Bob Schneider, Paul Ladd, Fred Norgard, Paul Kruse, Mike Donlin, Galen Nelson, Charles Conrad, John Fuhs.

PLAYER FROM THE DECADE
BOB JENSEN

Bob Jensen graduated from Harlan Community High School in 1969. During his senior year, his head coach was Terry Eagen, and his position coach was Curt Bladt—in his first year as offensive line coach. From a time span of thirty-eight years, Bob remembers, "Playing for Curt was the most fun I've ever had playing football. He would tell a joke at just the right time, could find humor in any situation, and has the greatest laugh of anyone I know. Of course, winning was fun, too. Once you play for Curt, you never forget him."

Bob Jensen in 1969

Bob played football at UNI (State College of Iowa at the time) for one year before an injury ended his career. He has been coaching football at Mt. Pleasant High School for thirty-three years—the last seventeen as head coach.

In the 1990s, when most schools were reluctant to play Harlan, Bob and Curt played four games against each other. Bob sagely says, "Why wouldn't you want to play the best to see what you've got?"

Bob adds, "Some coaches who don't know Curt are intimidated by him. But to know him is to love him. He would never run up the score on another team unless they said or did something that warranted it."

Bob learned three valuable lessons from Curt that he uses as a head coach:

1. **Toughness beats talent.** On the path to an Iowa-best eleven state Class 3A football championships since 1972, Harlan occasionally had the most talent. They always had the most toughness.

2. **Your classroom work is important.** Football is important. Doing well in the classroom is more important. If a Cyclone player's grades aren't up to snuff, they receive a friendly reminder from the coaching staff.

3. **Coach knows best.** There's not a lot of wiggle room with Curt Bladt or Bob Jensen. The players need to trust their coaches and be coachable. Bob remembers a "coach knows

Football and wrestling team physician, Dr. Joe Spearling, wearing his trademark bow tie

best" situation during a district wrestling tournament when Curt was an assistant coach. "I was wrestling against a guy from Tee Jay. I had a badly split lip that Doc Spearing had just stitched up. The Tee Jay guy was cross-facing me and purposely aggravating the injury for no good reason.

"I looked over at Coach Bladt, and he's giving me a 'bite him' signal. I couldn't believe what I was seeing, but I knew that coach knows best. So I bit him. At the end of the period, the guy got up, whacked me on the back of the head and was quickly disqualified. I won the match!"

Mark Kohorst, Iowa State University head coach Dan McCarney,
Curt Bladt (holding his National High School Football Coach of the Year
trophy), and Bob Jensen

Decade Conclusion

There were fifty-five years between Harlan's first undefeated team in 1906 and the second one in 1961. There were only ten years between the second one and the third one in 1971. The pace was picking up.

The 1970s were a time of change in many ways. One of the changes was the beginning of an Iowa state playoff system in 1972. The playoffs marked a change in the ultimate goal for a football team. Before then, the goal was to be undefeated. After that date, the ultimate goal was to win a state championship. As the decade changed, Harlan was poised to do just that.

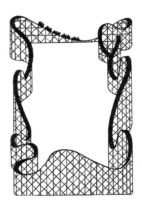

Chapter: 9
The 1970s

The Decade in Review: It's too bad there wasn't a state championship in 1971. The Cyclones were undefeated and had one of their most talented teams of all time. In 1972, considering what has happened since then, it's fitting that the Cyclones won the first Iowa 3A championship by beating Cedar Rapids Regis at Kinnick Stadium in Iowa City 14 to 12.

In 1974, Terry Eagen moved on to Marshalltown and Ken Papp was selected as Harlan's head coach. Ken's record was a solid 25 wins and 11 losses with no playoff appearances.

Curtis Melvin Bladt became Harlan's 27th head football coach in 1978. Even though the Cyclones lost their starting quarterback early in Curt's first season, Harlan finished with a 10 and 1 record. In the quarterfinal playoff game, Harlan Community bamboozled the belligerent, big-city boys from Urbandale on their home field 23 to 22. In the semifinals, the Cyclones lost 6-0 to Emmetsburg on a cold and windy day in Harlan.

Terry Eagen holding the 1972 state championship trophy

Ken Papp

81

1970

Curt's Comments

"In 1969, we had a game at Jefferson where both teams were part of an experiment to use half-inch spikes instead of the traditional three-quarter-inch spikes. It was a rainy night. We wore our half-inch spikes, but because of a 'communication mix-up,' Jefferson wore the three-quarter-inch ones. We were slipping and sliding all night long and lost 25-19. We remembered the 'mix-up' in 1970 and beat them 53-0."

1970 Scores (8-1)

Harlan 49	Audubon 0
Harlan 66	Carroll 0
Harlan 62	Denison 0
Harlan 53	Jefferson 0
Harlan 7	Lake City 19
Harlan 62	CB Lewis Central 6
Harlan 55	Perry 8
Harlan 49	Red Oak 0
Harlan 41	Sac City 14

Todd Nelson, first team all-state back,
breaks for a touchdown. Todd broke the school
rushing record for a season with 1,820 yards
—an average of 304 yards per game

1970 Team

Front row (*left to right*): *Bob Feser, Tom Gettys, Vern Nelson, Ron McCord, Jim Chipman, Joe Lauterbach, Farrell Zimmerman, Galen Nelson, Roger Jacobsen, Todd Nelson, Steve Klitgaard, Jeff Branstetter.* **Second row:** *Lee Barnett, Todd Plumb, Jan Jacobs, Craig Petersen, Cole Findlay, Bob Bogler, Mark Markham, Bruce Guyett, Mark Peterson, Steve Daeges, Steve Adams, Bob Norguard.* **Third row:** *Doug Deskin, Tim Conrad, Mike Sorensen, Ervin Erickson, Paul Ladd, Richard Ohlinger, Terry Morris, Robin Jacobsen, Randy Richards, Larry Petersen, Craig Noble, Dan D'Arcy.* **Fourth row:** *Ted Johnson, Kim Conrad, Greg Roecker, Ralph Doran, Ric Adams, Bob Schneider, Steve Oswald, Jeff Allen, Todd Petersen, John Kellen, Pat Arkfeld, Redge Pash, Sid Booth.* **Fifth row:** *Dennis Conrad, Don Beiderman, Jim Dodd, Jeff Kelly, Ken Rosman, Ric Sorensen, Mike Croghan, Dave Jensen, Jim Kruse, John Fuhs, Ric Tallman.* **Back row:** *Mike Leuschen, Jim Bruck, Bruce Poldberg, Joe Reinig, Curt Stephany, Jerry Falkena, Les Finken, Jeff Nelson, Paul Kruse, Roger Rust.* ***Coaches:*** *Mr. Gettys, Mr. O'Riley, Mr. Bladt, Mr. Eagen*

1971

Curt's Comments

"I will never forget our long trip to Knoxville that year. We rented a big Scene-a-Cruiser bus because of the three-hour ride. As we headed south on 59 toward I-80, I looked over the bus driver's shoulder, and this guy's doing eighty-five. We got to the game forty-five minutes earlier than planned.

"In the first three plays of the game, they lose their quarterback, tailback, and second team tailback. We scored all seven times we had the ball and led 49-0 at halftime. Their coach came up to me during the break and said, 'Please, call off the dogs.' We did and only won by 56-0."

1971 Scores (9-0, H-8, 1st)

Harlan 20	Atlantic 14
Harlan 49	Glenwood 13
Harlan 56	Knoxville 0
Harlan 35	CB Lewis Central 0
Harlan 56	Shenandoah 6
Harlan 49	Red Oak 7
Harlan 14	Carroll Kuemper 10
Harlan 42	Clarinda 6
Harlan 39	Creston 12

*Steve Daeges and Mark Petersen deflect a
Shenandoah pass*

1971 Team

Front row (left to right): *Mr. Gettys, Bob Schneider, Wade Jensen, Steve Daeges, Lee Ray Barnett, Bob Bogler, Kim Conrad, Bob Norgaard, Bruce Guyett, Tim Hodapp, Mark Petersen, Steve Oswald, Mr. O'Riley.* **Second row:** *Mr. Bladt, Roger Jacobsen, Jeff Branstetter, Doug Deskin, Joe Lauterbach, Dick Ohlinger, Dennis Petersen, Ron McCord, Farrell Zimmerman, Tim Conrad, Mike Larsen, Bob Feser, Mr. Eagen.* **Third row:** *Rick Adams, Jim Kruse, Paul Ladd, Lyle Lefeber, Roger Rust, Sid Booth, Greg Roecker, John Fuhs, Robin Jacobsen.* **Fourth row:** *Mark Sorensen, Craig Graeve, Todd Roecker, Ralph Doran, Dan D'Arcy, Brian Klindt, Ted Johnson, Todd Petersen, Craig Noble, Pat Arkfeld.* **Fifth row:** *Wayne Petersen, Rick Finken, Craig Oswald, Terry Barton, Tom Powers, Steve Goeser, Jeff Jacobsen, Rick Rasmussen, Dave Schneider, Randy Nowatzke.* **Sixth row:** *Jim Bruck, Dennis Conrad, Lee Knudtson, Gary Weihs, Tony Thielen, Mark Harris, Gary Jensen, Mark Conrad.* **Back row:** *Bruce Wigg, Slim Jim Norgaard, Gaige Petersen, Tom Murtaugh, Chuck Doran, John Kaufman*

1972

Curt's Comments

"During the regular season, we were playing at Atlantic in a big rainstorm. It was fourth and seven late in the ballgame. We gave the ball to Mike Larsen, who scored.

"I can still see in my mind the winning score in the championship game against Cedar Rapid Regis at Kinnick Stadium in Iowa City. Our fullback, Mike Larsen, knocked down two defenders, and Tim Conrad followed him into the end zone. That put us up by one. Our spotter, Gene Alvine, was shouting into our headsets, 'Call time-out and go for two!' It was so noisy we didn't hear him. We made the single extra point to go up by two, but they still could have defeated us with a late field goal. Luckily, they didn't, and we had our first state title."

1972 Scores (11-0, H-8, 1st)

Harlan 20	West Des Moines Valley 0
Harlan 13	Atlantic 12
Harlan 14	Red Oak 6
Harlan 28	CB Lewis Central 14
Harlan 48	Shenandoah 0
Harlan 28	Creston 3
Harlan 42	Clarinda 14
Harlan 42	Glenwood 12
Harlan 42	Denison 0
Playoffs	
Harlan 22	Cherokee 14
Harlan 14	CR Regis 12

Craig Noble goes head-over-heels for another Cyclone victory

1972 Team

Front row (left to right): *Craig Noble, Craig Oswald, Brian Klindt, Tim Guyett, Craig Graeve, Jeff Allen, Kim Conrad, Randy Nowatzke, Pat Arkfeld, Dave Schneider, Steve Oswald.* **Second row:** *Robin Jacobsen, Dan D'Arcy, Todd Roecker, Doug Deskin, Farrell Zimmerman, Terry Barton, Rick Rasmussen, Mike Linton, Mark Sorenson, Tony Thielen, Tim Conrad, Mike Larsen.* **Third row:** *Mike Maiwald, Wayne Peterson, Doug Poole, Tom Powers, Gary Jensen, Gary Weihs, Steve Goeser, Jeff Jacobsen, Tom Murtaugh, Mark Conrad, Dennis Conrad, Brian Peterson.* **Fourth row:** *Bob Clark, Phil Langenfeld, Randy Schnack, Paul Sorenson, Denny Peterson, Jim Noble, Dean Nelson, Al Mores, Brent Rasmusen, Mike Doster, Tom Garrison.* **Fifth row:** *Dave Jacobs, Pat Schuery, Rick Christiansen, Kent Morgan, Marc Roecker, Dave Falkena, Mark Thielen, Steve Holzer, Coach Terry Eagen, assistant coaches Curt Bladt, Gene Gettys, and Bill O'Riley, managers Rod Vanderheiden, Curt Wigg.* **Not pictured:** *Randy Laver*

1973

Curt's Comments

"Because of our school size, we were 4A in 1973. Our only loss was to Valley, 14-3. Mike Larsen gained forty yards on his three carries of the game, but had to leave because of an injury. It was our only loss in three years. We played a predominantly 3-A schedule, so that one loss was enough to keep us out of the playoffs."

1973 Scores (8-1, H-8, 1st)

Harlan 3	West Des Moines Valley 14
Harlan 28	Atlantic 0
Harlan 34	Red Oak 14
Harlan 7	CB Lewis Central 6
Harlan 30	Shenandoah 6
Harlan 10	Creston 7
Harlan 16	Clarinda 6
Harlan 35	Glenwood 6
Harlan 50	Denison 6

Bandit Dave Schneider makes a key tackle against Red Oak before Randy Nowatzke (71), Wayne Petersen (65), and Jeff Jacobsen (62) arrive to help

1973 Team

Front row (left to right): *manager Curt Wigg, Marc Roecker, Al Mores, Brian Peterson, Wayne Petersen, Jeff Jacobsen, Tim Guyett, Craig Graeve, Dave Schneider, Craig Oswald, Brian Klindt, Randy Nowatzke, Bob Clark, Gary Jensen, manager Rick Jacobsen.* **Second row:** *manager Larry Arentson, Mark Martin, Todd Roecker, Tony Thielen, Mark Sorenson, Terry Barton, Rick Rasmussen, Mike Linton, Tom Garrison, Steve Goeser, Mike Larson, Jim Noble, Denny Peterson, trainer Lindsey Vanderheiden.* **Third row:** *assistant coach Gene Alvine, assistant coach Curt Bladt, Larry Kenkel, Pat Schwery, Rick Christiansen, Randy Schnack, Brent Rasmussen, Mark Thielen, Mike Doster, Dean Nelson, Tom Murtaugh, Randy Laver, Doug Poole, Brad Norgaard, Phil Langenfeld, Dave Jacobs, Jeff Boltinghouse, Dan Frazier, head coach Terry Eagen, and assistant coach Gene Gettys.* **Back row:** *Andy Schwery, Bob Blum, Lee Schechinger, Greg Ouren, Charlie Leban, Craig Hodapp, Bill Heese, Garry Patten, Jeff Zimmer, Gary Jacobs, Rick Brown, Tom Leinen, Rick Graeve, Steve Mueller, Larry Wendt, Brian Kelley, Bob Klein, Shawn Byrnes, Ron Dotzler, Kevin Kaufman, Dan Smith, Mike Johnson, Kevin Moore, Mike Christensen*

1974

Curt's Comments

"This was Ken Papp's first year as head coach. We were ahead of the Valley boys 9-7 at halftime, but couldn't sustain our momentum and lost 26-9. That kind of set the tone for our 5-4 year."

1974 Scores (5-4, H-8, 3rd)

Harlan 9	West Des Moines Valley 26
Harlan 19	Glenwood 6
Harlan 13	Atlantic 26
Harlan 29	Red Oak 0
Harlan 12	CB Lewis Central 0
Harlan 17	Shenandoah 6
Harlan 9	Creston 6
Harlan 17	Clarinda 20
Harlan 7	Decorah 17

Getting to the outside is not always good,
as Shawn Byrnes is about to find out

1974 Team

Front row (left to right): Al Mores, Phil Langenfeld, Rick Christiansen, Jim Noble, Marc Roecker, Mike Linton, Denny Petersen, Brian Petersen, Mark Thielen, Dean Nelson, Tom Garrison. **Second row:** manager Larry Arentson, Bob Klein, Shawn Byrnes, Jim Buman, Pat Schwery, Mark Martin, Dave Shelton, Ron Dotzler, Tom Leinen, Brent Rasmussen, Brad Norgaard, manager Curt Wigg. **Third row:** manager Lindsey Vanderheiden, Larry Kenkel, Kevin Moore, Lee Schechinger, Steve Mueller, Rick Brown, Charlie Lehan, Rick Graeve, Kevin Krohn, Dein Thielen, Brian Kelley, Ross Jacobsen, manager Emory Arentson. **Fourth row:** assistant coach Gene Gettys, Dan Frazier, Bob Blum, Terry Rauterkus, Andy Schwery, Greg Ouren, Kevin Kaufman, Mike Weis, David Ohlinger, Scott Christensen, Scott Ross, Brian Hurd. **Fifth row:** assistant coach Gene Alvine, Jeff Weihs, Gary Schneider, Ron Doran, Dale Williamson, Jamie Adams, Sam Allen, Mark Kaufman, Phil Zimmerman, Jay Smith, Paul Dotzler, Mike Schwery. **Back row:** head coach Ken Papp, assistant coach Curt Bladt, Gene Langenfeld, Ron Fox, Tim Ernst, Kevin Crawford, Dan Schulte, Mike Garrison, Bruce Burger, Dave Finken, Tom Schwery, Jody Elliot

1975

Curt's Comments

   "We were getting closer to being a good team. During our 6-3 season, we lost two close ones to Atlantic and Creston before being blown out at Sioux City East."

1975 Scores (6-3, H-8, 3rd)

Harlan 17	Carroll Kuemper 6
Harlan 28	Glenwood 15
Harlan 0	Atlantic 6
Harlan 34	Red Oak 7
Harlan 18	CB Lewis Central 13
Harlan 29	Shenandoah 7
Harlan 18	Creston 19
Harlan 44	Clarinda 0
Harlan 12	Sioux City East 42

Junior back Sam Allen (30), the Cyclone's top ground gainer, gallops for a few more yards as Mark Martin (52) and Lee Schechinger (64) block

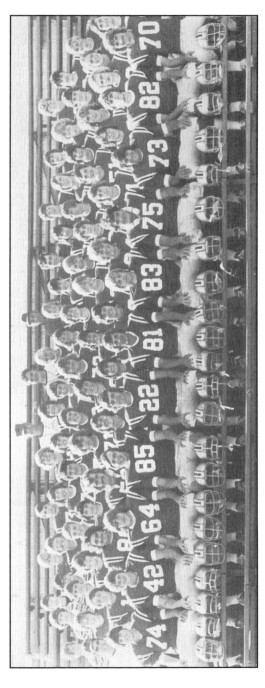

1975 Team

Front row (left to right): Larry Wendt, Tom Leinen, Lee Schechinger, Don Frazier, Brian Kelly, Kevin Moore, Rick Brown, Bob Klein. **Second row:** Coach Gene Alvine, Ron Dotzler, Bob Blum, Mark Martin, Kevin Kaufman, Charlie Lehan, Wayne Gearhart, Dean Theilen, Greg Ouren, Gary Patten, Steve Mueller, Shawn Byrnes. **Third row:** Tim Ernst, Ron Fox, Gary Schnieder, Brian Hurd, Ross Jacobsen, Kevin Crawford, Scott Christensen, Sam Allen, Mark Kaufman, Ron Doran, Dennis Wade. **Fourth row:** manager Rick Jacobsen, manager Emory Arentson, Gene Langenfeld, Mike Weis, Bruce Burger, Mike Garrison, Phil Zimmerman, Jeff Weis, Steve Petersen, Mike Rust, Gene Laver, Tim Thielen. **Fifth row:** manager Dan Petsche, manager Mike Wisenborn, Ric Pauley, Phil Arkfeld, Glen Schmitz, Jim Greer, Myron Bissen, Jim Kay, Kevin Coenen, Roger Blum, Curt Chadwick, Mark Jensen. **Sixth row:** trainer Lindsey Vanderbiden, Jerry Christensen, Mark Simms, Rick Reinig, Mike Schechinger, Mark Maxwell, Dave Schroeder, Ken Anderson, Nick Leinen, Jim Poepsel, Lynn Martens. **Back row:** coach Gene Gettys, coach Curt Bladt, head coach Ken Papp

1976
Curt's Comments

"We continued to improve, going 7-2. We lost another squeaker to Atlantic and lost to Sioux City East 30-12 at home. In those days, only eight teams qualified for the playoffs using a point system. We didn't have enough points.

"In the East game, we were pulling out all the stops. Rick Brown ran a fake punt for a long gain. The East players had set up a wall along the sidelines for their return guy. They didn't see it was a fake, and Rick ran right down the alley they created."

1976 Scores (7-2, H-8, 2nd)

Harlan 31	Carroll Kuemper 15
Harlan 28	Clarinda 14
Harlan 42	Glenwood 0
Harlan 14	Atlantic 21
Harlan 12	Red Oak 7
Harlan 58	CB Lewis Central 0
Harlan 10	Shenandoah 7
Harlan 22	Creston 3
Harlan 12	Sioux City East 30

Winning style in field goal kicking is shown by Pork (Mark Kaufman)

1976 Team

Front row (left to right): Phil Zimmerman, Gene Lengenfeld, Ron Doran, Bruce Burger, Mike Weis, Gary Schneider, Mark Kaufman, Dennis Wade, Mike Garrison, Ross Jacobsen, Kevin Crawford, Tim Ernst, Jeff Weihs. **Second row:** Scott Christensen, Rick Reinig, Myron Bissen, Mark Maxwell, Kelvin Coenen, Mike Schechinger, Steve Petersen, Jim Greer, Mark Jensen, Gene Laver, Mark Simms, Tim Thielen, Sam Allen. **Third row:** Glen Schmitz, Rick Pauley, Lynn Martens, Jack Bieker, Nick Leinen, Jim Poepsel, Mike Rush, Brian Hurd, Jeff Larson, Randy Bruck, Dave Schroeder, Stacy Hodapp. **Fourth row:** Galen Schmack, Skip Sorensen, John Murtaugh, Mark Stamp, Bill Murtaugh, Dave Martin, Dean Wilke, Paul Wingert, Dan Donlin, Mike McCoy, Mike Cambell. **Fifth row:** Tim O'Bryan, Jeff Wold, Blake Hibray, Jim Rau, John Fromm, Brett Rold, Paul Waltz, Dan Hardy, Mike Byrnes, Jeff Petersen. **Sixth row:** Mike Petersen, Rick Walter, Craig Davis, Phil Pedersen, Gaige Petersen, Scott Sojka, Scott Petersen, Kerry Boltinghouse, Randy Snyder. **Back row:** manager Ken Andersen, manager Terry Goeser, manager Dave Petersen, trainer Mike Weisenborn, manager Emory Arentson, coach Ken Carstens, coach Curt Bladt, coach Gene Gettys, head coach Ken Papp

1977

Curt's Comments

"This was Ken Papp's last year. We got beat pretty good by Atlantic and Shenandoah and were out of the playoff picture. We went up to LeMars for the last game of the season. They were favored to win, and we could have easily thrown in the towel. But the kids played their hearts out and beat them 29-7."

1977 Scores (7-2, H-8, 3rd)

Harlan 41	Carroll Kuemper 0
Harlan 12	Clarinda 7
Harlan 12	Glenwood 0
Harlan 7	Atlantic 30
Harlan 33	Red Oak 0
Harlan 26	CB Lewis Central 8
Harlan 7	Shenandoah 28
Harlan 45	Creston 6
Harlan 29	LeMars 7

Assistant Coaches Gene Gettys,
Curt Bladt, and Ken Carstens
gather for a quick strategy session
with head coach Ken Papp

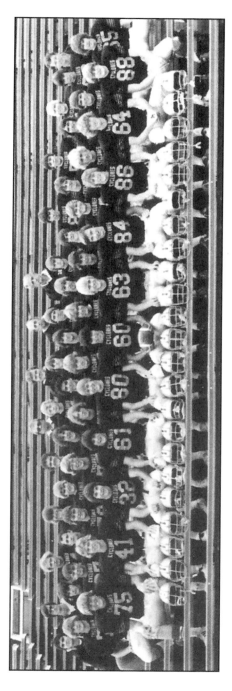

1977 Team

Front row (left to right): Rick Pauley, Rick Reinig, Mike Schechinger, Mike Rust, Steve Petersen, Mark Jensen, Mark Maxwell, Jim Greer, Jeff Larson, Nick Leinen, Todd Langenfeld. *Second row:* Dave Martin, Mark Simms, Dean Wilke, Lynn Martens, Myron Bissen, Stacy Hodapp, Jack Bieker, Gene Laver, Tim Thielen, Jeff Petersen, Mike Petersen, Mike Erickson. *Third row:* Mike Tamm, Jim Rau, John Murtaugh, Scott Petersen, Scott Sojka, Tony Hough, Mike Byrnes, Kerry Boltinghouse, Brent Gustason, Paul Waltz, Bill Murtaugh, Randy Schneider. *Fourth row:* Mike Weisenborn, Jerry Pauley, Tom Blum, Dave Kohles, John Fromm, Tim O'Bryan, Galen Schnack, Rick Walters, Kurt Block, Doug Graeve, John Neuenschwander, Ken Anderson. *Back row:* coach Ken Carstens, coach Curt Bladt, head coach Ken Papp, coach Gene Gettys

1978

Curt's Comments

"It was my first year as head coach. We only had two returning starters and only one big guy, Scott Sojka. Dean Wilke was our next biggest guy at about 185. To make matters worse, our starting quarterback, Jeff Petersen, got hurt in the first quarter of the first game. Our tight end, Mike Tamm, had to take over.

"In spite of all this, we went undefeated during the regular season. In our first playoff game against Urbandale, we were outweighed about forty pounds per man. Things weren't looking good after they scored on the first play of the game—a 60-yard run where their guy didn't even get touched. After the TD, one of our players came up to me and asked, 'Now what do we do?'

"I sagely answered, 'Tackle him next time.'

"The kids fought back. We scored late in the game to pull to within a point. We could have kicked a PAT, tied them, and gone into overtime; or we could go for two. Because of Urbandale's size advantage, we knew they could easily score rushing touchdowns in OT. I decided to go for two.

"I asked Russ Gallinger, 'What do think we should do—pass or run?'

"I'll never forget Russ's answer. He said, 'The pass looks bad and the run looks worse.' So I decided to go with 'bad' and called a pass. It was incomplete, but there was a pass interference penalty on the play. So we got another shot from the one-and-a-half yard line. This time we called a running play and made it over the goal line by a quarter of an inch. We won the game 23-22."

Senior Bill Murtaugh tries his best for some more yardage. He led the team in rushing with 873 yards

1978 Scores (10-1, H-8, 1st)

Harlan 14	Carroll Kuemper 0
Harlan 6	Creston 0 (ot)
Harlan 14	Clarinda 0
Harlan 18	Atlantic 0
Harlan 41	Glenwood 6
Harlan 14	Red Oak 3
Harlan 10	CB Lewis Central 0
Harlan 14	Shenandoah 7
Harlan 34	LeMars 0
Playoffs	
Harlan 23	Urbandale 22
Harlan 0	Emmetsburg 6

1978 Team

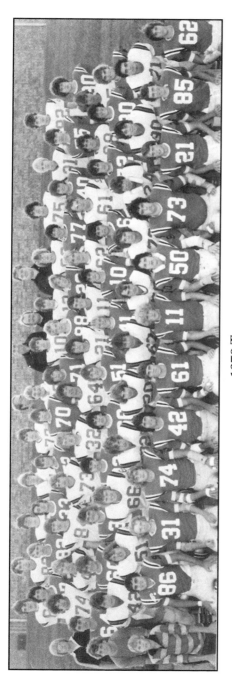

Front row (left to right): Kent Abrenholtz, Mike Tamm, John Fromm, Dave Martin, Bill Murtaugh, Galen Schnack, Jeff Petersen, John Murtaugh, Scott Sojka, Rick Walter, Mark Stamp, Mike Brynes. **Second row:** Scott Roecker, Ray Christensen, Ron Olson, Stacy Hodapp, Paul Waltz, Kerry Boltinghouse, Dean Wilke, Tim O'Bryan, Dan Donlin, Randy Snyder, Doug Graeve, Tony Hough. **Third row:** Gary Pauley, Jim Cave, Tom Blum, Kurt Block, Dan Wade, Pete Fromm, John Neuenschwander, Dan Jones, Jim Rau, Brent Gustason, Dan Kalal, Scott Petersen. **Fourth row:** Curt Olson, Mike Erickson, Mark Reinig, Terry Bettcher, Tom Schimerowski, Cole Custer, Dave Reinig, Dan Lehan, Paul Stewart, Frank Powers, Victor Brown, Allen Grote, Kevin Fries. **Fifth row:** Jeff Nelson, Phil Kenkel, Gerald Bogler, Randy Doran, Jay Tiarks, Bob Burgin, Kevin Kluver, Jim Baldwin, Craig Schuning, Bob Schechinger, Doug Schleimer, Dave Weis. **Sixth row:** Jay Schechinger, Howard Lansman, Chuck Kline, Gene Kruse, Bob Schimerowski, George Buthman, Chris Larsen, Bill Daeges, Brent Norgaard, Bill Rauterkus, Todd McKinney, Todd Kelly. **Back row:** Coach Carstens, Coach Getys, Coach Goettsche, Coach Bladt

1979

Curt's Comments

"We were 7-2, only losing close games to Atlantic and Shenandoah. That season, we started using an audible system where our quarterback could change the play at the line of scrimmage. Against Shen, we were close to scoring a game-winning TD near the end of the fourth quarter. Our quarterback audibled at the line of scrimmage, but our tailback didn't hear him correctly. Our QB went one way. Our TB went the other way. And we lost three yards on the play. We stopped using the audible system after that game. Lesson learned."

1979 Scores (7-2, H-8, 2nd)

Harlan 7	Carroll Kuemper 0
Harlan 35	Creston 15
Harlan 16	Clarinda 7
Harlan 17	Glenwood 7
Harlan 0	Atlantic 6
Harlan 15	Red Oak 14
Harlan 17	CB Lewis Central 15
Harlan 12	Shenandoah 14
Harlan 8	LeMars 0

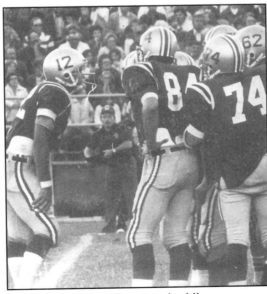

The offense in a huddle

1979 Team

Front row (left to right): *Howard Lansman, Brent Norgaard, Paul Stewart, Dan Jones, Ron Olsen, Doug Graeve, Ray Christensen, Kevin Fries, Alan Grote, Jay Christensen, Mark Reinig.* ***Second row:*** *Jim Cave, Bob Burgin, Gerald Bogler, Randy Doran, Jon Neuenschwander, Mike Tamm, Dan Kalal, Tom Blum, Kurt Block, Pete Fromm, Gary Pauley, Dean Stamp.* ***Third row:*** *Tom Schimerowski, Dave Reinig, Cole Custer, Chuck Kline, Todd McKinney, Bill Rauterkus, Chris Larsen, Jay Schechinger, Gene Kruse, Jay Koesters, Bob Schimerowski, Terry Bettcher.* ***Fourth row:*** *Bob Schechinger, Jim Baldwin, Dave Weis, Jay Tiarks, Dan Wade, Tim Peterson, Tim Waltz, Lon Lefeber, Jamie West, Ron McCall, Mike Jensen, Gary Buthman, Doug Schliemer.* ***Fifth row:*** *Brian Fries, John Stewart, Dave Schimerowski, Jim Stewart, Rich Leuschen, Grant Christensen, Frank Poepsel, Layne Hansen, Kevin Mills, Brent Zimmerman, Dan Martin, Dan McLaughlin, Pete Leinen, Tracy Stahl.* ***Sixth row:*** *Jim Weis, Corey Stanley, Todd Lauridsen, Doug Matthews, Don Fuhs, Tom Koos, Rich Bilenberg, Ron Grote, Tim Goeser.* ***Seventh row:*** *Coach Bill Hosack, Coach Ken Carstens, Head Coach Curt Bladt, Coach Arvid Goettsche*

PLAYER FROM THE DECADE
DEAN WILKE

Dean in 1978   *Dean today*

Today, Dean Wilke farms near Panama and surveys land. He and his wife, Laurie, have two sons who played for the Cyclones: Dan, who graduated in 2002, and Greg, who graduated in 2006. In his high school days, Dean saw an important transition in Cyclone football firsthand. In 1977, he played on the last team coached by Ken Papp. In 1978, he played on the first team coached by Curt Bladt. Dean says, "I noticed a difference right away. Curt was great at getting us motivated to play our best. He also didn't let us fight among ourselves at practice. Curt said, 'If you don't practice as a team, how are you going to play as a team on Friday nights?'"

Curt and the whole coaching staff do their best to attend all of the senior players' graduation parties. At Greg's party in May of 2006, Dean told his old defensive coordinator, Ken Carstens, "With all your temper tantrums, I thought you would have had a stroke by now."

Curt chimed in, "Ken is only acting when he does that."

Dean was thinking, "It sure seemed real to us when we were playing."

Dean says the most important thing he learned from his days as a Cyclone was the power of confidence. He and his teammates needed all the confidence they could muster in a playoff game against Urbandale in 1978. The big-city boys had six future Division I players on their roster. The David versus Goliath game ended in a 23 to 22 Harlan victory.

Decade Conclusion

Do you remember the classic children's book, *The Little Engine That Could?* The book is about a small railroad engine who needed to deliver a load of food and toys to children on the other side of the mountain. At first, the little engine couldn't pull the load up the mountain and was passed by many other bigger engines. But the little engine didn't give up and while repeating over and over again the words "I think I can! I think I can!" finally pulled the load up the mountain. On the way down the other side, the little engine gleefully shouted, "I thought I could! I thought I could!" The food and toys were delivered on time, and the little engine learned a valuable lesson.

The Little Engine That Could was first published in 1930. The author wrote the book to help children and their parents make it over The Great Depression mountain. In many ways, the book also describes the 1978 Cyclone football team. They thought they could, and they did. In the process, they set the stage for the Cyclones' breakthrough decade—the 1980s.

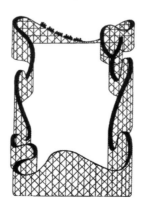

T
he Decade in Review: After failing to make the playoffs in 1980, the Cyclones pulled off a huge upset with a 7 to 6 overtime victory over their biggest rival, the Atlantic Trojans, in the first playoff game of 1981. Harlan Community went on to defeat Emmetsburg in the semifinals before losing a close game to Cedar Rapids Prairie in the finals, 13-7.

The years 1982, 1983, and 1984 were pure magic as the Cyclones won three consecutive state championships (HCHS 15 and Cedar Rapids Regis 14, HCHS 26 and Oskaloosa 0, HCHS 14 and Waterloo Columbus 13). The 1983 team was unscored upon in all three of its playoff games—winning them by a combined total of 103 to 0.

Three championships in a row is a tough act to follow. The 1985 and 1986 teams made it to the finals in the Dome, but lost to Pleasant Valley and Waterloo Columbus.

From 1981 through 1986, the Cyclones made it to the state finals each year. Six consecutive years in the championship game is another all-time Iowa record.

In 1987, Harlan Community won two playoff games before losing a squeaker in the semifinals to Estherville 7-6. The 1988 and 1989 Cyclones were state runners-up, losing to Decorah twice, 21-16 and 17-6. The totals for the decade include nine playoff appearances, five second place finishes, and three championships.

1980

Curt's Comments

"We finished 7-2 that year and learned a valuable lesson—one mistake can take you out of the playoffs. Against Lewis Central, we lost containment on one play and let their speedy halfback run around the end for a long touchdown. LC won the game 10-7. We've done a pretty good job since then not letting those kinds of things happen."

1980 Scores (7-2, H-8, 3rd)

Harlan 17	Carroll Kuemper 0
Harlan 13	Shenandoah 20
Harlan 7	Creston 0
Harlan 41	Clarinda 14
Harlan 14	Glenwood 0
Harlan 7	Atlantic 20
Harlan 20	Red Oak 0
Harlan 7	CB Lewis Central 10
Harlan 33	Denison 19

Chris Larson takes the opportunity to show his tackling ability

1980 Team

Front row (left to right): Cole Custer, Mike Jensen, Pete Leinen, Chuck Kline, Bob Schimerowski, Bob Burgin, Randy Doran, Jay Schechinger, Bill Rauterkus, Dan Jones, Jay Koesters, Gary Pauley, Pete Henscel. **Second row:** Tom Koos, Bob Schechinger, Gerald Bogler, Dave Weis, Todd McKinney, Howard Lansman, Gene Kruse, Chris Larsen, Jock Gettys, Dan McLaughlin, Don Fuhs, Bill Daeges, Ron Schmidt, Brent Zimmerman. **Third row:** Jim Stewart, Rod McCall, Chip Fletcher, Brian Fries, Doug Kenkel, Grant Christensen, Jay Tiarks, Lon Lefeber, Ron Grote, Rich Bielenburg, Sean Donlin, Dave Schimerowski, John Stewart. **Fourth row:** Tracey Stahl, Jim Weihs, Dan Martin, Tim Goeser, Layne Hansen, Jeff Nelson, Dan Wageman, Frank Poepsel, Steve Peake, Mick Tierno, Todd Kloewer, Kevin Mills, Steve Reid. **Fifth row:** Gary Buthmann, Gene Schmitz, Paul Mahlberg, Bill Defenbaugh, Doug Wade, Kevin Moore, Phil Schneider, Mark Kloewer, John Weilhs, Kevin Allen, Denny Combs, Ron Fields, Mike Christiansen. **Back row:** Coach Hoasack, Coach Carstens, Dave Petsche, Tom Ernst, Bill Kimmen, Doug Buman, Richard Jorgensen, Gaylen Boeck, Bill Behrendt, Coach Bladt, Coach Gallinger

1981

Curt's Comments

"1981 was our first time playing in the Dome. All of us were fresh off the farm, so to speak. As Cedar Rapids Prairie came trotting out on the field, we were shocked to see they had suited up a 6'5", 270-pound offensive and defensive lineman who had been injured earlier in the year. This was his first game back. We didn't have any game film on him. He completely changed the offensive and defensive line play.

"We were trailing 13-7 late in the game and had them pinned deep in their own territory. It was third and long. If we held them, they had to punt, and we would have a chance to win the game with a TD. They threw the ball (gutsy call), made a first down, and ran out the clock. Our boys played well, though."

Todd Lauridsen "breaks on through" the Atlantic line

1981 Scores (10-2, H-8, 2nd)

Harlan 28	Carroll Kuemper 26
Harlan 20	Shenandoah 6
Harlan 35	Creston 7
Harlan 17	Clarinda 15
Harlan 30	Glenwood 0
Harlan 6	Atlantic 28
Harlan 28	Red Oak 0
Harlan 21	CB Lewis Central 7
Harlan 32	Denison 6
Playoffs	
Harlan 7	Atlantic 6 (ot)
Harlan 10	Emmetsburg 7 (ot)
Harlan 7	CR Prairie 13

1981 Team

Front row (left to right): Grant Christensen, Rod McCall, Jim Stewart, Dan McLaughlin, Tom Koos, Pete Leinen, Kevin Mills, Todd Lauridsen, Mike Jensen, Gary Buhmann, Brent Zimmerman, Dave Schimerowski. **Second row:** John Stewart, Ron Grote, Phil Schneider, John Weihs, Todd Koos, Gene Schmitz, Mark Kloewer, Paul Mahlberg, Steve Peake, Rich Bielenberg, Lon Lefeber, Dan Martin. **Third row:** Bill Kimmen, Mike Long, Doug Wade, Bill Defenbaugh, Kevin Allen, Tom Ernst, Jim Lehan, Rick Nobel, John Bogler, Todd Kloewer, Doug Buman, Layne Hansen. **Fourth row:** Perry Sibenaller, Courtney Lawyer, Darin Jones, Tim Jacobsen, Larry Kintner, Mike Kloewer, John Barton, John Kruse, Darrin Thompson, Pete Finken, Scott Mahlberg, Jeff Swenson. **Fifth row:** Doug Mathiasen, Mike Glenn, Kevin Brus, Brian Coenen, Alan Patton, Curt Anstey, Troy Jacobsen, John Vance, Barry Norgaard, Tim Pauley, Bill Behrendt, **Sixth row:** Kathy Andersen, Jill Christiansen, Dan Taylor, Eric Luchsinger, Mark Buman, Rick Snyder, Ken Rau, Rod Hansen, Mike Christensen. **Back row:** Greg Bladt, Mike McCall, Coach Bladt, Coach Carstens, Coach Hosack, Coach Gallinger, Doc Spearing

1982

Curt's Comments

"In the championship game, we trailed Cedar Rapids Regis 14-0 at halftime. Superintendent Orville Frazier was so upset he left. He should have stayed. We scored two touchdowns in the last half to win the game 15-14 on the Swinging Gate two-point play after our second TD. On the last touchdown drive, Steve Peake ran the ball six straight times behind undersized and over-hearted John Weihs, who was lined up against a Division I Regis recruit."

1982 Scores (12-0, H-8, 1st)

Harlan 42	Carroll Kuemper 13
Harlan 28	CB Lewis Central 6
Harlan 34	Shenandoah 6
Harlan 35	Creston 0
Harlan 39	Clarinda 14
Harlan 48	Glenwood 6
Harlan 40	Atlantic 6
Harlan 62	Red Oak 6
Harlan 42	Denison 0
Playoffs	
Harlan 28	Webster City 6
Harlan 41	Fairfield 21
Harlan 15	CR Regis 14

At the close of the half, Paul Mahlberg intercepts the ball in the endzone to end the Fairfield threat

1982 Team

Front row (left to right): Galen Boeck, Chuck Assman, Phil Schneider, John Weihs, Bill Kimmen, Kevin Allen, Tom Ernst, Paul Mahlberg, Todd Kloewer, Mike Long, Steve Peake, Mark Kloewer, Gene Schmitz, Doug Wade, Bill Defenbaugh, Doug Buman. *Second row:* Mark Buman, Pete Finken, Darren Thompsen, Todd Koos, Troy Jacobsen, Curt Anstey, Scott Mahlberg, John Bolger, Rick Noble, Tim Jacobsen, Alan Patten, Mark Schmitz. *Third row:* Ken Rau, Courtney Lawyer, Mike Christensen, Tim Pauley, Mike Kloewer, Larry Kitner, Rick Snyder, John Kruse, Gene Gettys, Kevin Brus, Dave Kline, Scot Koesters, Mike O'Bryan, Dave Larson. *Fourth row:* Coach Bladt, Coach Gallinger, Barry Norgaard, Eric Luchsinger, Jeff Swensen, Danny Taylor, Rod Hansen, Jeff Wehr, Brad Svendsen, Brandt Ferry, Curt Andersen, Coach Carstens, Coach Hosack. *Back row:* Alan Jankiewitz, Jerry Kast, Dan Defenbaugh, Bob Klein, Ken Swanson, Dave Warner, Dan Schmitz, Richard Taylor, Leroy Garmen, Gary Hadley, Larry Kelly, Jason Hilsebeck, Brian Ernst

1983

Curt's Comments

"We had a lot of tough guys coming back from our 1982 championship team. We were undefeated for the year and unscored on in the playoffs. That's only happened one other time in Iowa in all the classes. In the championship game, Mike O'Brien replaced the injured John Bogler at tailback and promptly broke the Class 3A championship game rushing record with 188 yards. His record was broken eleven years later by our Kevin Kruse's 278 yards."

1983 Scores (12-0, H-8, 1st)

Harlan 34	Carroll Kuemper 22
Harlan 21	CB Lewis Central 0
Harlan 53	Shenandoah 0
Harlan 47	Creston 0
Harlan 39	Clarinda 14
Harlan 38	Glenwood 6
Harlan 28	Atlantic 6
Harlan 40	Red Oak 6
Harlan 49	Denison 0
Playoffs	
Harlan 49	Norwalk 0
Harlan 28	Webster City 0
Harlan 26	Oskaloosa 0

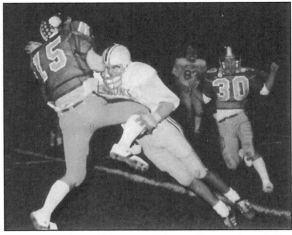

Stripping the ball from a Webster City receiver is first team All-Conference defensive end Scott Mahlberg

1983 Team

Front row (*left to right*): Perry Sibernaller, Mark Buman, Pete Finken, Larry Kitner, Jim Lehan, Scott Mahlberg, Mike Jones, Steve Lytle, Kevin Sprague, Tim Jacobsen, John Bogler, David Schmitz, Mike Kloewer, Darren Thomsen, Jon Kruse, Rick Nobel, Ken Rau. **Second row:** Rick Snyder, Gus (last name unknonw), Ken Schechinger, Brian Ernst, Rod Hansen, Bob Klein, Todd Koos, Tim Pauley, Jim Schmidt, Troy Jacobsen, Alan Patten, Kevin Brus, "Beaner" Gettys, Brian Coenen, Jeff Wehr. **Back row:** Mike O'Bryan, Jeff Swensen, Kurt Andersen, Gary Hadley, Rick Blum, Bill Schomers, Don Klitgaard, Brandt Ferry, Jason Hilsabeck, Dave Erlbacher, Lynn Schmitz, Pat Shelton, Richard Taylor, Mike Wilwerding, David Kline, Tim Kloewer, Dean Schmitz, Greg Lansing, Brad Svendsen. **Not pictured:** John Barton, Sam Graeve, Craig Wigness, Tracey Fink, Mark Hansen, Tracey Klein, Chad Kluver, Brian Leinen, Dirk Stamp, Steve Stessman, Ken Swanson, Tim Boettger

1984

Curt's Comments

"We had won thirty-one games in a row before we lost to Atlantic in the regular season. We came back and beat them 35-20 in the playoffs.

"My physician is Don Klitgaard. Do people in Harlan remember him for being the valedictorian of his senior class? Unfortunately, no. They remember him for picking up a fumble created by Pat Shelton late in the championship game against Waterloo Columbus and running it in for a touchdown.

"We called a timeout to get the boys calmed down. Then we kicked the pressure-packed PAT to win the game 14-13.

"On the video of Don's touchdown, you can

Don Klitgaard running for a touchdown past stunned Waterloo Columbus fans

see a Columbus assistant coach running down the sideline a few yards behind Don. In despair, he falls down at the twenty yard line. After a timeout and our extra point, you can still see him lying in the same spot on our kickoff. That's disappointment!"

1984 Scores (11-1, H-8, 1st, Tied LC)

		Playoffs	
Harlan 13	Carroll Kuemper 10	Harlan 35	Atlantic 20
Harlan 34	Red Oak 0	Harlan 28	Winterset 0
Harlan 26	CB Lewis Central 8	Harlan 33	Algona 14
Harlan 15	Shenandoah 6	Harlan 14	Waterloo-
Harlan 26	Creston 0		Columbus 13
Harlan 14	Clarinda 0		
Harlan 40	Glenwood 0		
Harlan 14	Atlantic 20		

Cyclones celebrate the winning touchdown

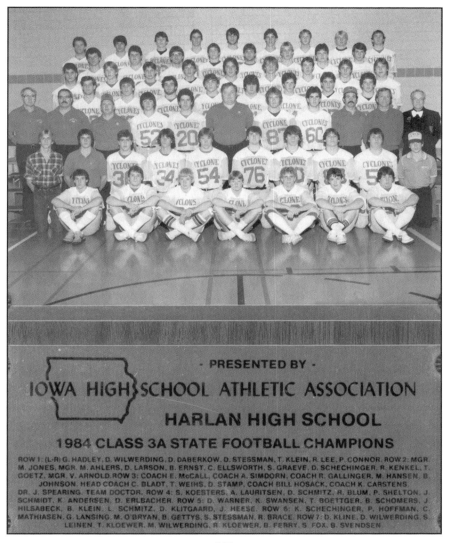

- PRESENTED BY -

IOWA HIGH SCHOOL ATHLETIC ASSOCIATION

HARLAN HIGH SCHOOL

1984 CLASS 3A STATE FOOTBALL CHAMPIONS

ROW 1: (L-R) G. HADLEY, D. WILWERDING, D. DABERKOW, D. STESSMAN, T. KLEIN, R. LEE, P. CONNOR. ROW 2: MGR. M. JONES, MGR. M. AHLERS, D. LARSON, B. ERNST, C. ELLSWORTH, S. GRAEVE, D. SCHECHINGER, R. KENKEL, T. GOETZ, MGR. V. ARNOLD. ROW 3: COACH E. McCALL, COACH A. SIMDORN, COACH R. GALLINGER, M. HANSEN, B. JOHNSON, HEAD COACH C. BLADT, T. WEIHS, D. STAMP, COACH BILL HOSACK, COACH K. CARSTENS, DR. J. SPEARING, TEAM DOCTOR. ROW 4: S. KOESTERS, A. LAURITSEN, D. SCHMITZ, R. BLUM, P. SHELTON, J. SCHMIDT, K. ANDERSEN, D. ERLBACHER. ROW 5: D. WARNER, K. SWANSEN, T. BOETTGER, B. SCHOMERS, J. HILSABECK, B. KLEIN, L. SCHMITZ, D. KLITGAARD, J. HEESE. ROW 6: K. SCHECHINGER, P. HOFFMAN, C. MATHIASEN, G. LANSING, M. O'BRYAN, B. GETTYS, S. STESSMAN, R. BRACE. ROW 7: D. KLINE, D. WILWERDING, S. LEINEN, T. KLOEWER, M. WILWERDING, R. KLOEWER, B. FERRY, S. FOX, B. SVENDSEN.

1984 Team

1985

Curt's Comments

"Our starting quarterback, Greg Lansing, got hurt in the quarterfinal playoff victory against Creston. We struggled offensively after that. We beat Webster City 3-0 in overtime in the next game. In the finals, a phantom holding call moved us out of field goal range. Pleasant Valley got the ball, kicked a field goal of their own, and beat us 10-7.

"Another lesson learned—the decision of the judges is final."

Fading back to pass is Greg Lansing, versus Atlantic in the playoffs. Lansing passed for 738 total yards, although he didn't play in the season's final two games

1985 Scores (11-1, H-8, 1st)

Harlan 20	Carroll Kuemper 0
Harlan 33	Red Oak 6
Harlan 28	CB Lewis Central 7
Harlan 36	Shenandoah 0
Harlan 38	Creston 14
Harlan 24	Clarinda 0
Harlan 32	Glenwood 13
Harlan 14	Atlantic 0

Playoffs

Harlan 33	Atlantic 21
Harlan 21	Creston 11
Harlan 3	Webster City 0 (ot)
Harlan 7	Pleasant Valley 10

1985 Team

1986

Curt's Comments

"Most games are decided on the field. The playoff game against Indianola was decided at halftime. We were trailing as we took the field to start the third quarter. Somebody in a tower that must have been one hundred feet up in the air threw a water balloon and hit me in the back of the neck. It was real cold that night, but I instantly became real hot. The coaching staff didn't see the bombing episode, but did notice a 'slight' change in my emotional state. We went on to win the game 26-14.

"We lost to an excellent Waterloo Columbus team 24 to 7 in the championship two games later."

1986 Scores (11-1, H-8, 1st)

Harlan 7	Carroll Kuemper 0
Harlan 21	Atlantic 7
Harlan 48	Red Oak 0
Harlan 17	CB Lewis Central 0
Harlan 14	Shenandoah 28
Harlan 20	Creston 18
Harlan 37	Clarinda 12
Harlan 50	Glenwood 13
Playoffs	
Harlan 9	CB Lewis Central 6 (ot)
Harlan 26	Indianola 14
Harlan 21	Webster City 10
Harlan 7	Waterloo Columbus 24

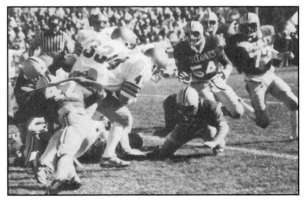

Reaching out a strong arm, Brad Johnson pulls down a Webster City Lynx

1986 Team

1987

Curt's Comments

"In 1987, the name of the game was adversity. We lost our starting tailback, Curt Jensen, for the year due to injury. In the semifinal game, after a three-hour road trip in the semifinals, we lost to a fired-up Estherville team 7-6. After the game, there was some finger-pointing going on between our boys. Another difficult lesson was learned. We win together, and we lose together. No one person is responsible for either.

"This was the last game for my oldest son, Greg, who was a starting offensive guard for us."

1987 Scores (10-1, H-8, 1st)

Harlan 7	Carroll Kuemper 0
Harlan 10	Atlantic 7
Harlan 13	Red Oak 6
Harlan 20	CB Lewis Central 10
Harlan 17	Shenandoah 14 (ot)
Harlan 26	Creston 12
Harlan 48	Clarinda 7
Harlan 49	Glenwood 7
Playoffs	
Harlan 17	Clarke (Osceola) 14 (ot)
Harlan 30	Pella 0
Harlan 6	Estherville 7

Because of an injury to Jerry Deren, sophomore Scott Arkfeld saw a lot of varsity action. Here, he receives instructions from Coach Bladt

1987 Team

Front row (left to right): *manager Theresa Kloewer, Jason Pauley, Troy Schulte, Jeff Kenton, Lance Grummert, Tim Miller, Scott Schiltz, Jamie Petsche, Steve Bails, Jeramy Kuhn, Todd Gross, Brian Petersen, Todd Hansen, Bryan Tiller, manager Theresa Jacobs.* **Second row:** *Doc Spearing, Marc Mores, Dale Schmitz, Corey Zea, Kerry Gual, Jamie Meuer, Jerrad Popp, Corey Sprague, Troy Bruck, Cory Carter, Paul Kenkel, Jeff Bladt, Todd Parkhurst, Kenyon DeHaan, Dana Tuma.* **Third row:** *Coach Bill Hosack, Steve Kluesner, Johnny Larsen, Carr Salvo, Kevin Schechinger, Brad Schuery, Coben Johnson, Kurt Jensen, Mike McCall, Ed Paden, Darrin Ellsworth, Jason Moore, Duane Brus, Alan Hall, Coach Russ Gallinger.* **Fourth row:** *Coach Ken Carstens, Chad Tremmel, Curt Schulte, Dale Fink, Steve Nichols, Brian Koesters, Greg Bladt, Jason Eckermann, Dave Blum, Stacy Treganza, Craig Jensen, Jim Springman, Mike Lambertson, Randy Zimmerman, Coach Curt Bladt.* **Fifth row:** *Jeff Chamberlain, Dave Schechinger, Scott Arkfeld, Jerry Deren, Brad Asmann, Mike Brinker, John Hemminger, Shawn Arkfeld, Jim Hanson, Gary Petersen, Chris Johannsen, Jeff Sonderman, Shawn Gessert, Tyler Jacobsen*

1988

Curt's Comments

"We were undefeated going into the championship game against Decorah. We were trailing by five points with time running out. We had the ball inside their five yard line, but they kept us out of the end zone. Sometimes in great games you're going to lose. Lesson learned? No regrets. We had our chance."

1988 Scores (11-1, H-8, 1st)

Harlan 20	Carroll Kuemper 6
Harlan 27	Glenwood 12
Harlan 27	Atlantic 14
Harlan 39	Red Oak 6
Harlan 41	CB Lewis Central 6
Harlan 20	Shenandoah 6
Harlan 49	Creston 13
Harlan 42	Clarinda 0
Playoffs	
Harlan 37	Glenwood 7
Harlan 28	Creston 6
Harlan 19	Spencer 10
Harlan 16	Decorah 21

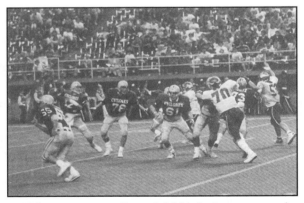

Helping to protect Scott Arkfeld during a pass rush are Tony Burger, Scott Baker, Chris Johannsen, and Scott Schiltz

1988 Team

1989

Curt's Comments

"We were undefeated going into the championship game against Decorah again. They beat us again, 17-6. I remember a punt return where my middle son, Jeff, blocked a kid and knocked him out of both his shoes. I've never seen that before or since. Luckily, the kid got up and came back into the game after the cobwebs cleared."

1989 Scores (11-1, H-8, 1st)

Harlan 34	Carroll Kuemper 7
Harlan 24	Glenwood 7
Harlan 42	Atlantic 0
Harlan 54	Red Oak 6
Harlan 42	CB Lewis Central 14
Harlan 39	Shenandoah 6
Harlan 35	Creston 14
Harlan 24	Clarinda 0
Playoffs	
Harlan 34	Denison 14
Harlan 45	Chariton 13
Harlan 21	Spencer 14
Harlan 6	Decorah 17

*Escaping the grasp of a Spencer opponent
is senior running back Cohen Johnson*

- PRESENTED BY -

IOWA HIGH SCHOOL ATHLETIC ASSOCIATION

HARLAN HIGH SCHOOL

1989 CLASS 3-A STATE FOOTBALL RUNNER-UP

FRONT ROW: DALE SCHMITZ, SCOTT HEESE, CHAD SONDERMAN, SHAWN ERLBACHER, MARK KLEIN, COREY SPRAGUE, TYLER PARKHURST, BRIAN SCHNEIDER. ROW 2: SEAN MONSON, TOM SCHUMACHER, CHRIS HOGZETT, BRAD ZIMMERMAN, TROY HODAPP, JASON CAIRNEY, AARON ANDERSON, JEFF BOLTON, ED BURCHETT. ROW 3: SHAWN PAGE, (MGR.), MARC MORES, (MGR.), KEVIN MUSICH, STEVE KLUESNER, DOUG WILWERDING, JEREMY OLSEN, CORY CARTER, TIM MILLER, MARTY BARNETT, RYAN DE HAAN, DARCI ZEA, (MGR.), BECKY SCHABEN, (MGR.). ROW 4: JEFF BLADT, ROGER GAUL, RYAN LOWE, PAUL KENKEL, SCOTT SCHILTZ, TROY BRUCK, LANCE GRUMMERT, MIKE BUCKLEY, KEVIN SCHECHINGER, COACH KEN CARSTENS. ROW 5: COACH CLIFF TAMM, JAY FREDERICK, TROY REIMER, TROY SCHULTE, JASON PAULEY, RANDY ZIMMERMAN, STEVE WEGNER, AARON STAMP, CORY BRINKER, JERRAD POPP, CHAD KENKEL, RYAN SCHMITZ. ROW 6: COACH AL SIMDORN, COACH CURT BLADT, CHUCK OBRECHT, SCOTT ARKFELD, KIRON ANDERSEN, JOHN LARSEN, JEFF SONDERMAN, STEVE WILWERDING, COHEN JOHNSON, COACH BILL HOSACK, COACH RUSS GALLINGER.

1989 Team

PLAYER FROM THE DECADE
PERRY SIBENALLER

Perry, his wife Susie (Tamm), and their two girls live in Overland Park, Kansas. Perry is the safety director for TransAm Trucking. Susie is a school teacher. After his Cyclone days, Perry played football at the University of South Dakota.

Perry in 1983   *Perry today*

Perry says he learned three valuable lessons from Curt and the entire coaching staff:

1. **Hard work creates long-term success**

   Perry says, "Everywhere you go, you see sports teams being successful for a year or two if they have a few talented players. To achieve long-term success like the Cyclones have, you've gotta put in the time and effort. In my last three years in high school, we lost two games. It took hard work to pull that off."

2. **Treat people right**

   "On teams, whether it's coaching a football team or running a trucking company, you have to treat people right. Give them high expectations to live up to. Give them the tools they need to do the job right. Curt has done that throughout his career."

3. **Hit the right buttons**

   "People respond differently at different times to positive and negative feedback. Curt was master at knowing when to get on players and when to back off. During my senior year, we beat Carroll Kuemper, but the score was way closer than it should have been. Coach Bladt really got on us. He forcefully communicated, 'You think you're so great. Just look at what they did to you!'"

Decade Conclusion

In the 1970s, the Cyclones won one state championship. In the 1980s, they won three. In the 1990s, the upward spiral continued for Curt and his boys.

T he Decade in Review: In 1990 and 1991, Harlan Community ran into two very good Spencer teams and was defeated in the semifinals of the playoffs both years. The Cyclones moved it up a notch in 1992 with a runner-up finish in the Dome, losing to Waverly-Shell Rock 14-6. In 1993, Curt's kids continued their climb by beating West Delaware 34-20 in the championship game.

After making it to the playoffs thirteen years in a row, Harlan went 7-2 in 1994—but missed the playoffs. The Cyclones bounced back in 1995, easily defeating West Delaware 27-7 for the championship.

On the frozen tundra of Central Lyon's field in 1996, Harlan lost a semifinal game 20-13. Two more first-place trophies were added to the Cyclone display case with state championships in 1997 (Harlan 14 and Decorah 7) and 1998 (the good guys 49 and Grinnell 7). The decade ended in 1999, with Harlan losing a quarterfinal game to Jefferson 6-0.

The final result for the 1990s was nine playoff appearances and four state titles. Not a bad decade's work.

1990

Curt's Comments

"In the playoffs, we went to Knoxville. They have the coolest high school stadium I've seen. It's constructed of big, stone blocks and was built in the 1930s by the WPA.

"We were undefeated until we met a very physical Spencer team in the semifinals. They had no weaknesses and kicked our butts all over the field."

1990 Scores (11-1, H-8, 1st)

Harlan 10	Denison 6
Harlan 36	Carroll Kuemper 6
Harlan 31	Clarinda 0
Harlan 7	Glenwood 0
Harlan 19	Atlantic 0
Harlan 19	Red Oak 6
Harlan 19	CB Lewis Central 0
Harlan 35	Shenandoah 6
Harlan 40	Creston 7
Playoffs	
Harlan 21	Denison 13
Harlan 49	Knoxville 26
Harlan 6	Spencer 31

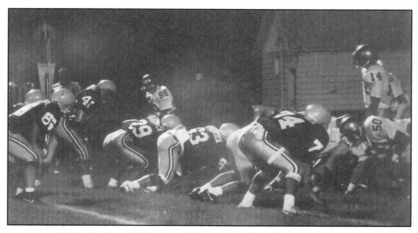

The Cyclone defense—Kevin Musich, Shawn Erlbacher,
Mike Buckley, Cory Brinker, Steve Wilwerding, Chad Sonderman,
and Doug Wilwerding—faces the Glenwood Rams

1990 Team

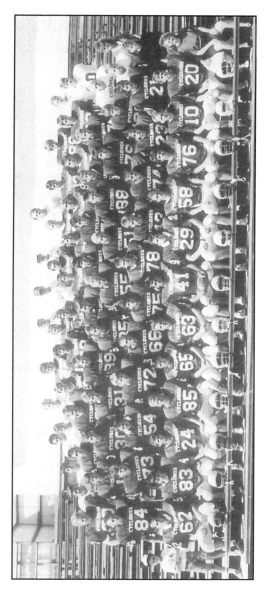

Front row (left to right): Chad Sonderman, Aaron Andersen, Brian Schneider, Steve Wegner, Doug Wilwerding, Shawn Erlbacher, Steve Wilwerding, Kevin Musich, Jeremy Olson, Tom Schumacher, Troy Reiner, Chuck Obrecht, manager Darci Zea. *Second row:* Jeremy Arkfeld, Todd Hendricks, Ed Burchett, Roger Gaul, Jeff Bolton, Chad Kenkel, Tyson Haas, Scott Heese, Cory Brinker, Dan Fuehrer, Chris Klitgaard, manager Becky Schaben. *Third row:* Doug Schneider, Chad Morgan, Chris Hogzett, Brad Zimmerman, Ryan DeHaan, Troy Hodapp, Kelly Green, Kiron Andersen, Trent Schuning, Tyler Parkhurst, Chad Manz, manager Vicki Tremel. *Fourth row:* Chad Schechinger, Jason Cairney, Jay Frederick, Ryan Schmitz, Marty Barnett, Stephen Gessert, Kelly Gaer, Troy Fink, Jason Kruse, Jeremy Briggs. *Fifth row:* Dave Nash, Jeff Buman, Stacy Doonan, Jamie Buckboldt, Josh Leinen, Greg Doonan, Steve Childs, Marv Kohles, Jason Gaul, Troy Kloewer, Jason Sporrer. *Sixth row:* Todd Johnson, Brian Andersen, Brandon Munson, Tracy Olson, Jesse Rose, Dallas Schwery, Kyle Funk, Dave Schechinger, Mike Petersen. *Back row:* Coach Russ Gallinger, Coach Ken Carstens, Coach Bill Hosack, Coach Curt Bladt

1991

Curt's Comments

"1991 was a weird year. We won eleven games, but the success was overshadowed by Jason Cairney's death in a car accident in the spring. Jason wore number 22. Maybe we were just looking for it, but the number 22 kept appearing on the scoreboard throughout the year—3rd and 22, a score of 22, or the clock stopping at 22 seconds. Every time that happened, the players would shout, 'Look, 22!' We all got a shot of adrenaline every time it happened. It was a strange feeling. By his absence, he was still playing. With the loss of Jason, we were again reminded that there are things a lot more important than football.

"In the semifinals, we suffered our worst loss in twenty-eight years. We trailed Spencer 41-0 at halftime. In the second half, they kept their first teamers in the game in an attempt to increase their lead to 50 points, so the game would end early. I don't blame them. In the playoffs, you need all the rest you can get. To our boys' credit, they kept their heads up, played a solid second half, and outscored Spencer 7-0 in the second half."

Scott Heese escapes the grasp of his opponent

1991 Scores (11-1, H-8, 1st)

Harlan 25	Denison 18
Harlan 23	Carroll Kuemper 21
Harlan 27	Clarinda 0
Harlan 40	Glenwood 16
Harlan 42	Atlantic 13
Harlan 51	Red Oak 6
Harlan 21	CB Lewis Central 20
Harlan 51	Shenandoah 0
Harlan 13	Creston 12
Playoffs	
Harlan 31	CB Lewis Central 27
Harlan 34	Creston 0
Harlan 7	Spencer 41

1991 Team

Front row (left to right): Jason Kruse, Troy Fink, Marty Barnett, Kelly Gaer, Trent Schuning, Kiron Andersen, Ryan DeHaan, Brad Zimmerman, Chris Klitgaard, Ryan Schmitz, Troy Hodapp. *Second row:* Mike Petersen, Dallas Schwery, Jesse Rose, Steve Gessert, Tyler Parkhurst, Chris Hogzett, Scott Heese, Jay Frederick, Cory Brinker, Barry Spencer, Tyson Haas. *Third row:* Dave Schechinger, Jeff Buman, Tracy Olsen, Brandon Monson, Jason Sporror, Steve Childs, Josh Leinen, Chad Schechinger, Jamie Buckholdt, Jeremy Briggs. *Fourth row:* Barry Sorensen, Michael Burger, Allen Leinen II, Mark Goetz, Jereme Chamberlain, Travis Rust, Nate Ahrenholtz, Brian Andersen, Stacy Doonan, Chad Manz, Greg Doonan. *Fifth row:* Mike Sonderman, Reid Johannsen, Kirk Graeve, Kevin Schaben, Jim Chamberlain, Kurt Kenkel, Walt Carter, Todd Bruck, Scott Burchett, Andy Sondag, Pat Etler. *Sixth row:* Ryan Kastens, Chris Cundiff, John Baratta, Clint Sonderman, Bob Bruck, Billy Wageman, Nate Christensen, Dan Schumacher, John Olsen, Toby Mosher, Todd Johnson. *Seventh row:* Ryan Wheatley, Matt Bartlett, Kent Bruck, Doug Blum, Roger Schumacher, Curt Schaben, Mike Frederick, William McDaniel. *Back row:* Kelli Blum, Vicki Tremel, Darci Zea, Coach Ken Carstens, Coach Curt Bladt, trainer Tim Kloever, Coach Russ Gallinger, Coach Bill Hosack.

1992

Curt's Comments

"We lost our last game of the season in a squeaker to Denison. In the playoff quarterfinals, we traveled to Norwalk. The visitors' benches were nothing more than wooden boards on concrete blocks. Somebody pulled off a sneaky pre-game trick by cutting one of the boards three-quarters of the way though from the bottom side. Coach Carstens was the lucky one to sit on the board. It collapsed, and he went rolling. Needless to say, it raised his level of concern, which he communicated to the team. Late in the game, we intercepted a pass in our end zone to preserve a 26-21 win.

"In the next game, we played our old nemesis, Spencer. We needed a win in the *best* way—not a win in the *worst* way. We got it 21-7. In the finals, we lost 14-6 to Waverly-Shell Rock."

Returning a kickoff is Jamie Buckholdt

1992 Scores (11-2, District, 1st)

Harlan 31	LeMars 21
Harlan 34	Carroll Kuemper 8
Harlan 34	Creston 7
Harlan 24	Clarinda 7
Harlan 41	Glenwood 12
Harlan 42	Atlantic 6
Harlan 51	Red Oak 17
Harlan 26	CB Lewis Central 16
Harlan 33	Denison 36
Playoffs	
Harlan 27	Johnston 9
Harlan 26	Norwalk 21
Harlan 21	Spencer 7
Harlan 6	Waverly-Shell Rock 14

1992 Team

1993

Curt's Comments

"In the regular season, Denison cleaned our clock to the tune of 36-10 in Harlan—not a pretty sight. I had a feeling we would see them again in the playoffs. We did—at their place. The view was better this time, as we pulled off a hard-fought 14-0 victory.

"The championship game in the Dome may have been our best example of a great game plan that was well executed. West Delaware won the state title in 1991 by beating Spencer—the team who clobbered us in the semifinals. West Delaware had six talented sophomores who started on the 1991 team. Now they were seniors!

"This is the game where Coach Carstens took away their short, slant passes and gave them the deep stuff. Our band of 5'4" defensive backs intercepted two slant passes and returned them for TDs—and their receivers were real tall. Lesson learned? Raw talent can be beaten with a great game plan, excellent execution, and hard playing."

Billy Wageman and Al Leinen are in pursuit of Lewis Central's star back, Mike Kell

1993 Scores (12-1, District, 1st)

Harlan 28	LeMars 0
Harlan 48	Carroll Kuemper 14
Harlan 23	Creston 21
Harlan 7	Clarinda 0
Harlan 16	Glenwood 7
Harlan 21	Atlantic 10
Harlan 56	Red Oak 12
Harlan 37	CB Lewis Central 34
Harlan 10	Denison 36

Playoffs

Harlan 31	Winterset 0
Harlan 14	Denison 0
Harlan 28	Boone 0
Harlan 34	West Delaware (Manchester) 20

- PRESENTED BY -

IOWA HIGH SCHOOL ATHLETIC ASSOCIATION

HARLAN
HIGH SCHOOL

1993 CLASS 3-A STATE FOOTBALL CHAMPIONS

FRONT ROW: (L-R) B. GALLINGER (BALLBOY), R. SCHUMACHER, K. GRAEVE, R. SCHWERY, S. DOONAN, K. GRAEVE, R. KASTENS, A. SONDAG, C. MILLER, L. OHLINGER (MGR), ROW 2: C. CARSTENS (BALLBOY), T. BLADT (BALLBOY), T. MOSHER, J. MANZ, D. SCHILTZ, T. FELDMAN, G. ADAMS, M. GOLTZ, A. GAUL, S. BURCHETT, M. MC KINNEY, J. ALDERSON (MGR) ROW 3: COACH K. CARSTENS, N. AHRENHOLTZ, S. SCHECHINGER, K. KENKEL, R. MAHLBERG, B. SCHMITZ, C. SONDERMAN, T. BRUCK, R. PLEAK, D. MAGES, COACH R. GALLINGER, T. ELSE (MGR), ROW 4: COACH B. HOSACK, J. GOESER, C. HANSEN, D. SCHUMACHER, J. PETERSEN, B. SORENSEN, B. WAGEMAN, R. KLINKEFUS, M. LEINEN, M. SONDERMAN, M. BURGER, ROW 5: C. RASMUSSEN, J. CHAMBERLAIN, M. HOGZETT, R. JOHANNSEN, W. CARTER, T. RUST, J. BLUM, J. CHAMBERLAIN, W. STEPHANY, C. CUNDIFF, COACH A. SIMODRN. ROW 6: COACH C. BLADT, B. KNAUSS, J. FISCUS, T. AHRENHOLTZ, A. LEINEN, J. OLSON, A. BURCHETT, J. KLOEWER, D. HAZELTON, N. CHRISTENSEN, J. BLUM, R. WHEATLEY, COACH J. PANEK

1993 Team

1994

Curt's Comments

"1980 was the last year we missed the playoffs. Fourteen years later, it happened again. We lost our third game of the year to Denison and our sixth game of the year to Glenwood—the only time that's happened in thirty-six years. It was obvious we weren't going to make it to the post-season. The kids could have packed it in at that point. But they didn't. They pulled together and pulled down Atlantic, Red Oak, and Lewis Central in the last three games. The Lewis Central game knocked them out of the playoffs.

"It's been said that 'pride goes before the fall.' In 1994, even though we lost two games and didn't make the playoffs, we never lost our pride, and we never fell."

1994 Scores (7-2)

Harlan 29	LeMars 0
Harlan 20	JSPC (Jefferson) 12
Harlan 3	Denison-Schleswig 18
Harlan 21	Carroll Kuemper 7
Harlan 35	Clarinda 6
Harlan 17	Glenwood 20
Harlan 22	Atlantic 12
Harlan 21	Red Oak 0
Harlan 17	CB Lewis Central 6

Yeah! Coach Bladt, Coach Gallagher, Jason Blum, and Jason Lensch celebrate a touchdown with the rest of the Cyclones

1994 Team

Front row (left to right): *Jeromy Kloewer, Jason Blum, Ron Mahlberg, Brad Schmitz, Colby Miller, Chad Hansen, Aaron Gaul, Jamey Petersen, Andy Burchett, Wil Stephany, Josh Goeser, Jason Manz.* ***Second row:*** *Danny Schiltz, David Mages, Kevin Graeve, Duane Hazelton, Jason Lensch, Mike D'Arcy, Eric Padget, Matt Leinen, Jared Blum, Andy Rouboff, Ron Schwery.* ***Third row:*** *J.W. Sorensen, Ryan Ohrtman, Justin Green, Nate Benskin, Tony Abrenboltz, Chad Freund, Jeremy Hess, Matt Hogzett, Ryan Brasch, Rob Klinkefus, Ted Feldman, Jeremy Nielsen.* ***Fourth row:*** *Harry Adams, Corey Rassmussen, Steve Schechinger, Jeremy Fiscus, Ryan Pleak, Aaron Schmitz, Brad Knauss, Doug Chamberlain, Larry Wendt, Matt Studer, Calvin Webr.* ***Fifth row:*** *Kevin Gittins, Jeremy Smith, Matt Martin, Billy Carpenter, Mark Hazelton, Eric Schulte, Adam Bentz, Brian Baxter, Bryan Buckholdt, Justin Cox, Josh Mellinger, Byron Bentzen, ballboy Tom Hosack.* ***Sixth row:*** *manager Jessica Troll, Dax Doran, Adam Schechinger, Jeff Schmitz, Kris Mickelsen, David Schiltz, Dayton Robinson, Shawn Heyderboff, Mark Schmitz, John Slaven, William Packard, Jeremy Schechinger; ballboy Brent Gallinger.* ***Back row:*** *manager Lisa Oblinger, Ross Burchett, Jake Fubs, Coach Gallinger, Coach Carstens, Coach Hosack, Coach Bladt, Coach Simdorn, Coach Tamm, Michael Schechinger, Mark Cogdill, manager Theresa Else, ball boy Todd Bladt*

1995

Curt's Comments

"Sometimes the second-best team in the state is right in your own backyard. That's what happened in 1995. Our district is always tough, but in 1995 it was the toughest. We beat Denison 2-0 in the regular season at our place and 10-7 in OT up there.

"In the championship game, West Delaware returned a punt for a touchdown to take a 7-0 lead. We scored twenty-seven unanswered points to win 27-7."

1995 Scores (13-0, District 1st)

Harlan 42	LeMars 14
Harlan 32	JSPC (Jefferson) 7
Harlan 2	Denison-Schleswig 0
Harlan 41	Carroll Kuemper 0
Harlan 35	Clarinda 0
Harlan 19	Glenwood 0
Harlan 33	Atlantic 13
Harlan 47	Red Oak 14
Harlan 20	CB Lewis Central 6
Playoffs	
Harlan 28	Creston/O-M 27
Harlan 10	Denison-Schleswig 7 (ot)
Harlan 10	Spencer 7
Harlan 27	West Delaware 7

Quarterback Rob Klinkefus looks downfield for an open receiver

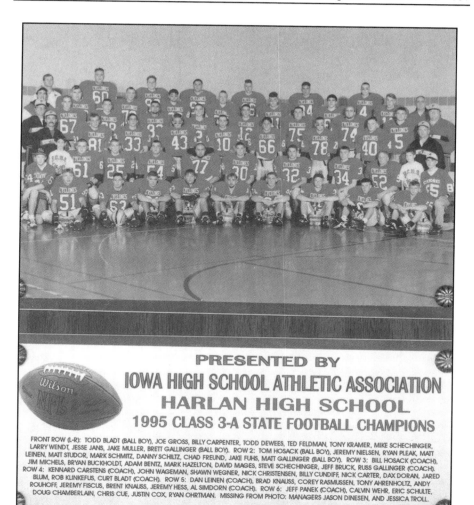

PRESENTED BY

IOWA HIGH SCHOOL ATHLETIC ASSOCIATION

HARLAN HIGH SCHOOL

1995 CLASS 3-A STATE FOOTBALL CHAMPIONS

FRONT ROW (L-R): TODD BLADT (BALL BOY), JOE GROSS, BILLY CARPENTER, TODD DEWEES, TED FELDMAN, TONY KRAMER, MIKE SCHECHINGER, LARRY WENDT, JESSE JANS, JAKE MULLER, BRETT GALLINGER (BALL BOY). ROW 2: TOM HOSACK (BALL BOY), JEREMY NIELSEN, RYAN PLEAK, MATT LEINEN, MATT STUDOR, MARK SCHMITZ, DANNY SCHILTZ, CHAD FREUND, JAKE FUHS, MATT GALLINGER (BALL BOY). ROW 3: BILL HOSACK (COACH), JIM MICHELS, BRYAN BUCKHOLDT, ADAM BENTZ, MARK HAZELTON, DAVID MAGES, STEVE SCHECHINGER, JEFF BRUCK, RUSS GALLINGER (COACH). ROW 4: KENNARD CARSTENS (COACH), JOHN WAGEMAN, SHAWN WEGNER, NICK CHRISTENSEN, BILLY CUNDIFF, NICK CARTER, DAX DORAN, JARED BLUM, ROB KLINKEFUS, CURT BLADT (COACH). ROW 5: DAN LEINEN (COACH), BRAD KNAUSS, COREY RASMUSSEN, TONY AHRENHOLTZ, ANDY ROUHOFF, JEREMY FISCUS, BRENT KNAUSS, JEREMY HESS, AL SIMDORN (COACH). ROW 6: JEFF PANEK (COACH), CALVIN WEHR, ERIC SCHULTE, DOUG CHAMBERLAIN, CHRIS CUE, JUSTIN COX, RYAN OHRTMAN. MISSING FROM PHOTO: MANAGERS JASON DINESEN, AND JESSICA TROLL.

1995 Team

1996

Curt's Comments

"In 1996, we had the coldest game I've ever played or coached in. We were in Rock Rapids playing Central Lyon in the semifinal game. A twenty-five-mile-an-hour gale out of the north was pelting us with freezing rain. It was so cold that several of our players suffered from hypothermia and couldn't remember the plays. We should have never taken the field that day. It was my call, and I blew it.

"Lesson learned—sometimes discretion *is* the better part of valor."

1996 Scores (10-2, District 2nd)

Harlan 17	Mt. Pleasant 14
Harlan 54	LeMars 13
Harlan 35	Glenwood 7
Harlan 24	CB Lewis Central 25
Harlan 31	Clarinda 6
Harlan 16	Atlantic 10
Harlan 37	Carroll Kuemper 0
Harlan 44	Creston/O-M 7
Harlan 42	Denison-Schleswig 17
Playoffs	
Harlan 48	Carroll 7
Harlan 36	Johnston 7
Harlan 13	Central Lyon/G-LR 20

On the run for a touchdown is
Mark Schmitz

1996 Team

Front row (left to right): Kevin Gittins, Tony Kruse, Todd DeWees, John Slaven, Jake Fuhs, Justin Cox, Eric Schulte, Doug Chamberlain, Billy Erlbacher, Matt Studer, Bryan Buckholdt, Adam Bentz, Jeff Bruck. **Second row:** David Hosack, Shawn Heyderhoff, John Wageman, Shawn Wegner, Michael Schechinger, Dax Doran, Mark Hazelton, Jesse Jans, Mark Schmitz, Nick Carter, Billy Cundiff, Jeff Schmitz, Joe Goss. **Third row:** David Witt, Brody Deren, Eric Chipman, Jim Michels, Jake Muller, Josh Feldman, Randy Buck, Brandon Swisher, Joe Lawler, Chris Cue, Jarred Behrendt, Russ Zimmerman. **Fourth row:** Todd Bladt, Dan Grabill, Kyle Ahrenholtz, Nick Christensen, Brent Knauss, Tim Hemminger, Mike Burchett, Eric Manz, Paul Bruck, Garrett Burchett, Kyle Schomers, Matt Schwery. **Fifth row:** Chad Plumb, Todd Sondag, Adam Studer, Rick Thompson, Tony Studer, Justin Conrad, Ben Hall, Ben Olson, Nate Schmitz, Carl Martin, Bob Greer. **Back Row:** Assistant Coach Russ Gallinger, Assistant Coach Dan Leinen, Assistant Coach Bill Hosack, Assistant Coach Al Simdorn, Ryan Fagan, Jason Conrad, Tim Jacobson, Regi Horsley, Chris Schweiso, Adam Pash, Head Coach Curt Bladt, Assistant Coach Kenard Carstens, Assistant Coach Jeff Panek, trainer Jessica Troll.

1997

Curt's Comments

"We lost to Creston in the regular season but bounced back to thump Lewis Central, LeMars, and Pella in the first three games of the playoffs. In the finals, we ran into our good friends from the northwest, the Decorah Vikings. These are the same guys who beat us in the championship games of 1988 and 1989. These were the final two years of their three consecutive titles—the only other team besides us to do that. Decorah had two sets of stud twins on their team—the Larson twins and the Fulsas twins. One of the Fulsas boys went on to be a heavyweight wrestler for the University of Iowa.

"As you might imagine, it was a very physical game. It was also the first championship game that one of my sons, Todd, competed in. We won a nailbiter, 14-7."

1997 Scores (12-1, District 1st)

Harlan 37	Mt. Pleasant 3
Harlan 21	LeMars 7
Harlan 43	Glenwood 0
Harlan 14	CB Lewis Central 10
Harlan 66	Clarinda 14
Harlan 31	Atlantic 8
Harlan 66	Carroll Kuemper 14
Harlan 17	Creston/O-M 22
Harlan 31	Denison-Schleswig 13
Playoffs	
Harlan 21	CB Lewis Central 16
Harlan 35	LeMars 14
Harlan 24	Pella 18
Harlan 14	Decorah, 7

Congratulating each other are
Ryan Fagan and Nick Carter

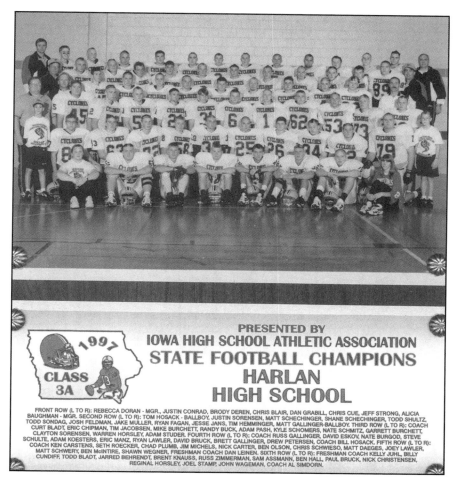

PRESENTED BY
IOWA HIGH SCHOOL ATHLETIC ASSOCIATION
STATE FOOTBALL CHAMPIONS
HARLAN
HIGH SCHOOL

CLASS 3A 1997

FRONT ROW (L TO R): REBECCA DORAN - MGR., JUSTIN CONRAD, BRODY DEREN, CHRIS BLAIR, DAN GRABILL, CHRIS CUE, JEFF STRONG, ALICIA BAUGHMAN - MGR. SECOND ROW (L TO R): TOM HOSACK - BALLBOY, JUSTIN SORENSEN, MATT SCHECHINGER, SHANE SCHECHINGER, TODD SHULTZ, TODD SONDAG, JOSH FELDMAN, JAKE MULLER, RYAN FAGAN, JESSE JANS, TIM HEMMINGER, MATT GALLINGER-BALLBOY. THIRD ROW (L TO R): COACH CURT BLADT, ERIC CHIPMAN, TIM JACOBSEN, MIKE BURCHETT, RANDY BUCK, ADAM PASH, KYLE SCHOMERS, NATE SCHMITZ, GARRETT BURCHETT, CLAYTON SORENSEN, WARREN HORSLEY, ADAM STUDER. FOURTH ROW (L TO R); COACH RUSS GALLINGER, DAVID ESKOV, NATE BURGOD, STEVE SCHULTE, ADAM KOESTERS, ERIC MANZ, RYAN LAWLER, DAVID BRUCK, BRETT GALLINGER, DREW PETERSEN, COACH BILL HOSACK. FIFTH ROW (L TO R): COACH KEN CARSTENS, SETH ROECKER, CHAD PLUMB, JIM MICHELS, NICK CARTER, BEN OLSON, CHRIS SCHWIESO, MATT DAEGES, JOEY LAWLER, MATT SCHWERY, BEN McINTIRE, SHAWN WEGNER, FRESHMAN COACH DAN LEINEN. SIXTH ROW (L TO R): FRESHMAN COACH KELLY JUHL, BILLY CUNDIFF, TODD BLADT, JARRED BEHRENDT, BRENT KNAUSS, RUSS ZIMMERMAN, SAM ASSMANN, BEN HALL, PAUL BRUCK, NICK CHRISTENSEN, REGINAL HORSLEY, JOEL STAMP, JOHN WAGEMAN, COACH AL SIMDORN.

1997 Team

1998

Curt's Comments

"In 1998, we lost to Carroll Kuemper 21-17 in Carroll. It's the only time they've defeated us in thirty-one tries. We learned a bit of a lesson that night about teamwork. We made some changes in personnel and spanked them to the tune of 27-0 in a quarterfinal playoff game.

"In the semifinal game, we met Central Lyon again. Instead of hypothermia, we experienced euphoria as we won 21-0 in the cozy confines of the UNI Dome. In the finals, Brody Deren went bonkers. Grinnell refused to come out of their eight-man defensive front, and we lit them up to the tune of 49-7. Brody played his finest game ever, passing for 275 yards in the first half. Ben Hall caught three TD passes."

Adam Studer congratulates Dominic Leinen on his block

1998 Scores (12-1, District 2nd)

Harlan 33	Boone 12
Harlan 47	LeMars 7
Harlan 50	Glenwood 0
Harlan 17	Carroll Kuemper 21
Harlan 22	Denison-Schleswig 7
Harlan 41	Creston/O-M 13
Harlan 50	Lewis Central 24
Harlan 55	Clarinda 0
Harlan 43	Atlantic 13
Playoffs	
Harlan 48	Carroll 6
Harlan 27	Carroll Kuemper 0
Harlan 21	Central Lyon/G-LR 0
Harlan 49	Grinnell 7

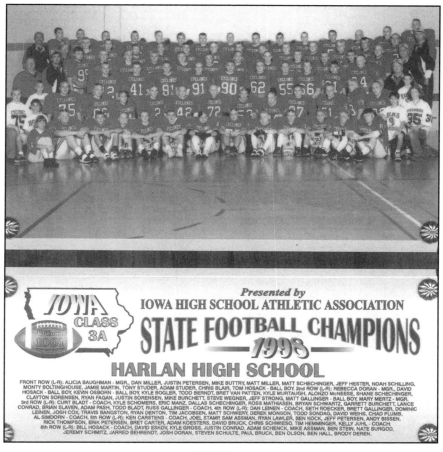

1998 Team

1999

Curt's Comments

"In the last game of our undefeated season, we were easily beating Atlantic. I told Russ Gallinger, 'Let's get Ryan (Lawler, our starting tailback) out of the game after the next play.'

"Ryan ran the ball for a substantial gain. As he ran past me back to our sideline, he said, 'Coach, I think I just broke my collarbone.'

"He was right. Without him we struggled offensively and lost in the second game of the playoffs to Jefferson 6-0.

"The lesson we learned is that there are some things in life you just can't control. 'If onlys'—'if only' I got Ryan out of the game sooner, we could have been state champions again—will drive you to drink. The trick is to realize that when these things happen, just get ready for the next play. It's the only thing you have any control over."

*Eager to block a
Kuemper player
is Monty Boltinghouse*

1999 Scores (10-1, District 1st)

Harlan 25	Boone 7
Harlan 30	LeMars 21
Harlan 40	Glenwood 0
Harlan 26	Carroll Kuemper 0
Harlan 35	Denison-Schleswig 34 (2ot)
Harlan 48	Creston/O-M 13
Harlan 35	Lewis Central 2
Harlan 37	Clarinda 0
Harlan 45	Atlantic 7
Playoffs	
Harlan 24	Adel-DeSoto-Minburn 7
Harlan 0	JSPC (Jefferson) 6

1999 Team

Front row (left to right): *Adam Koesters, Chris Blair, Seth Roecker, Justin Sorensen, Matthew Schechinger, Clayton Sorensen, Ryan Lawler, David Eskov, Brett Gallinger, David Bruck.* **Second row:** *Warren Horsley, Bruce Spray, Adam Schenck, Jon Troll, Matt Schmitz, Alonzo McNeese, Nate Burgod, Sam Assmann, Stephen Schulte, Chris Heese, Justin Petersen.* **Third row:** *Derek Monson, Cameron Kiersch, Brian Slaven, Monty Boltringhouse, Dominic Leinen, Kyle Murtaugh, Todd Berndt, Jeff Hester, Jeff Petersen, Ryan McDermott, Jared Lytle.* **Fourth row:** *David Weihs, Mike Thompson, Ben Stein, Ben Kock, Matt Miller, Kyle Goss, Steve Wener, Josh Cox, Ross Mathiasen, Ryan Denton, Rick Ohlinger, Josh Pedersen.* **Fifth row:** *Josh Doran, Bryan Schwartz, Bret Carter, Bobby Whitney, Noah Schilling, Jamie Martin, James Shields, Jay Wageman, Jesse Sporrer, Matt Lauterbach, Brent Schumacher, Andy Chamberlain.* **Sixth row:** *Kyle Bogler, Danny Miller, Lance Conrad, Jeremy Schmitz, Erik Petersen, Adam Gubbels, Mike Assmann, Nic Klindt, Todd Chamberlain, Dan Wilke, Kyle Manz, Heath Schechinger.* **Seventh row:** *Mark Schneider, Jason Leinen, Adam Nelson, Jesse Blaine, Andy Smith, Dan Salvo, Jeremy Svendsen, Paul Schenck, John Petsche, Brad Thygesen, Ben Pedersen.* **Eighth row:** *Jaime Schwery, Zach Daeges, Karl Fremel, Bob White, Coach Kenard Carstens, Coach Kelly Juhl, Coach Al Simdorn, Coach Dan Leinen, Coach Curt Bladt, Coach Russ Gallinger, Allen Assmann, Bret VanPatten, Dallas Schechinger.* **Back row:** *manager Gina Kenkel, manager Mark Frahm, manager Alicia Baughman, manager Mary Mertz*

PLAYER FROM THE DECADE
TODD BLADT

Todd Bladt is the player from the decade of the 1990s for two reasons:

1. He played high school football for his dad, which is always interesting and revealing.
2. He's an assistant football coach now.

The Brothers Bladt

Todd is youngest of the three Bladt boys. He graduated from high school in 1999. Brother Greg graduated in 1988. Brother Jeff graduated in 1990. As you can see in the photo below, they all wore the #64 for the Cyclones. Curt says the boys did that so their mother wouldn't be confused.

Like Todd, Greg and Jeff were also starters for the Cyclones and played in championship games—Greg in 1986 and Jeff in 1988 and 1989. Curt says, "All three of my boys were and are great kids—men any parent or coach would be proud to call son."

Jeff, Todd, and Greg Bladt

Brother Greg Bladt

Greg always wanted to be an Army Airborne Ranger. Because of a hearing and balance deficiency, he couldn't qualify. He used his dad's "next play" philosophy and spent six years as a small arms specialist at Camp Dodge in Des Moines. Greg went to college at Northwest Missouri State and Bellevue College. He is married to Tammy, who is the RN supervisor at Myrtue Memorial Hospital in Harlan. The couple has three children—triplets Drew, Haley, and Alex.

Brother Jeff Bladt

Jeff was a 3A first team all-state defensive tackle for the Cyclones. After attending Iowa Western Community College, he became a manager at Jim's Wholesale Meats in Harlan. His wife, Shilo, is marketing director for Concerned, Inc. They have two children, Hannah and Sam.

Goal Line Stand

Greg and Jeff were instrumental in creating Todd's toughness. The three boys used to play a game in the Bladt basement called Goal Line Stand. Todd would carry a Nerf football and attempt to score a touchdown by running over his two older brothers. I wonder if they would be willing to play the game now that Todd is 6'3" and 270 pounds?

The Bladt Family

Front row (left to right): Greg (with Drew), Curt (with Haley and Alex), Jeff (with Samuel), and Todd. Back row: Jill, Tammy (Greg's wife), Shilo (Jeff's wife), and Hannah (standing)

As you might imagine, with two older brothers, Todd always wanted to play for his dad. He remembers, "In a fifth grade English class, Brody Deren, myself, and about eight other boys made a pact by signing a sheet of paper stating that we were going to win the state football title our last three years in high school. We fell a little short of our goal. We only won the title our last two years—1997 and 1998."

When Todd was in eighth grade, Curt was head coach of the South Shrine Bowl team. One of the assistants was Bob Jensen, the coach of Mt. Pleasant High School and the Player from the Decade for the 1960s. Bob instructed Todd in the art of hiking the ball for punts, field goals, and extra points. Todd learned his lesson well and went on to be the long snapper in high school and at the University of South Dakota.

Like most coaches, Curt says, "I was harder on my sons than I was on anyone else."

Todd agrees, "He held us all to a higher standard."

Trough Time in Tivoli Fest Town

Keeping with the food theme of this book, Todd relates the following story: "For years, on the Thursday nights before games, Dad, many of the players, and I would drive to the Danish Inn Restaurant in Elk Horn (home of the Tivoli Fest) for their all-you-can-eat prime rib and crab legs buffet. The manager would see us walk in, roll her eyes, and seat us at a huge table in the back. After a while, she saw that we were at the crab legs section of the buffet so much that we were keeping the other customers away. So they started bringing us plates piled high with crab legs. Sometimes we would stay and eat over two hours. A couple of times they had to kick us out."

Eating prime rib and crab legs helped to build big linemen. It also helped build close-knit teams. Todd says, "Dad always stressed the team aspect of football. During the season, the team was always together."

Second Fiddle—for Now

As an assistant football coach at Abraham Lincoln High School in Council Bluffs, Todd constantly finds his dad's words coming out of his own mouth. Todd hears himself saying, "You can block anybody if you're motivated enough and use the right technique," and "You've gotta believe you can do it before you can do it."

As head coach, Curt Bladt has won an amazing 91% of his games. In his first year as an assistant, Todd's head coach was ejected from a game and was restricted from coaching the following week's contest. Todd took over and won the overtime game. That made his winning percentage 100%, which demoted Curt to the second-highest winning percentage in the family.

When asked about coming back to coach football in Harlan, Todd diplomatically replied, "It would be an adventure!"

Decade Conclusion

How can you top four state championships in a decade? The answer is get off to a fast start by winning three titles in the first six years of the next decade—which is exactly what the Cyclones have done in the 2000s.

Chapter:
The 2000s

12

The Decade in Review: As the new millennium rolled in, the Cyclone Express rolled on. HCHS was runner-up in 2000 and 2001. The 2000 playoffs were overtimeville for Harlan Community. They defeated Denison 30-24 in the quarterfinals in two overtimes and beat Grinnell 56-55 in four overtimes in the semifinals. Many fans of Iowa high school football consider this game to be the most exciting playoff game ever played. The 111 points scored in the Grinnell game is the most in the Cyclones' 110-year football history. Harlan Community lost to Clear Lake 23-20 in a three overtime championship game. Hey, maybe the boys were a little tired!

In the 2002 playoffs, the team made two *loooooong* road trips to MOC-Floyd Valley and LeMars, losing the second game 24-21. This would be the last time Harlan would lose a football game for three years—and counting.

The years 2003, 2004, and 2005 were a carbon copy of 1982, 1983, and 1984—two title trifectas. The 2003 season featured a title game that Curt calls his most exciting finish ever. Two Osborn-to-Applegate bombs in the last five-and-a-half minutes led to Cyclone state championship #9.

These two plays may have prompted Curt to comment on an interesting Russ Gallinger prediction. In the darker days of Curt's tussle with Miller-Fisher Syndrome, he was lying in his hospital bed at the University of Nebraska Medical Center. Russ visited him and whispered in his ear, "We'll be going to the Dome together again real soon."

Curt replied, "Make sure Applegate's on the bus."

Compared to 2003, the 2004 and 2005 title games were anticlimactic, as Harlan Community beat Decorah 42-7 and West Delaware 34-13.

2000

Curt's Comments

"In the fifth game of the year, Denison unloaded on us to the tune of 35-9 in Harlan. We came back and beat them in two overtimes in the playoffs.

"After we scored a TD in the third overtime of 'the playoff game that wouldn't end' with Grinnell, we were trailing by a point. I was considering going for two points for the win. I turned to ask our defensive coaches their opinion. They were all lying down on the 30-yard line.

"I asked them, 'What should we do?' They just shrugged their shoulders. Everybody was physically and emotionally drained."

2000 Scores (11-2, District 2nd, State 2nd)

Harlan 21	Boone 7
Harlan 48	Creston/O-M 35
Harlan 46	Glenwood 21
Harlan 16	Carroll Kuemper 13
Harlan 35	Denison-Schleswig 9
Harlan 39	Carroll 14
Harlan 47	CB Lewis Central 14
Harlan 62	Red Oak 8
Harlan 49	Atlantic 20
Playoffs	
Harlan 25	Boyden-Hull/Rock Valley 0
Harlan 30	Denison-Schleswig 24 (2ot)
Harlan 56	Grinnell 55 (4ot)
Harlan 20	Clear Lake 23 (3ot)

Preparing to defend for the Cyclones are Derek Monson, Ben Kock, Steve Wagner, and Kyle Gross

2000 Team

2001

Curt's Comments

"We had a game at Creston that was rained out. We blocked a punt on the first series of the game and had a first-and-goal. Then the storm hit. The lightning was so bad it was like mid-day on the field. Eventually the storm dumped six inches of water. We could have driven back and played the next day, but it was a non-district game, so we just canceled it.

"Our first playoff game was in Orange City. Al Simdorn is from that part of the state and has gotten all our assistant coaches hooked on Dutch letters pastries. Al knows every bakery known to mankind in northwest Iowa. He drove real fast to get to the game so we could visit them all and load up the bus with as many pastries as we could.

"We finished second in the district thanks to a 26-7 loss to Coach Dave Wiebers' bunch from Denison. In the playoffs, we evened the score with a 21-7 victory at home. After beating Grin City (Grinnell) in the semifinals, we lost a 12-9 nailbiter to a new opponent (Western Dubuque) in the finals."

Receiving the play call from Coach Gallagher is Jeff Deren

2001 Scores (10-2, District 2nd, State 2nd)

Harlan 28	Boone 7
Harlan —	Creston/O-M (rained out)
Harlan 35	Glenwood 25
Harlan 45	Carroll Kuemper 15
Harlan 7	Denison-Schleswig 26
Harlan 44	Carroll 14
Harlan 44	Lewis Central 16
Harlan 2	Red Oak 0 (forfeit)
Harlan 30	Atlantic 7
Playoffs	
Harlan 42	MOC-Floyd Valley 13
Harlan 21	Denison-Schleswig 7
Harlan 20	Grinnell 13
Harlan 9	Epworth, W. Dubuque 12

2001 Team

Front row (left to right): Brent Schumacher; Heath Schechinger; Andy Chamberlain, Allan Assmann, Colby Pash, David Maxwell, Matt Lauterbach, Rick Ohlinger, Adam Gubbels, Dan Wilke, Jesse Sporrer, Josh Pedersen, Jason Leinen. *Second row:* Spencer Wegner, Mike Schneider, Ryan McDermott, Mark Staiert, Jaime Schuery, Karl Freml, Paul Schenck, Jeremy Svendsen, Jesse Cantrell, Kyle Manz, Todd Chamberlain. *Third row:* Travis Hilgartner; Bobby Leuschen, ALex Schomers, Brock Swisher; Tyler Muller, Ryan Coenen, Andy Petersen, Mike Martens, Chuck Baughman, Brett Bogler, Jeff Deren. *Fourth row:* Danny Assman, Jake Smith, Tyler Henscheid, John Henscheid, Ryan Lee, Paul Schechinger; Tom Hosack, Matt Allen, Michael Kelley, Jared Noack, Randy Kaufmann, Richard Graeve. *Fifth row:* Dan Erickson, Ben Arentson, Warren Rauterkus, Adam Schwery, Matt McDermott, Lucas Von Glan, Jason Burger, Adam Bissen, John Martin, Tobey Jacobsen, Aaron Hansen, Charles Behrendt. *Sixth row:* Ross Larsen, Trent Hampton, Jason Petersen, Aaron McCutcheon, Sean Lawler, Jacob Lynch, Jeff Bissen, Joel Osborn, Kyle Martin. *Back row:* manager Dewayne Kenkel, Coach Bladt, Coach Hosack, Coach Juhl, Coach Leinen, Coach Simdorn, Coach Carstens, Coach Gallinger, manager Gina Kenkel

2002

Curt's Comments

"2002 was a disappointing and a great season rolled into one. We were undefeated going into the last regular season game at Atlantic. They had two Division I players on their roster—quarterback Brett Meyer and lineman Tom Schmeling. Both went on to be starters for Iowa State. In overtime, Atlantic kicked a field goal. On our possession, we had a kid streaking toward the end zone for a touchdown when an Atlantic kid made a big play by punching the ball out and causing a fumble.

"Incidentally, Atlantic's coach, Gaylord Schelling, and all the coaches in our district are great guys. We all get along well.

"The Atlantic loss meant we had to take the long and Dutch letters–filled trip to Orange City for our first playoff game. We won a tough game by seven points. Five days later we were in LeMars and lost the quarterfinal game 24-21 to a gritty group of kids."

2002 Scores (9-2, District 2nd)

Harlan 55	Mount Pleasant 6
Harlan 31	Carroll 20
Harlan 55	Glenwood 0
Harlan 31	Denison-Schleswig 14
Harlan 41	Lewis Central 7
Harlan 55	Red Oak 0
Harlan 48	Carroll Kuemper 0
Harlan 31	Creston/O-M 7
Harlan 21	Atlantic 24 (ot)
Playoffs	
Harlan 24	MOC-Floyd Valley 17
Harlan 21	LeMars 24

Making the tackle for the Cyclones are #6 Paul Schechinger and #34 Tyler Muller

2002 Team

Front row (left to right): *Jake McElroy, Tyler Muller, Bobby Leuschen, Danny Assman, Brett Bogler, Jake Smith, Spencer Wegner, Brock Swisher, Andy Petersen, Mike Schnekler, Jeff Deren, Chuck Baughmann.* **Second row:** *Travis Hillgartner, Matt McDermott, Adam Schwery, JP Henscheld, Alex Schomers, Tyler Henscheld, Dan Erickson, Ryan Coenen, Tom Hosack, Paul Schechinger, Mike Kelley, Jared Henscheld.* **Third row:** *Tobey Jacobsen, Aaron McCutcheon, Sean Lawler, Warren Rauterkus, Ben Arenston, Randy Kaufmann, Joel Osborn, Jeff Bissen, Kyle Martin, John Martin, Chris Sorensen, Matt Andersen.* **Fourth row:** *Jeremy Clark, Brandon Burmeister, Jason Hastert, Ross Hastert, Greg Applegate, Kevin Kruse, Eric Lauterbach, Andy Schneider, Michael Leinen, Nick Schaben, Jordan Petersen.* **Fifth row:** *Sam Arentson, Dusty Bruck, Lawrence Rasmussen, Matt Gallinger, Trent Svendsen, Garrett Rauterkus, Greg Knudsen, Joel White, Jason Petersen, Luke Von Glan.* **Sixth row:** *ball boy Willie Baughman, manager PJ Wegner, Matt Barelson, Matt Gubbels, Wyatt Flint, Chuck Bebrendt, manager Patrea Nelson, manager Jake Andersen.* **Back row:** *Coach Ken Carstens, Coach Bill Hosack, Coach Al Simdorn, Head Coach Curt Bladt, Coach Russ Gallinger*

2003

Curt's Comments

"We were undefeated going into the championship game in the Dome against Mt. Vernon. It was the strangest atmosphere in our locker room at halftime. Even though we were leading by a touchdown, the boys were emotionally down. I told them something I tell all my teams, 'No matter how good you are, somebody is going to test you at some point in the season.'

"We were being tested all right. After taking a 17-0 lead in the first half, Mt. Vernon outscored us 35-6 to take a 35-23 lead with 5:38 left in the game. Everybody remembers the offense scoring on two big pass plays of 80 and 67 yards. What most people don't remember is that we had to stop them after our two TDs. And we hadn't been doing a good job of that for most of the game. Our defensive lineman, Dan Erickson, made big play after big play, and Ben Arentson intercepted a pass on their last possession to seal the deal."

Jeff Bisson makes his way toward the end zone

2003 Scores (13-0, District 1st, State 1st)

Harlan 29	Mount Pleasant 0
Harlan 28	Carroll 21
Harlan 46	Glenwood 7
Harlan 31	Denison-Schleswig 6
Harlan 49	Lewis Central 8
Harlan 61	Red Oak 6
Harlan 42	Carroll Kuemper 14
Harlan 54	Creston/O-M 0
Harlan 48	Atlantic 21
Playoffs	
Harlan 35	Dallas Center-Grimes 14
Harlan 63	Creston/O-M 22
Harlan 62	LeMars 21
Harlan 38	Mount Vernon 35

2003 Team

2004

Curt's Comments

"In 2004, we were undefeated and untested during the regular season. Remember my line, 'No matter how good you are, somebody is going to test you at some point in the season.' Our test in 2004 came in the first playoff game against MOC-Floyd Valley. On a very slippery Merrill Field against a very slippery team, we passed our test 52-43. The total score of 95 is by far the most points put on the board in a non-overtime game in our history.

"In our march to the 3A state championship, we defeated Denison, Waukee, and Decorah by a combined score of 128 to 24."

Kevin Kruse dodges Decorah defenders in the championship game

2004 Scores (13-0, District 1st, State 1st)

Harlan 52	Norwalk 17
Harlan 48	Webster City 6
Harlan 48	Glenwood 7
Harlan 41	Carroll 7
Harlan 42	JSPC (Jefferson) 0
Harlan 14	Lewis Central 2
Harlan 42	Denison-Schleswig 0
Harlan 49	Atlantic 13
Harlan 42	Creston/O-M 7
Playoffs	
Harlan 52	MOC-Floyd Valley 43
Harlan 35	Denison-Schleswig 0
Harlan 51	Waukee 17
Harlan 42	Decorah-North Winn. 7

2004 Team

2005

Curt's Comments

"In the third game of the season, Carroll jumped out to a 14-0 lead in the first quarter. We came back and won 42-20.

"We received a big wake-up call from a very tough Winterset team in our first playoff game. We scored the last 10 points of the game to win 23-13.

"The atmosphere at Merrill Field for our next game against Waukee was wild. The crowd of over five thousand packed both stands and completely surrounded the field—six to eight fans deep in most places.

"They scored ten straight points just before halftime to make a game of it at 17-10. Then, on the last play of the first half, Shawn Doran hit Jared Boysen with a perfectly thrown ball to give us a two touchdown lead.

"At halftime, I told the boys another one of my favorite lines, 'If you win the first three minutes of the second half, you have a good chance to win the game.' It doesn't guarantee it, but it sets the tone for the rest of the game. They listened to me. We scored on our first possession to go up by 21. They never recovered, and we prevailed 48-17.

"We were leading West Delaware 13-6 in the championship game. Our spotters up in the press box played a big part in helping us go on to win the game 34-13. They saw that the Vikings were playing a defense that left them at a disadvantage to a certain type of play. The spotters sent me a note explaining the disadvantage. The note ended with the words, 'You will know what to do.' We did and pulled away for a three TD win."

The Cyclones' run of championships continues in the Dome

2005 Scores (13-0, District 1st, State 1st)

Harlan 37	Norwalk 7
Harlan 60	Webster City 0
Harlan 38	Glenwood 7
Harlan 42	Carroll 20
Harlan 31	JSPC (Jefferson) 0
Harlan 43	Lewis Central 7
Harlan 49	Denison-Schleswig 14
Harlan 48	Atlantic 34
Harlan 37	Creston/O-M 7
Playoffs	
Harlan 23	Winterset 13
Harlan 48	Waukee 17
Harlan 35	LeMars 21
Harlan 34	West Delaware 13

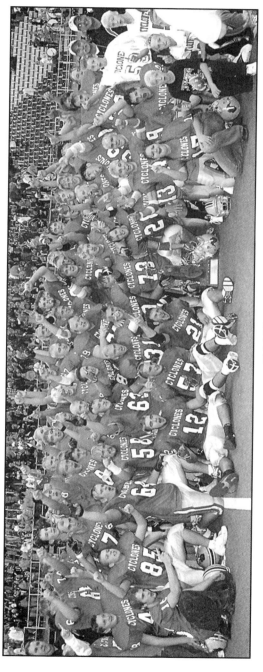

2005 Team

Adam Musich, Kevin Osborn, Tony Kenkel, Brett Stein, Ryan Clements, Lucas Larsen, Sam Brummer, Todd Schwartz, Zack Martens, Ben Bieker, Shaun Doran, Brady Greer, Hyle Haake, Chris Courtney, Brett Gubbels, Josh Edgecomb, Kevin Gries, Chris Jensen, Mark Blum, Jimmy McKean, Brad Blum, Brandon Cairney, Jason Weis, Kurt Chamberlain, Jared Boysen, Tyler Kloewer, David Hosack, Jonathon Davis, Garrett Clayton, Zach Stewart, Alex Hooge, Carl Schnack, Colton Chambers, Derrick Schwery, Cody Petersen, Michael Kruse, Jordan Schechinger, Anthony Lefeber, Tyler Murtaugh, Andrew Jensen, Zach Baer, Richard Petersen, Lucas Harding, Nick Hughes, Dennis Gubbels, Kyle Tearney, Jorge Hansen, Brad Schechinger, Nicholas Freml, Troy Langenfeld, Cory Bogler, Zach Kaufman, Curtis Schumacher, Chris McClain, John Kohorst, Brandon Bogler, Dan Smith, Ryan Wegner, David Plugmann, Stephan Erlbacher, Nathan Harris, Tyler Stahl, Derek Pauley, Derek Buman, Jake Laver, John Vorrath, Ben Hansen, Daniel Hoch, Nathan Andersen, Ross Andersen, Neil Gross, Doug Bissen, Mitchel Petersen, Keith Leinen, Zach Green, Adam Leinen, Randy Doran, Mike Schoemann, Greg Wilke

PLAYER FROM THE DECADE
SHAWN DORAN

How would you like to follow Joel Osborn, the record-setting Cyclone quarterback, who set state records for touchdown passes in a season (42) and passing yards in a season (3,254)? In the fall of 2004, that responsibility was accepted by Shawn Doran. Twenty-six consecutive wins and two state championships later, the 5'10", 170-pound signal caller proved he was more than up to the task.

Shawn Doran

Like so many Harlan players, Shawn's brother, Josh, played for the Cyclones. Of course, Shawn went to all his games, which whetted his appetite to play for Coach Bladt.

Shawn says, "I couldn't wait for game day to see Josh play. I went to every game expecting them to win."

In his junior year, Shawn completed 51% of his passes for 1,750 yards, ran for 485 yards, and scored eighteen touchdowns. Also on the team that year was half-back Kevin Kruse, who rushed for 2,011 yards and 41 touchdowns.

With no Kruser in the backfield for his senior year, there was added pressure for Shawn to perform. He was more than up to the task when he completed 60% of his passes for 1,274 yards, ran for 815 yards, scored eighteen touchdowns, and guided the Cyclones to their third state title in a row. Strangely, Shawn wasn't selected to the all-conference first team by a vote from the Hawkeye Ten coaches. Coach Bladt mused, "He ran past the other teams' players so fast that I guess their coaches didn't see him."

Shawn loves how Coach Bladt makes football fun (of course, winning 26 games in a row and two state championships helps too). From the senior steak feed at Curt's house and the potluck dinners before playoff games to the seven-on-seven drill and scrimmages in practices, Curt knew that a season lasting almost four months needs to be made enjoyable.

Three Valuable Lessons

Shawn says he learned three valuable lessons that he will take with him through life:

1. **"Never give up."** Shawn saw this one firsthand when he visited his coach in the hospital while Curt was fighting to recover from Miller-Fisher Syndrome.
2. **"Play each down like it's your last one."** Harlan doesn't always have the biggest, strongest, and fastest kids on the football field, but they almost always have the most motivated. Shawn is a perfect example of this. "He plays with a little bit of an edge, and that rubs off on the other guys," says Coach Bladt. "He's just a tough nut."
3. **"Put in the extra time. It will make a difference in the end."** Shawn says, "We were always prepared to play the game. We always had back-ups if the other team did something out of the ordinary."

Before home football games at Merrill Field, the opposing teams and the Cyclones dress in adjacent locker rooms at the Veterans Memorial Building adjacent to the field. Shawn remembers a time when the opposing team was whooping and hollering next door. Being the motivational expert he is, Coach Bladt said, "Be quiet. Do you hear that noise? Now, listen to the sound in our locker room. This is the quiet sound before a tornado hits."

The Doran's Field of Dreams

In the memorable movie, *Field of Dreams,* the voice in the cornfield whispers to the Iowa farmer, "If you build it, he will come." The farmer did build it (the baseball diamond), and his father did come.

Harlan Community High School and Coach Curt Bladt have built it too: a football program that is admired throughout the state of Iowa and beyond, a program dripping with tradition that attracts talented and committed players from throughout the school district to the Merrill Field of Dreams to play for the Cyclones. Players like Shawn Doran, who just happens to grow nine acres of sweet corn with his parents and sister, Ashley, on their farm southwest of Harlan.

Shawn plans to continue growing. He is following his coach's footsteps by attending Morningside College on a football scholarship and wants to teach high school vocational agriculture after graduation.

Shawn Doran with his sister, Ashley, and parents Shirley and Ralph

Thank God for Good Parents

In seventh grade, Shawn played quarterback on the B team. Because he didn't make the A team, he questioned going out for football the next year. In typical fatherly fashion, his dad, Ralph, proclaimed, "You're going out for football."

His mother, Shirley, was a huge supporter of Shawn's athletic career, too. In the summer before Shawn's senior year, Shirley was told she needed open-heart surgery. Not wanting to be a distraction to her son, she waited until after the season was over to have the surgery. Shawn led his team to the 3A state championship on the third Saturday in November. Shirley had her open-heart surgery the following Wednesday and is doing fine today. How's that for a dedicated family— a family like the Cyclone football player families who preceded Shawn Doran and those who will surely follow?

Merrill Field of Dreams

In *Field of Dreams,* Doc Graham, the character played by Burt Lancaster, tells Ray Kinsella, the character played by Kevin Costner, "We just don't recognize the most significant moments in our lives when they're happening. We walk by them like they were strangers in the night." How true.

In this section, you met The Players on every Curt Bladt-coached team. They all briefly danced under the lights of Merrill Field on a few Friday evenings. Like most 16-to-18-year-old kids, they probably didn't recognize the significance of those moments as they occurred. As adults, I have a strong feeling they do now.

An Ordinary Place?

On the surface, the Harlan Community School District looks like an ordinary place filled with ordinary people. While driving through the town of Harlan, the small villages surrounding it, and the rolling Iowa countryside, nothing really jumps out and screams at you.

But, lying underneath that silent surface are the keys to success in any of life's endeavors, the keys that allows ordinary people in ordinary places to accomplish extraordinary things, the keys that unlocks the magic of The Cyclone Way:

The Expectation of Excellence

Cooperation

Hard Work

Curt Bladt's life is a shining example of this triad of qualities in action. But his example is way more than *what* he does—coach football well. It's *who* he is. In the next section, you will take a closer look at The Person Curtis Melvin Bladt really is.

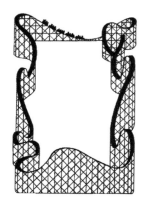

It's easy to be spoiled by success. As Cyclone fans, sometimes we need to take a step back, take a panoramic view of Curt's coaching career, and appreciate how unusual the journey has been.

- Only two of eight district teams (25%) make the playoffs each year, so it's usual to be sitting at home in November. As a head coach, Curt's teams have been playoff-bound an unusual 25 out of 28 years (89%).

- The odds of winning your first playoff game against teams that finished first or second in their district (the cream of the crop) is 50%. Curt has won an unusual 26 in a row (100%).

- In a 64-team class, the odds of making it to the championship game are 3%. Curt's teams have done it an unusual 18 out of 28 years (64%).

- In a 64-team class, the odds of winning the championship game are 1.5%. Curt's teams have done it an unusual 10 out of 28 years (36%).

- You would think a team would win about half of its playoff games. Harlan Community's record is an unusual 74 wins and 15 losses—83%. The 74 wins are by far the most for any Iowa school in any class.

- Curt's teams have won eight out of ten overtime games against teams that scored just as many points as the Cyclones did for the previous 48 minutes. Very unusual.

- Of the top twelve career leaders in PATs for the state of Iowa in all classes, an unusually high number of five kicked for Harlan.

#4	Kyle Martin	151 PATs	2001–2003
#5	Jamie Martin	145 PATs	1998–2000
#7	Zach Kaufman	128 PATs	2004–2005
#9	Chris Hogzett	118 PATs	1989–1991
#12	Billy Cundiff	113 PATs	1995–1997

All of the above players kicked during Curt Bladt's tenure as head coach. That's a lot of touchdowns, folks.

- Through the fifth game of the 2006 season, the Cyclone football team has put together a 44-game winning streak. This is the longest winning streak since Iowa went to a playoff system in 1972. Very, very unusual.

- The Iowa record for regular season games without a loss is held by Harlan—66 consecutive games from 1985 through 1992. Very, very, very unusual.
- It's typical to win about 50% of your games. Curt's teams have won an unusual 91%. This is the highest career winning percentage for any high school coach in Iowa history.

It's interesting to note the Cyclones' basketball coach, Mitch Osborn, has a record of 448 wins and 87 losses in his twenty-two year career at three schools. This is an average of over 20 wins per year. Mitch's 84% career winning is also the highest career winning percentage for any high school coach in Iowa history. The two people with the highest career winning percentages coaching at the same time at the same school? Unusual times four!

The unusual results chronicled above don't happen by accident. They are due to a very unusual *place* (the Harlan Community School District), a very unusual group of *players*, and a very unusual *person,* who had very unusual *preparation.* In this section, you will dig deeper into what makes Curt Bladt tick.

In Chapter 13, you will learn Curt's Eight Keys to Coaching Success. In Chapter 14, you will see how Curt defeated his toughest opponent—Miller-Fisher Syndrome. In Chapter 15, you will discover the surprising events that occurred in the year beginning September 1, 2005. And finally, in Chapter 16, Curt will answer twenty-seven questions you've been dying to ask him.

Chapter: 13
Eight Keys to Coaching Success

Charles Poore once said, "There is nothing quite so complicated as simplicity." I agree. That's why, in this chapter, I will attempt to uncomplicate the eight simple keys Curt uses to unlock the vault of high school football success. These same keys can be used in any business or any life. The eight keys are:

1. Treat Everyone Well
2. Keep It Simple
3. Care About the Kids
4. Effectively Motivate the Players
5. Focus on Action, Not Results
6. Focus on the Past, Present, and Future at the Right Times
7. Stress Teamwork
8. Have Fun

Key #1: Treat Everyone Well

The most important word in Key #1 is "everyone."

Curt says, "We have lots of social diversity here in the Harlan Community School District. Because of the variety of life experiences I've had, I can talk with and relate to anybody."

> *"Some people are born on third base*
> *and go through life thinking they hit a triple."*
> **—Barry Switzer**

All the "Treat Everyone Well" stories I've collected about Coach Bladt would fill a book by themselves. In an attempt to keep you from having a hernia carrying this one, I've included a few of the best examples:

- Long-time KNOD sports director Ron Novotny tells this story: "When Curt's son, Todd, was playing for South Dakota University, Curt would often leave for Todd's game

Ron Novotny

171

real early on Saturday morning or right after the Harlan game on Friday evening. Curt would *always* stop and call me at 8:15 a.m. sharp to do an interview on the previous night's game."

• Curt helps judge the Apple Pie Contest every year at the Shelby County Fair. Typically, fifty to seventy pies are entered. According to Dave Webber, sportscaster for WOWT television in Omaha, Curt is an apple pie connoisseur.

"Curt will cut out a one-inch square piece of the pie, stick his nose in the hole, and take a deep whiff of it. Then he studies the pie. Finally, he tastes a piece and savors it. If he likes the pie, he will signal me. In an effort to preserve my waistline, he narrows it down to ten or so pies before the Shelby County Mother of the Year and I jump in."

Curt with Dave Webber

Sharon Petersen, the Apple Pie Coordinator at the Fair, has this to say about Curt's gastronomic exploits:

"Apple Pie Morning at the Shelby County Fair has been in existence for over twenty years. During the past fifteen years, we have invited Curt Bladt to serve as one of our judges. After the pies are judged, they're served to the three hundred or more senior citizens who attend.

"We've found that Coach Bladt is not only a winner at coaching football, but he's also a great taster and judge of apple pies—over one thousand pies and counting! Judging with Curt is Dave Webber, a sportscaster at WOWT-TV in Omaha, and the current Shelby County Mother of the Year.

"When Curt was very ill and in the hospital, Dave Webber took an apple pie to him. There's a definite camaraderie between those two. They love to ham it up at Apple Pie Morning, and the crowd loves them.

"Yes, Coach Bladt is not only a master in his coaching profession, but also a willing guy who just happens to love apple pie. He's loved by the seniors of Shelby County, who enjoy coming to Apple Pie Morning to see who is the champion apple pie baker."

CoachBladt.com website posting
Name: Mark McLaughlin
City, State: Harlan, IA
Date: 12/15/2004

What's always fascinated me about you is that, for as tremendously successful as you are, you've never taken yourself seriously.

Coach, you build loyalty and esteem from others because of the way you treat them—with respect. You've left an indelible mark on people. And just so everyone knows, we shared a near-death experience together on a trip to a class in Council Bluffs. It wasn't a car that swerved in our path, or the deer that bounded across the road in front of us. It was the tears in my eyes from laughing so hard that very nearly took us down that embankment—something about the Jerry Springer Show, a goat, and a strange family member.

Get better and take care of yourself. The kids need you here, and frankly, I need a good laugh again.

- Dave Koos tells a story about when he and Larry Miller were announcing a state title game at the Dome in Cedar Falls (commonly known as Merrill Field East). The State Athletic Association had just changed its postgame interview guidelines for coaches. They were now asked to go immediately to the Association media room. Previously, they could do their usual interviews with local media first.

Dave Koos and Larry Miller

Dave and Larry were sitting in their broadcast booth after another Harlan victory, wondering if an assistant coach would make the trek up the Dome steps. Just then, they saw Curt huffing and puffing in their direction. When he reached the broadcast booth, Dave mentioned that he was supposed to be in the media room. Curt replied, "I'll tell you what. Those guys want to talk to me once a year. You guys are here every week." Dave also says that Curt Bladt is a sportscaster's dream to interview. "Curt's like the Energizer Bunny. All you have to do is turn him on with a question and let him go. In fact, if you don't ask him a question, he will ask his own question and then answer it!"

- Here's another story from Dave Koos. After Curt had won his 200th game, Dave said to him, "'You know, your cap would sure look good in my cap collection.' Curt took it off, signed it, and gave it to me on the spot."

- One Friday night, official Tom Fuller and his crew were listening to a scoreboard show on the radio while driving back from officiating a game that didn't involve Harlan. The announcer was interviewing Curt about the team Harlan had played. Instead of just repeating the standard lines about how hard the other team played and how well they were coached, Curt went on and on about the character of the other team and what a great guy the opposing team's coach was. Randy says that interview may seem like a small thing, but it reveals the man Curt Bladt truly is.

- Tom tells another story about a time fifteen years ago, when his crew wanted to work a Harlan game. All they asked for was one game. Curt agreed and said, "Give us your best game, and you may get our vote for officiating in the playoffs."

  During the game, Tom noticed Curt was on the field and told him to get back on the sidelines—which Curt did. Then Curt went out on the field again. Tom immediately threw his flag and penalized Harlan fifteen yards.

  After the game, the officials were changing their clothes in the Harlan coaches' locker room. In walked Coach Bladt. Tom was thinking, "Oh man, here it comes."

  Curt walked up to him, puts his hand on Tom's shoulder, and said, "Finally, an official who has enough guts to flag me." The crew got Harlan's vote for the playoffs and has worked several championship games.

- One summer day in the early 1980s, Curt and the University of Iowa's current head coach, Kirk Ferentz, were playing together in a golf tournament in Holstein. During the round, a violent storm started to move in that caused all the golfers to dash back to the clubhouse—except two, Curt and Kirk.

  Here's how Kirk remembers it: "Curt was my eyes and ears that day. While everyone else scurried for cover, we just sat back and watched the storm. After a minute or so, Curt said, 'Now it's time to move.' Curt drove our cart back to the clubhouse and backed it into an L-shaped cove that was made of cinder block and had a roof. We just sat and watched the storm. Curt wasn't nervous at all.

"In addition to tree limbs flying by, the keg started to roll away. My first reaction as a football coach was to yell, 'Fumble! Fumble!' Curt and I recovered the fumbled keg and rolled it to safety."

But a wayward keg wasn't all the dynamic duo rescued that day. The storm turned into a tornado and tore off the roof and ripped up the walls of a nearby house. The house belonged to a man named Hoolie, who played in Kirk and Curt's foursome. After the tornado passed by, the two brave suds-savers and a group of men ran to the house and helped pull Hoolie's wife and daughter from the wreckage.

- Offensive coordinator Mark Kohorst came to Harlan Community High School from Carroll Kuemper. One reason he did was because, "Harlan runs a classy football program. If they're way ahead in a game, they never rub your nose in it. The coaches get the young kids in quickly." On a personal level, Mark says, "It's a privilege to work under a guy like Curt. He's a coach's coach and like a second dad to me. I consider myself to be one of the luckiest guys in the world."

Curt Bladt, University of Iowa head coach Kirk Ferentz and Mark Kohorst

- Dave Wiebers, Denison's head coach, says, "Curt is down-to-earth. He has the old Iowa mentality. We talk before and after each game. He's the same friendly guy win or lose. The great thing about Curt is success hasn't changed his personality."

> **"The man who complains about the way the ball bounces
> is likely the one who dropped it."**
> **—Lou Holtz**

- Gene Johnson, the wife of Cyclone ex-football coach and athletic director Swede Johnson, remembers that Curt and Jill used to take them to Harlan's state basketball games. At the end of Swede's life, Curt would often visit him in the hospital. He was also with Swede when he died at home and delivered the eulogy at Swede's funeral. Gene says, "Curt can be very strict with the boys, but he is very kind to everyone."

Gene and Swede Johnson

- Curt has earned the respect of the younger kids at school. One year, only ten eighth grade boys went out for the track team. Curt got all the eighth grade boys together and told them, "You need to go out for track. It will help you excel in all sports." Another twenty immediately changed their plans.
- Many HCHS kids who go on to play for Curt at an earlier time in their lives sat on his lap during the holiday season and told him want they wanted for Christmas. No wonder they grow up to respect the guy.
- Because he treats everyone well, Curt has earned the respect of the entire Harlan community. Official Tom Fuller tells the following story about a play in the 2005 championship game in Cedar Falls: "West Delaware had the ball, and their quarterback got flushed out of the pocket and was running down the sideline right in front of Harlan's bench. I saw the player barely step out of bounds. Just after I blew my whistle, a Harlan player leveled the kid. Two flags immediately went up. The Harlan crowd, who couldn't see that the West Delaware player had stepped out of bounds, started yelling and booing. The noise was so loud I could feel it vibrate in my body. Curt saw the play, whirled around toward the stands, and thrust both his arms up in the air. The crowd *immediately* became silent. Then Curt looked at me and winked. It was the strangest thing I've ever experienced. It just shows the influence and respect Curt has from the Harlan fans. They revere the guy."

Key #2: Keep It Simple

Curt Bladt is not a complicated guy. What you see is definitely what you get. He has an amazing ability to focus on a few simple, but vital, aspects of communicating with people and coaching a football team.

The Rule Book

Unlike Howard Justice, Coach Bladt's freshman coach in high school, Curt's rule book is really thin. It contains four words:

DO THE RIGHT THING.

Curt says, "Players know what's right and wrong. It's a waste of everybody's time to spend 300 pages trying to spell it out for them."

Of course, the players must follow the high school's good conduct policy. If a player breaks a rule, Curt insists upon what he calls "timely admission." The player must call a school administrator or Curt within twenty-four hours of the infraction.

Weight Training and Conditioning

Many other schools in Iowa have mandatory weight training and conditioning programs. Harlan doesn't. Curt explains: "If the guys have the motivation, they'll do it on their own—which they usually do. And if a guy doesn't, the rest of the guys will let him know about it."

One time, when a junior high football coach was running his team too much, Curt told him, "Take it easy on them. I just want a lot of tough kids who can take three quick steps. Besides, little fat kids don't like to run and might quit the team—and little fat kids grow up to be big tough kids."

The Playbook

The Cyclone coaches have offensive and defensive playbooks, but Curt doesn't give them to the players. He tried that early in his career with little success. Now the coaches demonstrate the offensive plays and the various blocking options to the players. Then the team runs the plays until they get them right.

The Cyclones go into the first game with thirty or forty offensive plays, which can be run from multiple formations. The kids have run many of these plays since they were seventh graders. At the end of the season (often thirteen games), the team is running the same thirty or forty plays.

Curt doesn't change offensive and defensive systems every time a new one comes along. Instead, the coaches mold the system to match the players' talents. In 2003, the team featured the passing of Joel Osborn; in 2004 the power running of Kevin Kruse; and in 2005 the option attack, with several players sharing the load.

Defense, Defense, Defense

The first rule of real estate is location, location, location. Curt's first rule of high school football is defense, defense, defense. Extremely talented offensive players, the kind that can put big numbers on the scoreboard, come along every once in a while. Over the long haul, defense is what creates year-in-and-year-out consistency. As Curt says, "We've traditionally emphasized defense, and it's not very often that we have to outscore somebody to win."

Curt also keeps his practices simple. At most practices, the Cyclones:
1. Spend ten minutes stretching and jogging
2. Work on special teams for twenty minutes, in this order:
    *   kickoff team
    *   kickoff return team
    *   punt team
    *   punt return team
    *   PATs
    *   field goals
3. Split into offensive and defensive teams to run drills, practice plays, and review situations

Productive Practices
"The will to win is important,
but the will to prepare is vital."
—Joe Paterno

On Tuesday, Wednesday, and Thursday, Curt and the staff run their favorite drill—the Three-on-Three. Between cones set about five yards apart, three offensive blockers face off against three defensive players. A back runs behind the offensive linemen between the cones with the goal of making it through.

Curt says, "Football is simple. It comes down to blocking and tackling. Most games are won or lost in the trenches. I like the Three-on-Three Drill because it separates the wheat from the chaff. It's easy to see who your players are."

"Some people try to find things in this game that don't exist.
Football is only two things—blocking and tackling."
—Vince Lombardi

Once a week, the team runs an overtime drill in which the first team offense squares off against the first team defense. Just like real overtime, the offense gets the ball on the defense's ten yard line with four chances to score. It's no wonder Harlan has won eight out of its ten playoff games.

The final regular season game is on Friday. Then the Cyclones typically have playoff games on Wednesday, Tuesday, Monday, and Saturday. Because of the frequency and intensity of the games, the coaches turn down the intensity of practices during the playoffs.

One Not-So-Simple Play

Even though Curt and his assistant coaches keep their defensive and offensive plans simple, they're not afraid to run an exotic play every once in a while. In the 1982 championship game against Cedar Rapids Regis, Harlan won the game 15-14 with the aid of a play called the Swinging Gate. After a touchdown, most teams, including Harlan, kick the ball through the goal posts for one point. If you run or pass the ball and cross the goal line, you get two points. The Swinging Gate is a tricky extra point running play.

With Harlan's Swinging Gate play in the Regis game, the ball, the snapper, the holder, and the kicker were where they "should" be—right in front of the goal posts. The rest of the team was lined up way off to the right side of the ball. Instead of hiking the ball between his legs as he usually does, the snapper flipped the ball across the front of his body to a player in the group on the right side of the ball who ran it in for the game-winning two points.

Here's what's interesting and revealing about the Swinging Gate play in the Regis game. The team rehearsed the play every day at practice because it's difficult to do correctly. The players have to be lined up in a precise way to avoid a penalty and the "go ahead" for the play is signaled in by Curt at the last second. All year long, the kids screwed up the play in practice. Something always went wrong. Offensive Coordinator Russ Gallinger remembers, "We assistants thought practicing the play was a waste of time. In the end, Curt was right. The play won us the state championship."

> ### "The difference between ordinary and extraordinary is that little extra."
> #### —Jimmy Johnson

Three Yards and a Cloud of Dust

After the Mt. Vernon championship game in 2003, the team was eating at a restaurant in Ames. Harlan had just won another state title with 140 yards of passing on their last two plays. Curt and Russ were recalling the plays, and Curt said, "Passing just scares me to death."

Curt is definitely from the Woody Hayes "three yards and a cloud of dust" school of football. He says, "When you pass the ball, three things can happen. And two of them (incompletion and interception) are bad."

In the summer of 1980, Russ Gallinger was coaching a softball game at Lewis Central. Before the game, he was talking to Lewis Central's head football coach, Steve Padilla. Russ told him, "I'm going to be the new offensive coordinator."

Steve shot back, "Oh *&%#, now I'm going to have to worry about the run *and* the pass!"

Key #3: Care About the Kids

Curt has been known to yell at the players and occasionally swear a little. The following story illustrates what I'm talking about. In a game at Merrill Field, the Cyclones were leading by six points late in the game. The other team was driving down toward the goal line. Their quarterback dropped back and threw an incomplete pass, but the clock didn't run during the play. Then the same thing happened again on the next play. Curt spun around and yelled up at the clock operator, "Swede, start the *#^@ing clock!"

The Harlan crowd stayed strangely silent for a second. Then half of them turned around and yelled at Swede, "Yeah Swede, start the *#^@ing clock!"

At some schools in certain areas of the country, the coach would be fired for shouting something like that. Why doesn't Curt get in much trouble? Because everyone knows he cares about the kids.

Assistant coach Al Simdorn explains: "Curt's a blue collar coach. He relates to all the kids. He'll yell and scream at the kids at practice and then pat them on the back on the way to the locker room. He goes to a lot of the other sporting events and school activities and encourages kids to play other sports."

Curt and his assistant coaches know plenty about the game of high school football. But players don't care how much coaches know until the players know how much the coaches care. Curt cares about his players.

Dave Koos sums it up by saying, "Curt is loyal to a fault. When there's a choice between starting a talented sophomore or a senior with similar ability, most coaches play the sophomore to give him experience for his two years ahead. Curt always starts the senior and gives him the most playing time. He rewards the kids who pay the dues."

> *"Treat a person as he is,*
> *and he will remain as he is.*

Treat him as he could be,
and he will become what he should be."
—Jimmy Johnson

Former Cyclone head coach Terry Eagen probably gave the best description of Curt when he said, "Curt is big in every way—the man, the voice, the laugh, and the intense emotions. But always, at the base of things, he clearly cares about the kids."

Harlan Community High School principal Kent Klinkefus adds, "Whether it's being Santa Claus during the holidays or championing the underdog in the classroom or athletic field, Curt deeply cares about kids."

And his players care about Curt.

"A coach's greatest asset is his sense of responsibility—
the reliance placed on him by his players."
—Knute Rockne

Always the philosopher, Coach Bladt says, "We coaches are all in the same business—the business of trying to create successful men. I hope all Cyclone players move on to satisfying, high-income occupations…so they can afford to pay for my Social Security."

Key #4: Effectively Motivate the Players

One of the Six Building Blocks of Cyclone Football Success is Tough Kids. Having a bunch of tough kids isn't enough, however. The tough kids have to be put in the correct system and be motivated to play together and play hard. Curt and his team of assistant coaches have three basic strategies to motivate the players:

1. Play lots of kids
2. Know how and when to motivate them
3. Inspire them on game day

Play Lots of Kids

As Terry Eagen succinctly says, "Success begets success." The boys growing up in the Harlan Community School District see the success of the Cyclones. They attend the games and experience the winning atmosphere. They're coached by their high school heroes in the fifth and sixth grade flag football league. They want to be part of the Cyclone tradition when they reach seventh grade.

To accommodate all these kids, Harlan typically plays two platoon football beginning in seventh grade. Two platoon football means the kids play on offense *or* defense (not both), which allows up to twice as many kids to play in each game— twenty-two to thirty players if the game is close, and all of the players if the game isn't. In the varsity game, Curt tries to get all the seniors into every game. "They've busted their butts for six years and put up with me for three. They deserve it!"

Playing a lot of kids from the beginning is important because, as Curt says, "You never know who will become a great football player. Sometimes it's the one you least expect."

Curt's favorite example of this was a player named Bob "Snooky" Norgaard. When Snooky was a freshman, he couldn't walk and chew gum at the same time. In his early years, the coaching staff had to be resourceful in creating practice drills to protect him so he wouldn't get hurt. When he showed up for the first practice as a senior, his body had matured, and his coordination had improved. In addition, after three years of being pushed around in practice, Snooky had developed a real mean streak in him. It was payback time. In his senior year, Snooky was a starter and honorable mention all-state.

Curt notes another advantage. "When you play two platoon football, if a kid gets hurt, you only have to replace one position. If a kid plays both offense and defense, and he gets hurt, you have to replace two positions."

Playing two platoons also helps keep the players stay fresher for playoffs at the end of the year. "This time of year, they're a whole different team," says Waukee head coach, Scott Carlson, after being defeated by Harlan 48-17 in the 2005 quarterfinal playoff game at Merrill Field.

Even when the Cyclones lose a lot of key players due to graduation, they don't rebuild their team the next year. They reload. There are three reasons why this happens:

1. During the regular season, most of Harlan's games have been won about halfway through the third quarter. Curt takes out his offensive and defensive starters and replaces them with the JV teams. And against whom are the JV teams playing? The opponent's first teams. So Harlan's kids have game experience against the other school's best players *before* they become starters. That's quite an advantage.

2. The JV squads practice with and against the best team in the state four afternoons a week.

3. Harlan typically plays thirteen games a year (nine regular season and four playoff) when most schools only play nine. The extra four games provide

an additional half season of practice and exposure to big games in the playoffs.

Know How and When to Motivate Them

Curt has a very simple motivational plan. "I don't treat all the kids the same. Some kids need a kick in the butt every once in a while. Others need a pat on the back. Even if I do kick them in the butt, I try to find a reason to pat them on the back before they leave practice."

> *"Coaches who can outline plays on a black board are a dime a dozen. The ones who win get inside their players and motivate."*
> **—Vince Lombardi**

Inspire Them on Game Day

High school principal Kent Klinkefus remembers his son, Rob, telling him, "I can't wait to go to practice the Thursday before a game. At the end of practice, Coach Bladt will say something or tell a motivational story. We leave sky-high!"

Rob graduated from HCHS in 1996 and went on to become the quarterback at Buena Vista. His first year there, he noticed that, "These guys don't know what it is to win and commit to win." It's difficult to leave a program led by a person like Curt Bladt and go somewhere else where the expectations are lower.

Curt says this about his pre-game talks to the players. "They're totally off the cuff. I try to grasp the moment and say the right thing."

If you've ever seen a Harlan Cyclone kickoff team in action, you will understand the following motivational strategy. Curt tells his team early in the year, "I don't care if you're 120 pounds or 220 pounds. If you're aggressive on the kickoff team, we coaches will find you some playing time." The result on game night: eleven kamikazes on the field relentlessly slamming into the opposing team.

CoachBladt.com website posting
Name: Brad Norgaard
City, State: Phoenix, Arizona
Date: 01/14/2005

Coach—
You are truly an inspiration to everyone you come in contact with. I know you were for me. You taught us all to "bear down," nothing was insurmountable, and if you want it bad enough, to go and get it.

At times, when things get tough, I can hear you say dig deeper, try harder, and extend yourself. You lived this philosophy and all of your students and players on the field adopted your enthusiasm and energy.

As you taught us, "'Can't' isn't a word."
Keep pushing, Coach.

Dave Webber, WOWT's sportscaster, says Curt is successful because he has a six step plan:

1. He knows high school football backwards and forwards.
2. He understands kids and what motivates them.
3. He is an excellent teacher of the game.
4. He expects kids to do correctly what he teaches them.
5. If they do it wrong, he barks at them during practice and winks at them afterward.
6. If they do it right, he barks at them during practice and winks at them afterward.

John Naughton, a sportswriter at the *Des Moines Register* for eighteen years, makes a revealing point about Curt. "Curt is always very warm and cordial with the press and has a great sense of humor. He's competitive, but he doesn't take the angry motivational approach like some coaches."

Key #5: Focus on Action, Not Results

Many coaches focus on *results*, such as winning the game or making it to the playoffs. The problem with results is you don't always have total control over them. There may be a game where the other team's talent level is much greater than yours. If you both play with the same extremely high levels of motivation, the other guys are going to win most of the time.

You *do* have total control over your actions—the intensity and precision with which you play. Curt says it this way: "I never talked to the kids about winning the game. I tell them, 'Play as hard as you can, for as long as you can, and let the chips fall where they may.'"

CoachBladt.com website posting
Name: Matt Lauterbach
City, State: Sioux Falls, SD
Date: 12/17/2004

Football and coaching aside, and after looking down this list of people wishin', hopin', and prayin' for you to get well, I think that is a testimony in and of itself of how many people's lives you have impacted.

Some play football sure, but only a few. The rest know you for your big smile, jolly, roaring laugh, and your witty humor.

Coach, you're great on and off the field, a true champion both at Merrill Field East and in life. It has been my pleasure to know you and form a relationship with you as a friend, a coach, and as a person.

You never asked us to win, not once. You always told us two things, "Do your best, and let the chips fall where they may." The other was, "Don't worry about what happened on the last play, you focus on the next play."

Well coach, life has handed you lemons, I think your next play should be to make lemonade. Do your very best at beating this thing, and the chips will fall where they may. Let's just say, those chips falling, well, they seem to land on your side.

Wishin', hopin', and prayin' for you coach with all my heart. Stay strong, live well…Loberdoc

Do the Correct Actions

Curt also knows the correct actions to take. Dave Koos, football commentator on the KNOD broadcasts from 1982 through 2000, says, "Curt knows as much about offensive line technique as anyone walking. All season long, you can see the Cyclones have much better footwork. If he wanted to, Curt could easily have been a major college offensive line coach. Maybe even an NFL line coach."

Dave used to watch game film with the coaching staff. Here's what he said about the experience: "The coaches would watch an offensive play that didn't work. With twenty-two players on two teams running all over the place, Curt would always know what went wrong on the first viewing. The guy has a photographic memory."

At a time when Harlan was dominating Hawkeye Ten football, the conference's athletic directors and superintendents were having a discussion about whether to allow opposing teams to videotape their opponents. Harlan Community's superintendent, Orville Frazier, was really in favor of the idea but argued against it because he knew everyone would want to do what Harlan didn't want to do. The final vote was nine to one with Orville's vote being the only negative one. After returning home, he is reported to have said with a wink, "Give our coaches a week to look at the other team in action? That's just not fair."

Key #6: Focus on the Past, Present, and Future at the Right Times

Football players can focus on plays and games in the past, the plays and games that are happening now, or the plays and games in the future. Knowing when and how to do each is an art Curt teaches all his players. He says, "Look back to the past to learn what worked and what didn't. When the play is happening (the present), focus on your responsibility. After a play is over, immediately think 'next play' (the future)."

That's why Curt is constantly telling his team: "Forget what happened on the last play—whether it was good or bad. Forget how the game is going to turn out—whether we win or lose. Focus on the next play only."

The next play principle applies to football and to life. Curt sagely says, "The next play for a high school senior is going to college or developing a trade."

Like all great coaches, Curt also stresses taking one game at a time and not looking ahead to a future "big" game. His strategy must work. He has never lost two consecutive games as a head coach.

Key #7: Stress Teamwork

In Harlan, if you aren't a team player, you don't play. It's as simple as that.

In *Bernie Saggau and the Iowa Boys*, author Chuck Offenburger reports how he heard this reply when he had a conversation with Curt about teamwork: "We have never really focused on one person," Bladt said. "We never just feature one player. We try to have everybody be a team player and a contributor."

Here are three things Curt does to reinforce the teamwork concept:

1. Many schools award a helmet sticker when a player or small group of players achieve an accomplishment. This leads to some players having lots of stickers on their helmets and some players having none or just a few. The Cyclone helmets all look the same—the only sticker is one of a cyclone.

2. Another way Curt supports the team concept is by having different team captains for each game. With that plan, every senior gets a chance to represent the Cyclones at the pre-game coin flip at least once.

3. Curt effectively demonstrates the team concept when accepting awards. He constantly uses the word "we" when talking to reporters. The "we" is his entire coaching staff, in particular, and the entire Harlan Community, in general.

"People who work together will win,
whether it be against complex football defenses,
or the problems of modern society."
—**Vince Lombardi**

Key #8: Have Fun

If you've been around him long enough, you know that Curt believes life should be fun. He also believes coaches should make football fun for their players. Curt tells this story about the University of Southern California (USC) football coach, John McKay: "I was watching a football game on TV in the 1970s. It was a huge game, and USC was behind with just a couple minutes left. During a timeout just before a crucial fourth down, John came on the field to talk with his quarterback, who had screwed up big time on the previous play. It amazed me that Coach McKay was smiling as he talked with the kid."

"His approach worked to perfection, as he got his quarterback to focus on the next play—the only one that could affect the outcome of the game. The result of John's conversation was a confident, in-the-moment quarterback who directed a successful play, which led to a USC victory. I thought to myself, 'This is what we need to do in Harlan.'"

The following is from *Bernie Saggau and the Iowa Boys,* by Chuck Offenburger:

"…[W]e try to make it as fun as we can," Bladt said. "We're always throwing some little game or gimmick into our practices, just for fun."

And, as serious and focused as he and his assistants are on the sidelines during games, many fans are shocked when they see Harlan's players arrive for state championship games at the UNI-Dome in Cedar Falls. It has become another Harlan tradition that if the team reaches the finals, the players do crazy things with their hair—wild braids, Mohawks, handprints-shaved-on-their heads, and many different shades of red.

Jeff Deren styles Joel Osborn's
hair before the big game

"I know they all love to do that, so I just tell them that if they want to do that, as silly as it looks, that's fine with me," Bladt said. "A lot of other things might upset me, but that doesn't. I do remember, though, that when my own youngest son was playing in his senior year, he came out with a handprint on his head, dyed red, and I thought, 'Oh, God!' But, you know, if they have fun doing that, and it builds a little more camaraderie on the team, why not?"

Here are some other examples of Curt's humorous approach to life:

- In an interview after the quarterfinal playoff game against Waukee that Harlan won 48-17, Curt mentioned this about a last-minute 85-yard touchdown run by the opponent's first team against the Cyclone's third and fourth teams: "I think we had a couple of cheerleaders out there at cornerback."

  Curt later said, "Those 'cheerleaders' of ours will be varsity players in one or two years. They will draw upon that game experience of playing in front of five thousand fans. What did the other team's back-ups learn?"

- Before a big game with Lewis Central, Curt and the Titans' head coach, Steve Padilla, were joking around as usual at midfield. Officials Randy York and Ron Tryon wanted to get in on the fun. Randy relates, "As we were walking up to them, we put on big, thick Poindexter glasses at the last second and tapped the coaches on the shoulders. Curt turned around, busted out laughing, and said, 'This is just perfect. I always thought you guys were blind. This may be the first time you see the game clearly.'"

- Randy tells another story where Curt, Steve Padilla, and the officials had just finished their pre-game meeting at the center of the field. As the officials walked away, Curt yelled at them so Steve could easily hear, "Are you guys still coming over to my house for barbeque after the game?!"

- Randy's officiating partner, Tom Fuller, tells another story about a game where Harlan was way ahead. The JV team was playing and about to score a touchdown. This would increase Harlan's lead to over fifty points, which would stop the game. Curt yells, "Tom, my boys are holding out there! You've got to do something about it!" Of course they weren't, and Tom didn't.

- In the late 1960s, there was a pipe bomb incident in Harlan where no one was injured, but someone could have been if circumstances had been different. Russ Gallinger remembers, "It was three days after the incident. A bunch of teachers were sitting around talking in a basement room of the old high school. Curt was outside the room. He opens the door a little and tosses in a six-inch section of metal pipe onto the concrete floor. It scared the #@*% out of us. Curt thought it was hilarious."

- Curt usually gets roped into being part of pep rally skits before championship games. One year, complete with pink dress, wig, and rolled-up hosiery, he hilariously played the part of The Good Fairy from Cycloneland who spread pixie dust wherever she went.

  In another skit, Curt played Dorothy, a young girl who searched for The Wizard in the Land of Ooh and Ahh, while dragging a stuffed dog around the stage.

- Curt's fun-loving attitude rubs off on his assistant coaches. At a game in Denison, all the Harlan coaches were giving the refs some heat about the quality of their officiating. The coaches had already received one 15-yard penalty. A second penalty called on any of the Cyclone coaches would result in Curt being thrown out of the game. In the third quarter, one of the officials was fed up and shouted at the Harlan bench, "One more word out of anybody over here, and you're [Curt] gone!"

  Without missing a beat, Ken Carstens shot back, "Does that mean if I call you an *#! #@*^, the fat boy goes?" Ken later said the risk was worth it because it was a free shot at the official and Curt at the same time.

- Curt's fun-loving attitude also rubs off on his players. Dave Wiebers, head coach at Denison for nineteen years, says, "Curt passes his sense of humor on to his players. They play hard. They play clean. They play relaxed and aren't all stressed-out about the games."

CoachBladt.com website posting
Name: Kathe Stewart
City, State: Urbandale, IA
Date: 12/15/2004

Coach,
So sorry to hear you are not feeling well, but I know you will be back to normal before long. No one was ever able to keep you down for long! You have a lot of people praying for you and you are in my daily prayers.

I wanted to tell you about a funny story that my family often talks about when we reminisce about our school days. I was in your high school biology class, and we were dissecting pigs—or I should say, YOU were doing the dissecting and we were watching you. You were up in front of the class with your gloveless fingers covered in pig guts reading from the biology book. Well, it came time to turn the page. The page wouldn't turn. So, you calmly LICKED YOUR FINGER and turned the page. Half the girls in the class almost their lost their stomachs. My family still gets a kick out of that story!

Get well soon—We all miss you!

- In his sophomore biology classes, one of Curt's students fell asleep. Instead of immediately waking him and getting on his case, Curt had all the other kids tiptoe out of the room when class was over. When Curt left, he turned out the lights and shut the door. The boy woke up ten minutes later, smiled, shook his head, and went to lunch—late.
- Curt can find humor in most any situation. When Carroll Kuemper defeated Harlan for the first and only time, Curt told a reporter, "Even a blind sow finds an ear of corn every once in a while."
- Since 1980, Curt has worked on Tom Paulsen's farm east of town. Tom says, "Curt is the wind-rowing champion of Jackson Township. He takes one bolt off the machine and instantly turns into the greasiest man on earth. But he loves every minute of it. When Curt's here, we laugh all the time. Even when things aren't going well, we laugh."
- When Curt's first granddaughter was born, he went in to see Superintendent Bob Broomfield and confessed, "I'm a little concerned about the baby. We Bladts aren't exactly known for being cute."

Maybe the Bladt boys aren't known for being cute. They are very well known for being great coaches and fantastic people. However, even if you're a fantastic person, undeserved and life-threatening events can occur—as you are about to discover.

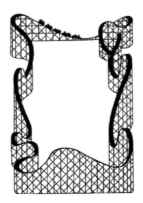

Chapter: 14
Defeating Miller-Fisher Syndrome

Sometimes life changes with the blink of an eye—literally. It was December 4, 2004, the morning of the Cyclone Invitational Wrestling Tournament. For a week, Curt had had a bad cold and persistent cough. When Curt opened his eyes that morning, he saw two of everything. The only way Curt could defeat the double vision was by closing his left or right eye. At breakfast, nothing smelled or tasted good, and he couldn't focus at a distance.

Being the trooper he is, Curt went to the high school that morning and conducted the seeding session. During the day, the symptoms gradually got worse. At 3 p.m. Curt said to himself, "I've gotta get out of here."

His son, Todd, took him to Myrtue Memorial Hospital, where he was seen by one of his former players, Dr. Don Klitgaard. At first, they thought it might be a stroke. After staying in the Harlan hospital overnight, Curt was taken to the University of Nebraska Medical Center (UNMC) in Omaha by ambulance.

For the next five days, Curt's symptoms worsened. He had severe headaches. "Like my head being in a 55-gallon drum being hit by somebody with a sledgehammer!" He couldn't get his eyelids to open on their own, so he had to use his fingers to open them. His face was sagging, and he had difficulty breathing and walking.

It took his physicians five days to diagnose his symptoms. They had to rule out stroke, meningitis, and botulism, which have similar symptoms. Finally, the diagnosis was made. Curt had a rarely occurring variation of Guillain-Barré Syndrome called Miller-Fisher Syndrome. With Guillain-Barré Syndrome, the symptoms start in the feet and work their way up the body. With Miller-Fisher Syndrome, the symptoms start in the head and work their way down.

CoachBladt.com website posting
Name: Eric Lauterbach
City, State: Harlan
Date: 12/19/2004

I don't think you'll be going anywhere. God is having too much fun watching you win, and the devil knows he couldn't handle your coaching.

A *coachbladt.com* website was created by Ruthanne Grimsley to keep every-one updated on Curt's condition. The following, slightly edited messages were periodically placed on the website by Curt's daughters-in-law, Shilo and Tammy Bladt, assistant wrestling coach Tony Hough, and family friend Ruthanne Grimsley. Also included is a newspaper article by *World-Herald* sportswriter Kevin White.

Sunday, December 12, 2004

Thank you everyone for sending your thoughts and prayers to Curt and our family. He is hanging in there, although not thrilled to be so far from home and all his grandbabies.

Curt's condition is a disease called Guillain Barré Syndrome (GBS). The Channel 6 news will be interviewing Dr. Fayed (Curt's doctor, head of Neurology) today for information on Curt's condition. I look for it on today/tonight's news. I understand GBS to be that Curt's antibodies are at war with his body. This condition basically tricks your defense system into believing that the body tissues are bad. So it turns against itself, attacking its own tissue. The symptoms are very stroke-like. His vision and speech are impaired, motor skills have decreased, breathing quite labored, and in a lot of pain in his head and neck. He is in serious condition, but stable.

The treatment is called plasmapheresis. This process removes your blood and spins it to separate the red blood cells from the plasma. The plasma (which houses the antibodies) is then discarded, and the red blood cells are put back in along with saline to replace the fluids along with "super-plasma" to hopefully re-direct his system. In order to maintain a controlled (disease-free) environment, they will be keeping him at UNMC until they feel he is completely treated. This will likely take quite a while, as they expect 10–14 treatments. He is to have one every other day. We hope to have him home by Christmas. But if not, we'll just keep the tree up until he is home! We know that he is in the best possible place that he can be and being cared for by the best possible neurological staff in the area.

Curt's first treatment was Friday, and it went well. Jeff was down yesterday and said that he seemed to be a little better, joking with the hospital staff in true Coach Bladt spirit. We are so thankful.

—Shilo Bladt

Monday, December 13, 2004, P.M.

I just spoke to Jeff (Curt's son). Curt is much the same as yesterday which is a good thing as yesterday was a very good day. He is a bit tired today, but still reacting well to treatment. He is very grateful for all of the cards, thoughts, and prayers people are sending his way.

I have printed everything I have received from email and via the contact form and guest book on this web site. I will take them to Curt today. He will enjoy all of the email so much.

—Shilo Bladt

Monday, December 13, 2004

Saw Curt and Jill yesterday morning, and he was doing considerably better. Friday afternoon he wasn't so good. It seems now he is more comfortable and his breathing is more steadily. I told him we swept Kuemper in wrestling and boys/girls basketball, and he gave me the thumbs up. Told him we have Lewis Central this week in basketball and a duel with Clarinda in wrestling. He seems to like to know what's going on all the time at HCHS so we are all keeping him posted. Hopefully he will get out of intensive care this week and be doing better. This is serious, and I think this will take some time. Will keep you posted.

—Tony Hough

CoachBladt.com website posting

Name: Hannah and Samuel Bladt
City, State: Harlan, IA
Date: 12/15/2004

'ampa Curt (& "ma Je-ull), Sammer and I sure do miss you guys an awful lot. We saw your picture last night on TV and wished you were here to watch football with us.

I'm getting very good at tackling—I'll show you when you get home. Mommy said your head is feeling better—I'm very glad. I told her my head is better too. Keep feeling better so that you can come home and see us very soon, o.k.?

We love you!

—Hannah (& Sam)

CoachBladt.co website posting

Name: Drew, Haley, and Alex Bladt
City, State: Harlan, Iowa
Date: 12/15/2004

Hey Grandpa,
We sure miss you. We have been waiting to snuggle up on your chest to take a nice cozy nap. Drew enjoyed crying to you last night on the phone. We can't wait to see you. We love you bunches!!!

Wednesday, December 15

Jeff and I saw Curt last night. He had just been moved out of ICU and into his own room—with a nice, big, comfy bed I might add! He had just received his

3rd treatment and was pretty tired, but is still responding very well. Curt was in good spirits, laughing, and telling jokes.

We brought with us all of the emails and postings from the guestbook—all 225 of them. Jill read them to him after we left. He and Jill are just so touched by all of the nice thoughts and prayers and good karma that people are sending their way. We also gave Curt the wrestling stats that John M. dropped off so that he would be up to date on what's going on there.

—Shilo Bladt

December 15th article in the Omaha World-Herald
Good News for Bladt: Condition Improving
by Kevin White, World-Herald Staff Writer

If Curt Bladt ever questioned his impact on Harlan Community High School, it was answered in one day.

About 24 hours after a website, *CoachBladt.com,* was established to update the ailing football coach's condition, more than 200 messages had been posted. They'd come from alumni in Arizona, North Carolina, New York, and even Mongolia. They'd come from former classmates, football officials, and coaches in every corner of the state. They'd come from people Bladt has never met. "Some," said Curt's son, Jeff, "say, 'We've never met you, but we know who you are and we want you to get well.'"

The well-wishers received good news Tuesday. Bladt, the most successful prep football coach in Iowa history, was upgraded from serious to fair condition at Nebraska Medical Center in Omaha. He has been hospitalized with a rare neurological disease.

One of his physicians, Dr. Pierre Fayad, said Bladt likely would be leaving the intensive care unit for the neurological ward either Tuesday or today.

"He's a tough guy, but it's a situation that needs a lot of patience," Fayad said. "He's getting better, but it's a slow process—we're talking about weeks and months. But he's heading in the right direction."

Bladt, 60, has been diagnosed with Miller-Fisher syndrome, a variant of Guillain-Barré (Ghee-YAN Bah-RAY) syndrome. It's a disease that causes the immune system to attack the nerves, resulting in a loss of muscle function. With Guillain-Barré, the disease starts in the feet and works its way up the body. Miller-Fisher syndrome begins in the nerves of the face and moves down.

Fayad said the chief concern is when the disease passes through the breathing muscles and chest area. Patients have to be monitored carefully during the process. He said Bladt's breathing is becoming less problematic, but that complications such as infections, high blood pressure, and blood clots are a concern.

Bladt is undergoing an extensive blood-cleansing treatment that attempts to prevent the loss of nerve function.

Jeff Bladt said the most difficult things for his father are the discomfort in his neck and head area, and not being able to go to wrestling meets. Curt Bladt is an assistant wrestling coach at the school.

Harlan hosted the Cyclone Invitational on Dec. 4, and that's where Jeff Bladt said his father realized he was suffering from more than a cold. "He went to yell something at one of the guys," Jeff said, "and he couldn't get it out."

In 27 years as the head football coach at Harlan, Bladt has a mark of 288-31, including 17 championship game appearances and nine titles. He was an assistant on the first of Harlan's state-record 10 championship teams.

He's also made an impression as a teacher. One of the messages posted on his Web site Tuesday came from Tyler Gubbels of Earling, a student in Bladt's first-hour biology class:

"We need you back in school. It is not the same without you. Hope it is not long before you can teach your next biology class. Hopefully you are feeling better. I will keep you in my prayers."

Another, from 11-year-old Brandon Weis of Earling:

"I hope you beat the disease so that one day I could play for you."

Before Bladt's illness, many had wondered how long he would continue to teach and coach. In an interview last spring, Bladt said he didn't have any immediate plans to walk away from any of his duties.

Joe Lauterbach, a Harlan attorney who has had sons go through the Cyclone program, said Bladt's short absence has left a void in the entire school system.

"He's more than just a football coach," he said. "He's like everybody's favorite uncle. The kids miss him at school, his wit, his sense of humor. He's irreplaceable."

Thursday, December 16

Curt was looking a little better last night. He was sitting up in a bed that basically turns into a recliner chair. He frequently sat forward on his own though. He still seems sleepy. Guess he can open his eyelids a slit. He is suppose to encourage himself to open them manually to "train the brain that they still work" as Jill says.

His speech is still garbled, difficult to understand at times. It seems like he only talks when he really has something to say. Tom Paulsen is going down in the morning (Thursday) so Jill can come home for some things. She said that Todd is going to spend some time down there this weekend so that she can get some of her Christmas shopping done. She plans on staying all the nights.

—Tammy Bladt

CoachBladt.com website posting
Name: Scott ('79) and Kerry Peterson
City, State: Hewitt, Wisconsin
Date: 12/17/2004

Trivia question: Over the last 30 years, how many times has Coach Bladt yelled this to a HCHS wrestler: "Get up! Get up! GET UP!"

Now it is our turn to give you our encouragement! Here's to a speedy recovery, Coach, and Merry Christmas

Happy New Year to you and Jill and your family from all your fans.

Wednesday, December 22
Not a lot of change on Curt since Thursday; some very gradual improvement, but enough that they transferred him to Immanuel Medical Center to begin rehabilitation therapy late yesterday afternoon. He is still quite weak, still has the double vision, and gets pretty dizzy when he is up, even for a little while. But, that the doctors feel he is ready for rehab is a gigantic step forward, and we are very grateful for this.

We have not heard yet how long he will need to stay at Immanuel, but I think he will be there through the New Year.

—Shilo Bladt

Thursday, December 23
Curt was transferred to Immanuel Medical Center in order to begin rehabilitation therapy and was very excited to get a jump on his recovery.

However, yesterday doctors discovered a blood clot in his leg. They did an ultrasound for more information and found it to be much bigger than they thought. He had surgery this morning to put in a filter which will hopefully deter any pieces that may break off of the clot from finding their way to his heart or brain. As a result, therapy is on the backburner for now as he is on bed rest for seven to ten days.

Curt is pretty bummed out about the setback. Being hospitalized over the holidays was bearable when he thought he was ready for rehab, but now it is pretty depressing for him.

On a positive note, Curt's coordination and nervous system seem to be improving, and he continues to be very thankful for all of the tremendous support he has received from all over the country. The cards and emails mean so much to him. He and Jill continue to read them between visits from friends and family.

On behalf of the Bladt family, thank you so much for thinking of us and sending your thoughts and prayers our way. Thank you also to the Harlan School System, community volunteers, Booster Club, and football boys for all of your fundraising efforts, Ruthanne for your terrific work on the website, and also to the pom pon girls for the babysitting—it is much appreciated!

Everyone please have a safe, happy, and healthy Christmas from the Bladts!

—Curt and Jill
Greg, Tammy, Drew, Haley, and Alex
Jeff, Shilo, Hannah, and Samuel
Todd and Angela Palma

Thursday, December 30
As for Coach, he is hanging in there. Christmas was tough. Not so much fun being in the hospital over the holidays, but we all took turns Christmas eve and Christmas day so that family would be around the whole time, but he was still pretty worn out (from the procedure to halt the blood clot) and bummed out (about the setback). He just really wants to come home.

On a positive note, he is recovering well from the clot, and did not have to be on bed rest nearly as long as they projected. He has been up in a wheelchair the past three days, down to the cafeteria for ice cream, and was able to sit in on a TEAM meeting on Tuesday. He has also been walking with a walker around the unit. His appetite is also improving.

Curt's physiatrist (a specialist in physical medicine and rehabilitation) is very optimistic that he will be coming home soon. He will require quite a bit of physical and occupational therapy to regain his strength and motor skills and should be able to do that here at MMH on an outpatient basis. It also helps that Curt and Jill's house is a ranch style layout with all the essentials on one floor.

Physically, in order for him to come home, he needs a bit higher of a score on the OT/PT assessment that they conduct on him daily. An example is that for walking, he needs to be able to walk with a walker (unassisted) for 15 feet. Yesterday he was up to 75 feet.

He continues to improve more and more every day; he just wears out easily right now. It's been hard on him to lie in bed for weeks when he is used to being so active. According to his doctor, you don't really get "cured" of Guillain Barré Sydrome. Your recovery is gauged more on how much you are able to bounce back from the disease. They are very happy with Curt's progress in this department.

Because of the possibility of future blood clots, Curt will need to be on a blood thinner (Cumaden) for some time. Doctors need to make sure that he has the correct level of this drug in his system before they send him home. Too little of the drug and he develops clots. Too much of the drug, and he is unable to clot at all. Once they get him leveled off, and he is able to return home, he will require weekly blood draws to monitor the drug.

We are very happy with the direction that things are taking. A few weeks ago, things were so very bad. It is just so awesome to have things improving at the rate that they are. Curt's a tough cookie, and he's not letting this thing get him down! Thanks again everyone for the thoughts, prayers, and words of encouragement. Please keep them coming. You gotta have faith!

—Shilo Bladt

Tuesday, January 4, 2005
Good Morning! Curt and Jill were out all of yesterday afternoon for tests. I didn't want to update you until I knew for sure what was going on with Curt's leg. It has been hurting him the last two days. We got ahold of Jill last night and it turns out that there is not an infection in his leg (thank goodness), but that it is still the blood clot that is paining him.

Doctors will continue to monitor him, but it will delay his return home. Jill also thinks that Curt had a touch of the flu over the weekend because he just wasn't feeling very well. As a result, he hasn't been able to be up and working on physical therapy much the last couple of days. Jill said that he was feeling a bit better last night and hoped to be up more today. He gets kinda bummed when he isn't able to do as much. Medically, his Cumaden levels are balancing out and his liver enzymes are closer to where the docs want them to be.

He still presents with some paralysis in his face and isn't yet able to move his eyes. But he can see, and his appetite is increasing a little every day. Ice cream always sounds good! He's been watching the games this week. Due to the weather, we weren't able to watch the Hawkeyes with him on Saturday, but I'm willing to bet that his whole wing of the hospital heard him during the last minute of the game! Needless to say, he was quite pleased with the outcome.

His doctors continue to be optimistic that he will be able to come home soon.

—Shilo Bladt

Thursday, January 6
Good afternoon. I talked to Greg and Todd today, and it sounds like Curt is continuing to show improvement. He has been feeling better and was able to be up quite a bit more the last couple of days, which means that he has been working quite a bit on his OT and PT so that he can come home. Doctors continue to be optimistic that it will be soon.

Jill has been staying with him through the wintry weather. She has not been out on the roads and the rest of us are just hunkering down and waiting on updates—but we will be ready to go just as soon as the doctors say come and get him! It appears that winter is finally here. We have been very fortunate up until this week regarding the weather. It has made it much easier for Jill and the boys to be down there as much as possible.

Thank you so much to whomever cleared all of our driveways today—it is very much appreciated!

—Shilo Bladt

Friday, January 7
Shilo just called and Coach Bladt arrived home this evening. She said he hasn't been this comfortable in the last five weeks. Tom Conroy at FMCTC has graciously offered Curt the use of a laptop computer, and FMCTC is donating Internet services to Curt & Jill throughout the duration of his convalescence at home (which we hope is a very short time).

—Ruthanne Grimsley for Shilo Bladt

Friday, January 14
It's good to have him home, and he is so glad to be there! He loves his big comfy chair and appreciates all of the visits from folks since he has been home.

FMCTC brought the laptop by the house and set him up with the best screen for him (with the impaired vision, the bigger, the better) and all of the instruction that he will need to keep in contact with well-wishers, so please keep the messages a coming!

Curt attends a rigorous therapy session three mornings per week for about four hours at a time. He has PT, OT, speech and any lab work that is necessary at that time as well. He really likes the therapy staff at MMH. He then is pretty exhausted and rests in the afternoon.

Thank you so much to all who have assisted and continue to volunteer in giving him a lift to and from the hospital. You are very much appreciated and he appreciates the company.

Jill took him for a little jaunt around town after therapy on Monday and he enjoyed being out and about. You lose touch so easily when you are away from home as long as he was.

—Shilo Bladt

Monday, January 17
Curt was ready to get out of the house so they came over for meatloaf—his favorite!

A fourth grade student (Tyler Johannsen) stopped by our house last night to interview Curt for a school project. Curt told him about the website and showed him the stats page for his report. He (Curt) is pretty darn tickled with the response.

Curt looked really good last night and said that he felt pretty good too. He played with the kiddos and watched some football with Jeff. He said that therapy is going well, but that it definitely wears him out. He will continue to go three times per week until his docs at Immanuel say otherwise.

—Shilo Bladt

Monday, February 7
On Saturday night, we had all of the Bladts over to our house to celebrate our "Christmas," since Curt was in the hospital over the holidays. It was very nice.

There was, of course, way too much food and a lot of good conversation and a whole bunch of babies!

Curt and Jill worked the wrestling meet that day, so he was kinda pooped out by the end of the evening, but a good time was had by all. He is just improving so much every time I see him. He now walks unassisted—no more walker, and his speech is so much better. Therapy is going very well, and he continues to go three times per week. He also had a very good report from the doctor at Immanuel last week.

I really think that he is just enjoying getting out and about these days.

—Shilo Bladt

Curt, Jill, and the grandbabies celebrate a belated Christmas

Tuesday, March 15
Curt and Jill stopped over last night to play with the kiddos, and he is just doing fantastically, and he looks great too!

His physical therapy is complete, and he is attending the fitness center three days a week while Jill is at work to keep up with his rehab. He will continue with speech therapy for another month. He has hit major milestones every time we see him! He can smile now and he can wink, and it's great to see him doing both! As you all know, his smile is quite contagious.

These accomplishments are huge when you haven't been able to do them for a while! Curt has also been going to school for an hour and a half every day to work with shot and discus track participants. He and Jill have been attending basketball games, wrestling meets, and even the state wrestling tournament in Des Moines as well as doing a bit of babysitting for the grandbabies!

He is also looking quite trim, having lost and kept off 50 pounds! His vision is also improving, and he can even read a little for short amounts of time. So please keep posting to the site because he really enjoys hearing from everyone! He still isn't able to drive and so he can use a ride every now and then when Jill is working.

The family as a whole continues to feel incredibly blessed that things have worked out the way that they did and that Curt continues to improve every day. We are so very grateful!

—Shilo Bladt

Friday, July 22, 2005
LETTER FROM COACH BLADT:

Friends—
We have been overwhelmed by the outpouring of concern shown by the number of cards, letters, emails, and visits that we have received during my recent illness. I feel very blessed, as the power of prayer that so many of you have expressed to me surely did work wonders. We thank God every day for the caring community that surrounds us. Very few people ever learn how many lives they have touched. I am one of the lucky ones.

What a tremendous job Ruthanne Grimsley (Harlan's Citizen of the Year) did in creating this website that has made it possible for people in all parts of the world to communicate with us.

Shilo and Tammi Bladt (daughters-in-law) did a great job updating and informing people of my improving medical condition.

Speaking of updates, I'm feeling good and doing well as I look forward to the upcoming football season. The U.S.D. summer camp and our own preseason Camp of Champions in August are close enough that you can just about hear the pads crackin' already.

One of the things that hasn't returned is my ability to whistle. Maybe this fall will be the first time EVER that I'll have to wear a whistle around my neck—one more thing to keep track of every day. Does anyone know where I can get one of those darn things?

We can't say thank you enough for the things that people have done for us. We love you all and may God bless!

Friday, August 26, 2005
UPDATE FROM COACH BLADT:

Friends—
If you see me running around town in a golf cart, there is a good reason for that. I am presently in an Immobilizer as I have suffered an insufficient fracture of the medial femur condyle—a/k/a a broken leg. Doctors think that the steroids I had to take when I was sick with GBS might have weakened the joints, contributing to the cause of the fracture.

It was either the immobilizer or a full body cast. I begged for mercy and got the immobilizer for the next 3 weeks or so. So I will be utilizing the golf cart for trips to and from school and during practice! Please don't run over me!

Not the World's Greatest Patient

Curt describes his hospital stay this way, "I wasn't the world's greatest patient." On his first night in Immanuel Hospital, Curt asked the nurse for his usual night-cap of a sleeping pill and pain medication. The nurse said she couldn't do that because the doctor didn't leave orders for the medication.

Curt responded, "Can you get me my pants? I'm going to get a cab and go to a drugstore. Then I'm going home."

A few minutes later, the nurse returned with the medication.

Putting a Bad Situation in Perspective

In typical Curt fashion, he downplays his experience with Miller-Fisher Syndrome. He said, "No matter how bad things seem, there is always someone who has it worse." Curt then told a story about former HCHS principal Merle Deskin. Merle was in the final stages of his battle with cancer. Despite his condition, Merle had never missed a day of school. He and Curt were chatting in the teachers' lounge one day. When the conversation was over, Merle popped two white pain pills into his mouth and then asked Curt, "Would you help me up? There are kids out there who need me."

Merle Deskin died two weeks later.

A few years later, Merle had the best seat in the house as he proudly looked down on his son, Doug, and watched him catch a pass, break free from his defender, and race into the end zone just before halftime to help give Harlan Community High School its first state football championship.

Merle Deskin

There are some moments in life we never forget—defining moments that change how we approach the world from that moment on. That day in the teacher's lounge with Merle was a defining moment for Curt. He knew there were thousands of kids who would need him, too. He was right.

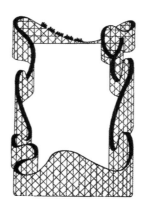

Chapter: 15
A Most Rewarding Year

In December of 2004, when Curt was lying in his bed at the UNMC with an exploding head and a sagging face, he was at the deepest valley of his life's roller coaster ride. Little did he know at the time, the year beginning September of 2005 would be the most rewarding one of his life—twelve months that would take him to the pinnacle of the high school football coaching profession.

At the end of October 2005, the Cyclones were undefeated coming into the playoffs. Their first playoff game was a bump and grind. They bumped up against a surprisingly tough Winterset squad and ground out a 23-13 victory.

In the quarterfinals, Curt's Crusaders walloped the Waukee Warriors 48-17. The next game was at the Dome against LeMars—the last team to defeat the Cyclones three years and 37 games before. A win would move Harlan Community into the finals for a chance at three-fer madness—back-to-back-to-back 3A state championships. The win would also be Curt's 300th as a head coach.

The following edited article by Mike Oeffner in the November 17, 2005, issue of the *Harlan Tribune* recaps the historic game:

BLADT NOTCHES 300TH CAREER WIN

CEDAR FALLS—Already Iowa's most successful high school football coach in terms of winning percentage (.906), state titles (9) and playoff wins (71), Curt Bladt can now add the elite 300-Win Club to his lengthy list of accomplishments. Whether he wants to talk about it or not.

Bladt's Harlan Community Cyclones gave the 28th-year head coach win number 300 with a 35-21 victory over Le Mars on Monday in a Class 3-A playoff semifinal at the UNI-Dome. Bladt's record at HCHS now stands at a glossy 300 wins, 31 losses, including 71-15 in playoff games. The Cyclones will seek the school's 11th state football championship overall, and Bladt's 10th, in Saturday's state title game versus West Delaware.

"That's not a goal—it's just to go out and have some fun and let the kids play hard, and they've been doing that," Bladt said Monday.

Always one to put the emphasis on his players, Bladt tried his best to avoid talking about the 300th win, which only four other coaches in the state have accomplished.

"(Number 300) was in the back of my mind, but you know how many times I mentioned it this week? Not once," he said. "We tried to keep it on the low-key and focus on what we had to get done today. We knew it was going to be a tough contest, so we were real happy with the outcome."

"(Win) 301 is going to be tougher to get because we've got to step up one more rung on the ladder, and from what I understand, Manchester, West Delaware is a very salty team."

After being hospitalized with the nerve disorder Miller-Fischer Syndrome, last December, there were concerns that Bladt might not be able to return to the sidelines this season. A rapid recovery quickly dispelled those thoughts, however, and Bladt says talking to previous victims of the same affliction helped raise his spirits.

"There was a point where I didn't know if I was up or down, but I always had the inkling that I would be back," he said, "especially talking to other people that have been in similar circumstances. They gave me all kinds of pump up and said it will get better in a hurry, and certainly it did."

Previous Iowa high school football coaches to surpass 300 wins are listed below:

- Dick Tighe, 350 wins, 134 losses and 8 ties—winning percentage of 72%
- Duane Twait (retired) 339 wins, 63 losses and 2 ties—winning percentage of 82%
- Jim Bellamy, 314 wins, 126 losses and 4 ties—winning percentage of 71%
- Tom Stone, 305 wins, 72 losses and 1 tie—winning percentage of 81%
- Curt Bladt, 300 wins, 31 losses and 0 ties—winning percentage of 91%

Championship #11

On Saturday, November 19th, while Dick, Jim, and Tom were sitting at home, the Cyclones were cavorting in the cozy confines of the UNI Dome. They were about to win championship #11, give their coach one more win, and continue A Most Rewarding Year.

The following edited article by Mike Oeffner from the November 22nd issue of the *Harlan News-Advertiser* recapped the game:

Title Town Three-Peat, Chapter 2:
Cyclones win third straight title 34-13 over West Delaware

This one's for you, Coach Bladt. A 10th state football title as a head coach and number 11 for the school—both Iowa all-time bests. Signed, sealed, and delivered by the 2005 Harlan Community Cyclones.

The above sentiment was a common theme among HCHS players following Saturday's Class 3-A championship game at the UNI-Dome, and for good reason.

It's been less than 11 months since Cyclone head football coach Curt Bladt lay in a hospital bed and waged a winning battle against the rare nerve disorder known as Miller-Fischer Syndrome. It's only been about three months since Bladt learned that a fractured lower femur would force him to ride a motorized cart on the sidelines for much of the season. On Saturday, the No. 1-ranked Cyclone football team thanked their coach for his perseverance.

Once again dominating in the third quarter, HCHS controlled the football for much of the second half to post an impressive 34-13 win over No. 4 West Delaware of Manchester in a title clash of 12-0 teams.

The victory was the 39th straight for HCHS, spanning a state-unprecedented three consecutive 13-0 seasons. The Cyclones are now the first football team in the state with a pair of championship three-peats, matching the run of HCHS titles from 1982 to 1984. Decorah (1987–1989) is the only other Iowa school to pull off such a feat.

"We wanted to win this for Coach Bladt, with all the trouble that he went through," said HCHS quarterback Shawn Doran, who threw a pair of touchdown passes on the day. "He bounced back and was able to coach us, and we just wanted to do it for him."

Cornerback Jonathon Davis, who tied a 3-A state title game record with two interceptions, shared Doran's viewpoint. "It meant a lot for us to get a championship for (coach)," he said. "We didn't know if he was going to be back to his full self, but he came back, and it was great to win one for him."

Bladt—now 301-31 as the Cyclones' 28th-year head coach, fielded post-game questions with his oldest granddaughter, Hannah, age 4, alertly listening from his lap. He called this year's four-game title run as enjoyable as any of the previous nine.

"It's a lot of fun to be able to be out there and be on sideline, to be with the kids," Bladt said. "It does keep you young, and it keeps you excited. I guarantee you my blood pressure is pretty high today. It's just a wonderful thing for the kids and the parents and the community."

Asked about possible retirement on the horizon, Bladt didn't blink. "The only thing bad about today is it's the last game of the season, and you've got to sell these guys a diploma, walk them across the stage, and start all over again," he said. "I don't like starting all over again, but we've got some core people that are coming back, and hopefully we can chip something together so we can put 11 on the field next year."

Saturday's victory marked the third time HCHS has won a state title at the expense of West Delaware—all three games decided by at least 14 points—but there was nothing easy about it.

Added Blum: "When you think about it, 39 straight wins is pretty much unheard of. You don't really think about it that much, but you go out day by day and try to get better and get better and get better. And when you do get better, stuff like this happens."

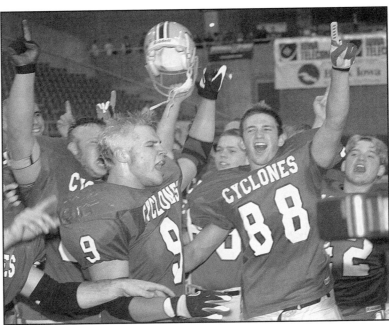

HCHS seniors Todd Schwartz (9) and Adam Leinen (88) lead the post-game celebration after Saturday's 34-13 win over West Delaware

The Rewarding Year Continues

In early 2006, Curt received the State of Iowa USA Football Champions Award. The award is designed to "recognize the efforts of those who have made a significant contribution to football at the youth, middle school, and high school levels."

Curt Comes Back for More

It would have been really easy for Curt to quit teaching and coaching in 2005 after winning two consecutive state championships and defeating Miller-Fisher Syndrome. He came back to both.

It would have been even easier to hang up the whistle after the 2006 season when the Cyclones won state championship #3, and Curt won the National Coach of the Year Award. He came back to coaching—just like he always asks his players to come back.

"Coach Bladt Is Retiring? The End of the World Is Near!"

In the summer of 2006, because of contract technicalities, Curt was forced to resign his coaching position when he resigned his teaching position at HCHS. This caused a considerable number of Cyclone supporters to freak out. Coach Bladt explained the situation with his typical comic flare on the *coachbladt.com* website.

June 2006

I have been asked by several people about my recent decision to retire from the Harlan Community School District. So, to set the record straight, I have totally retired from teaching and coaching at HCHS. Retiring from teaching does not rule out coaching "if" an individual would choose to do so, AND, "if" there is a vacancy in the sport of choice. This fall, there will be two coaches on the Harlan Community staff who have elected to do just that in football, one in Varsity and one in the Junior High.

As for things for me to consider, I have eliminated Professional Triathlon Competition, Alaska Crab Fisherman, and Wal-Mart greeter from the "things to try" list. All too dangerous.

Now that I'm retiring, my wife has informed me that she too will be cutting back on her "honey-do" list. In the future, she will only have me do things that start with "T", such as The dishes, The laundry, The yard work, etc.

This spring has been, and will be, an exciting time. On April 24th, I received a ring presented by the IFCA at the Iowa Football Clinic in Iowa City, symbolic of last Fall's 3-A football championship. At Iowa State University, the IFCA will present me with a regional and state 3-A Coach of the Year Award. A week later, the Iowa Chapter of the National Football Foundation and College Hall of Fame will be presenting me with an overall State Coach of the Year Award. Finally, in late June, I will be a finalist for the National High School Athletic Coaches Association National Coach of the Year.

This is only possible because of the hard work and dedication of all of our coaches and players who have over the years developed the tradition of Cyclone Football. They all have ownership of these awards! Thanks to the coaches and players and all the loyal fans for their support over the years. And thanks again to Shilo and Ruthanne for maintaining this website.

—Coach Curt Bladt

The Peak of the Ride

Eighteen months after the lowest point on Curt's roller coaster ride, he reached the peak when he received the 2006 National Football Coach of the Year Award presented by the National High School Athletic Coaches Association in a ceremony in Branson, Missouri.

Ever the praise-spreader, Curt had this to say about the award, "I felt that *we* had a decent shot. This is an award you don't win by yourself. It takes a good group of assistant coaches, and players who are dedicated over the long haul. There's also great community support…the band always puts on a show, and it takes all those things together to create a winning attitude."

Curt accepting his national coach of the year award

National Coach of the Year ring

Surprise, Surprise, Surprise! They Hired Him Back

According to state law, the head coaching position was posted. Dave Koos jokingly remarked that the job posting may have read, "If you haven't won ten state championships, don't apply."

Curt reapplied for the position on July 3rd. He was rehired on July 5th. This shows that Activities Director Mitch Osborn is a shrewd judge of talent.

So, What's Next?

What do you do when your kitchen shelves are getting empty? You restock them. That's the same thing the Harlan Cyclones will do in 2006—just like they've done for decades. That's the great thing about each new year of high school football. The only certainty is uncertainty.

However, there *are* a few certainties about those mesmerizing fall evenings at Merrill Field. The Harlan Community faithful will pack the stands. The band will put on a sensational show. The American Legion will unfurl its gigantic American flag. The Cyclone special team kamikazes will run down the field on their first kickoff like a pack of possessed pumas. The players will shout, "Next play!" as they break their huddles. And Coach Curt Bladt will be stalking the sidelines.

2006 Harlan Cyclones

The Harlan Newspapers

For 110 years, the Harlan Newspapers have been doing a superb job of covering Cyclone football. In 1975, my dad, Bob Booth, encouraged a young high school student named Alan Mores to write the Merrill Field article you read in Chapter 5. Now, Alan is helping me with this book. It's funny how life goes in circles.

I played football with his brother, Steve, in the early 1960s. Their father, Leo, was the publisher of the Harlan Newspapers from 1939 until his retirement in 2002. Now his sons are co-editors. I would like to thank Steve, Alan, managing editor Bob Bjoin, sports editor Mike Oeffner, and fact checker Maggie Hatcher for their assistance in writing *Let the Chips Fall Where They May.*

Bob Bjoin　　*Mike Oeffner*　　*Maggie Hatcher*

The Mores Family
Front row (left to right): Suzie (Mores) Laney,
Irene Mores, Leo Mores, Barbara (Mores) Johnson.
Back row: Steve and Alan Mores

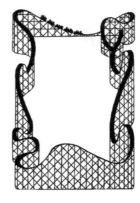

Chapter: **16**
Twenty-Seven Questions

What thoughts, ideas, memories, beliefs, and values are ricocheting around the cavernous confines of Curt's cranium? You're about to find out as he answers twenty-seven questions.

Question #1: What do you do to relax?

"Jill and I play with and baby-sit the grandkids. Before and during the season, I watch a lot of game film. I do a little woodworking—shelves and stuff for the house. Every year, I make key holders for the graduating senior football players. I'm a homebody, so we don't go out much."

Coachbladt.com website posting
Name: Demes Diogenes
City, State: Brazil/Ceará/Fortaleza
Date: 12/17/2004

Dear Coach Bladt,
Jeff, Mom, and Dad told me about the bad news, but i am sure you will get better relly soon, I know that i never was a good football player but you always make me feel like the best, i loved when you yeal with us, and had um day that i will not ever forget was that game against Denison at Harlan when you start to talk with us and you crye was the first and only time i saw this strong and awesome guy crye in the all time i live there and that make me feel that he loves all this boys like his sons.

Coach i am praying for you get better and i am sure that you will be better really fast and please make this guys work rarder like we did. I steel using the keep Keys that you maked to me.

Thanks for everything you did to me Coach.

Love you,
Demes (your only Brazilian player)

Question #2: What was the best decision you've made as a coach?

"My best coaching decision was to let the assistant coaches have responsibility for their areas. At first, I probably tried to do too much."

Question #3: What was the best decision you've made in your life?

"Without a doubt, my best decision was to marry my wife, Jill. If I were her, I would have kicked my butt out a long time ago. She puts up with a lot of stuff and does it with a smile. Jill always laughs at my jokes even though she's heard them a thousand times. She's only missed a couple of games in all the years I've been coaching."

Question #4: What was the single biggest play in your coaching career?

"The 1984 championship game was a tough one. We were trailing Waterloo Columbus late in the game 13 to 7. As time was winding down and emotions were running high, referee Smokey Barr came to the Cyclones defensive huddle and said, 'Don't lose your heads out there. Anything can happen.'

"It did. Pat Shelton tackled a Columbus kid real hard and knocked the ball loose. Don Klitgaard scooped up the fumble and ran it in for the winning touchdown."

This is the same Don Klitgaard who became the physician who first saw Curt in the hospital.

That play was also the genesis of another Harlan tradition. Marching Band Director Lee Nelson remembers that the band knew eight bars of the song "Superstar." They played it during a timeout shortly before Klitgaard's winning score. Through the years, "Superstar" has become the theme song of the band and all Harlan athletics.

Question #5: What do you like the least about coaching?

"It's gotta be the season-ending injuries. The kids put so much effort and time into the game and, with the injuries, they can't live out their dreams."

Question #6: What do you enjoy most about coaching?

"Seeing the kids grow right before your eyes. We always ask them, 'Did you grow today?' Growth is the key to life. If you don't, somebody else did, and they're catching up to you."

Question #7: What was the biggest mistake you almost made in your career?

"In 1978, I considered quitting teaching and coaching to sell Morman's Feed. I'm real glad I didn't. Money isn't everything, or even the most important thing. And the most important thing is doing the right thing."

Question #8: Which team are you proudest of?

"I'm proud of all the teams I coached. But the 1994 team, the one that finished 7-2 and didn't make playoffs, would have to be on top of the list. It was certain we wouldn't make the playoffs fairly early in the season. The kids could have given up, but we won our last three games and knocked Lewis Central out of the playoffs."

> *"The greatest accomplishment is not in never failing,*
> *but in rising again after you fall."*
> **—Vince Lombardi**

Question #9: What was the most exciting finish of a game you coached?

"Wow, we've had a lot of them, but my choice would have to be the 2003 championship game with Mt. Vernon."

Below is an edited article aptly written by Mike Oeffner that appeared in the November 25, 2003, edition of the *Harlan News-Advertiser:*

Air Harlan Reaches Cloud Nine
CEDAR FALLS—If just one thing is remembered about the 2003 Harlan Community football team, let it be the Cyclones' ability to strike quickly and with jaw-dropping magnitude.

On a championship afternoon at the UNI-Dome here Saturday, the reality of that ability was driven home loud and clear in the final five minutes, 38 seconds of a classic, 38-35, Class 3-A title game win over Mount Vernon.

HCHS quarterback Joel Osborn, the state's new single-season passing leader, fired two late touchdown passes to Greg Applegate, and the Cyclone defense came up with two huge stands to clinch the school's state-leading ninth championship in 17 title-game appearances. Ben Arentson's interception with 1:06 remaining sealed the deal and allowed HCHS to run out the clock, beginning a raucous celebration on the field and in the stands.

Joel Osborn and Coach Curt Bladt
share a congratulatory hug after the win

"It was kind of amazing," said HCHS Head Coach Curt Bladt. Facing their largest deficit of the season—35-23—with less than half a quarter of game time remaining, the Cyclones turned what would have been one of the most devastating losses in the storied program's history into what will certainly be remembered as one of the most thrilling wins.

Down 12 and outscored 35-6 since early in the second quarter, the same Cyclones who (had) outscored their first three playoff opponents, 160 to 57, suddenly found themselves between a rock and a hard place. Three offensive plays, 148 passing yards and two TDs later, top-ranked HCHS protected a three-point lead and the third-ranked Mustangs tried to figure out what happened.

Moments later, the 13-0 Cyclones celebrated their first state title since 1998 while Mount Vernon (11-2) struggled to swallow its second straight runner-up finish since moving to Class 3-A.

"Words can't even describe it," said Cyclone defensive end Dan Erickson. "It's the most amazing feeling I've ever had in my life, so I can't really explain it."

HCHS wide receiver/cornerback Randy Kaufmann may have summed it up best. "It was frustrating getting down," he said later, "but like the coaches said before the game, the team that plays together this whole game is going to win it, and we stuck together and it worked."

After Mount Vernon halfback Jacob Craig's fourth TD of the game put the Mustangs up 35-23, the ensuing kickoff sailed into the end zone for a touchback, giving HCHS the ball at its own 20. Kaufmann was just one of the Cyclone players involved in a play that would instantly turn the momentum of the game.

The call from the sidelines was "reverse-pitch-pass," a gimmick play pulled out of the bag about once a year by Cyclone offensive coordinator Russ Gallinger. Set up by a regular flanker reverse earlier in the game, the play started with a toss to tailback Kevin Kruse, who in turn handed the ball to Kaufmann coming back toward the middle of the field. Kaufmann flipped the ball back to Osborn, who lofted a perfectly-thrown pass down the sideline to Applegate, who had gotten behind the safety.

Applegate hauled in the pass near midfield, ran right over the only Mustang defender in his way and proceeded into the end zone for an 80-yard touchdown catch. "We've run that play probably at least once each practice for the last eight weeks," Gallinger said. "I kept telling [our guys] there will come a time when we're going to run this play…and I couldn't think of a better time to run it."

Applegate, who caught a combined 13 passes for 302 yards and four TDs in his first two games ever at the UNI-Dome, had plenty of time to watch the long throw into his hands before making the catch and turning up field. "I'm thinking either I'm going to be a hero, or I'm not going to be a favorite," he said of waiting for the ball to come down. "I have to [thank] the coaches and Joel for just putting faith in me to make that catch."

But the task at hand for Harlan was hardly over. The Cyclones still trailed, 35-30, and the pressure was now on the defense to stop a powerful Mount Vernon rushing attack that had generated touchdowns on five of its last six drives. It took only five plays for HCHS to force a punt, however, and the ball was back in the hands of the offense with 2:51 to go.

Once again, the Cyclones wasted little time. On second and 15, Osborn found a well-covered Applegate on a "backside six" route to the same area of the field he had made his TD pass minutes earlier. As he has done so many times this season, Applegate simply out-jumped and out-willed the defensive back for the football, making an outstanding grab near the 40 and sprinting the rest of the way to complete a 68-yard touchdown.

Kaufmann's two-point PAT catch restored Harlan's lead to three with 2:36 to play as a sea of red-clad Cyclone fans roared. Craig gained 14 yards on a fourth-and-12 to keep Mount Vernon alive, but with time running out, the Mustangs were out of their grind-it-out comfort zone. Erickson sacked the elusive Steve Kreinbrink twice on the final drive before hurrying the Mustang quarterback on his final pass toward the sideline.

Arentson, who just happened to be in the neighborhood, took it away from two Mount Vernon receivers for his first career interception. Two snaps later, HCHS prepared to host its championship trophy. After the game, Bladt was asked if he had ever coached a title game win that was so dramatic. "Not to come from that far behind with that little time to go," he said. "To play as well as we did all year, then to lose the championship game would have been a real stroke in the noggin. We've lost some like that, too, so I guess what comes around goes around down there. If you make a few mistakes, the other team capitalizes because they're all pretty good at that point."

"I was getting a little frustrated and getting down on myself, but I knew I had to keep my head up, keep grinding, and something would happen," Kevin Osborn said. "Everybody was just thinking now is the time, we've got to go, this is it…it's do or die right here, and we got it."

Erickson, who along with Adam Schwery led HCHS with 16 tackles, said the offense's dramatic touchdowns helped the defense rise up. "We were giving up way too many yards, we just weren't doing our job," he said. "The offense just kept us in the game and we came back and made a huge stop."

Erickson, in particular, played like a man possessed in the final few minutes. "I just knew I had to do it, it's my time," he added. "This is probably the last time I put on pads so I had to make it my best."

Question #10: What was your saddest moment as a coach?

"There were two of them. The first was Mick Tierno dying of cancer in 1982. I visited Mick in the hospital in the winter. He looked me in the eye and said, 'Coach, I'll be back to play for you next fall.' Mick was a fighter to the very end. He died two days later. You never forget moments like that.

"The second was Jason Cairney dying in a car accident in the spring of 1991. I was working in the garden. My son, Jeff, called me and said, 'Dad, are you sitting down?' After Jeff told me the news, I did sit down and was unable to stand on my own for several minutes.

"Mick and Jason were both great kids."

Mick Tierno *Jason Cairney*

Question #11: Who was your most unusual player?

"We've had a few who were wired up a little differently. David Klein, who graduated in 1985, was probably at the top of the list. He talked all the time. David would never shut up. We played him on offense *and* defense so we wouldn't have to put up with him on the sideline."

Question #12: Can a coach "will" his team to win?

"In order to accept the coach's will, the players have to will themselves. I just tell the kids, 'Play as hard as you can for as long as you can.'"

Question #13: What was your biggest upset?

"Our biggest upset was when we beat Atlantic on their home turf in the 1981 playoffs after they beat us 28 to 6 in the regular season at our place. One of the keys to victory was Ken Carstens figuring out how to stop their counter play. They pulled a tackle to lead the play. Ken just had our defensive tackles go with him and run the ball carrier down from behind. That wasn't easy to do as they had the Behrens twins running the ball, and they were the conference 100- and 220-yard dash champions.

"We were in overtime after four scoreless quarters. We had the ball first. One of my offensive linemen, Mike Jensen, told me we could run a play further inside than we usually did. Luckily, I listened to him. We scored a touchdown on our first play. They scored too, but Casey Hayes missed the extra point. He had made thirty-five in a row before that. That stunning 7-6 upset set the stage for our success in the following years."

As told by his father, Dave, Harlan's quarterback that year, Tom Koos, remembers the two 1981 meetings with Atlantic well. The Monday after the first game where the Cyclones lost by three touchdowns, Tom came home from practice and said, "That's the best practice I've ever been to. The coaches played the game film and showed us where we were just a little out of position on several key plays. There wasn't any shouting or finger-pointing. They just showed us what we needed to do differently the next time we played them. Then Coach Bladt said something I will never forget, 'We will see them again this year, and we will beat them.'"

Question #14 for Jill Bladt: What's it like raising three football players with the head coach in the house?

"It was surprisingly normal. We never talked about football at the dinner table. In fact, we never had a real football in the house until our youngest son, Todd, was a freshman—and only then because he was an offensive center and did the long snapping. Curt and I raised three boys and fifteen of their friends. We loved almost every minute of it."

Question #15 for Jill Bladt: What fact would people be surprised to know about Curt?

"He has a beautiful voice. He sang in the church choir for fifteen years in Exira."

Question #16: Which player got the most out his natural ability?

"We've had a lot of players through the years who played close to their potential, but the one who sticks out in my mind is John Weihs. He was an offensive guard who maybe weighed 165 pounds dripping wet. In 1982, we were playing Fairfield for the right to go to the state championship game. All the 'experts' said they were going to clobber us. They had a stud all-state linebacker who must have weighed 235. John just chewed his ankles off. We won the game 41-21."

Question #17: What is your favorite movie? Why?

"I love Mel Brooks' movie, *Young Frankenstein,* because of the wild humor."

Question #18: Fill in the blank. The game of football is really like (what?)."

"The game of football is really like life because no matter what you do, there's no substitute for hard work."

Question #19: Who is the greatest football coach of all time at any level? Why?

"That's a tough one. The Chicago Bears coach, George Halas, and the Green Bay Packers coach, Vince Lombardi, come to mind.

"I heard Grambling University's coach, Eddie Robinson, speak a couple of times. I'm really impressed with the man. He had the ability to take disadvantaged youth and get them to play hard and work together as a team. At one time, I believe he had more players in the NFL than any other college coach.

"Maybe the greatest coach is actually a bunch of people I don't even know—people who have taken a team from being a perennial loser to a perennial winner by instilling teamwork, hard work, and commitment."

Question #20: If you were an animal, which one would you be?

"I would be an eagle. They're high on the food chain. They're pretty, and they stand for something. And if you don't stand for something, you'll fall for anything. I believe you should always stand for doing the right thing."

Question #21: What was the most exciting game you coached?

"The multi-overtime game with Grinnell in 2000 was the most exciting. It just wouldn't end!"

The following edited article by Mike Oeffner in the November 16, 2000, edition of the *Harlan News-Advertiser* contained the account of the thrilling game:

Four Overtime Win a Classic; HCHS over Grinnell 56-55

CEDAR FALLS—Aspiring football coaches should be required to pass one last course before applying for their first job. Winning Overtime Playoff Games 101. The instructors: Harlan Community Head Coach Curt Bladt and assistant coaches Russ Gallinger, Ken Carstens, Bill Hosack and Al Simdorn.

The Cyclones improved their record in playoff O.T. games to 8-0 under Bladt Monday with an indescribable 56-55 quadruple-overtime victory against previously undefeated Grinnell. It was truly an epic Class 3-A playoff semifinal that the thousands of UNI-Dome patrons on hand will talk about for years.

"They oughta charge the fans again when they leave from this one, because it was a tremendous football game," said a weary Coach Bladt, following a game that exceeded three hours in length.

With the game tied 28-28 at the end of regulation, neither team could stop each other in the extra sessions, and both kickers were perfect on P.A.T.s. In high school overtimes, each team gets four downs from the 10-yard line until the tie is broken after both teams have had a series. After the Tigers' fourth O.T. score brought them within 56-55, Kyle Gross broke through Grinnell's line and made the game-winning play, deflecting Derrick Clark's P.A.T. kick enough to knock it short and to the right.

"I knew that with Dominic (Leinen) coming in, all the focus was on him," Gross said. "I just lined up head up on a guy and they gave me a gap and I got through and got a hand on it."

Gross fell over another player after the block and didn't actually see the ball fall short, but it didn't take him long to realize what had happened. A defensive tackle for the Cyclones, Gross was glad to avoid another overtime or two.

"I think we could have kept going for a while, but not too much longer," he said. "We had enough heart to keep going and we knew what we had to do."

The block gave Bladt a sense of relief.

"That was our only chance to [end it], try and get in and block the point. The way they were moving the football, the way we were moving the football, we could have been here until [Tuesday] morning," said Bladt.

The 111 combined points set an Iowa high school playoff record, and the four overtimes tied a playoff record accomplished on two other occasions. Bladt was elated and exhausted at the same time, as were the players.

"I didn't know how long we were going to have to play until that [block] happened," he said.

"The old heart is just a pitty-patting a little bit right now, but we've got to group up and get ready to play. We've got about five days to get ready for the next one back in here."

> *"I firmly believe that any man's finest hour,*
> *his greatest fulfillment of all he holds dear,*
> *is the moment he has worked his heart out in a good cause*
> *and lies exhausted on the field of battle—victorious."*
> **—Vince Lombardi**

Question #22: What is a little-known fact about you?

"My weight is ideal for a man 8'4" tall."

Question #23: Fill in the blank. "When it comes right down to it, coaches are (what?)."

"Coaches are big kids who never grew up. We all suffer from chronic arrested development."

Question #24: What was the funniest thing that happened at practice?

"There have been many. Some of them are unprintable. The one I remember was a day when our first team offense was scrimmaging our second team defense. The offense was lackluster at best, so we kept them banging heads. Our first team defense came over and began giving the quarterback, Jerry Deren, some heat because they wanted practice to end on time. Sometimes our practices get feisty. We like it that way.

"Jerry was getting madder and madder. He finally called his own number and broke into the secondary like a mad Brahma bull and headed straight for an undersized defensive back. Just before a collision for the ages, the little guy stepped aside like an intelligent bullfighter. Jerry stumbled and went face-first into the turf.

"When he got up to a chorus of whoopin' and hollerin', the space between his face mask and helmet was packed full of sod. Everybody cracked up. The embarrassment must not have done permanent damage. Jerry went on to graduate from the U.S. Naval Academy and became a Blue Angel pilot."

Question #25: What are three basic principles you use as a foundation in life?

1. "If you want people to respect you, respect them first."
2. "Practice humility. After you score a touchdown on the football field or in life, keep your helmet on."
3. "Learn from the past. Then focus on what's coming up next."

Question #26: What was your most emotional moment as a coach on the field?

"When Todd, my last son, played the last play of his last game."

Curt and Todd after the last play

Question #27: How do you want to be remembered?

"I want to be remembered as a team player—at home, at school, and on the football field. Just a guy making his way through life. A guy with a humble beginning and, hopefully, a humble ending. Someone who just rides a pale horse into the sunset."

POSTSCRIPT

In the opening of the classic television sports program *ABC's Wide World of Sports,* host Jim McKay asserts, "Spanning the globe to bring you the constant variety of sport…the thrill of victory…and the agony of defeat…the human drama of athletic competition."

As you read this book about Curt Bladt and Cyclone football, I hope you experienced the human drama of athletic competition played out through one man's life. I hope you experienced laughter, inspiration, and sadness. I hope all these things because that's the way life is. It's a roller coaster ride with high peaks, low valleys, and lots of unexpected twists and turns in between.

But every peak and valley, twist and turn teaches a valuable lesson that allows you to "Do The Right Thing" more effectively as you progress further down the track. On your wild ride, take Coach Curt Bladt's advice. "Play as hard as you can for as long as you can," and then…"Let the Chips Fall Where They May."

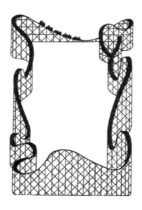

If you would like additional copies of this book and DVD, visit **www.coachbladt.com** or call (712) 755-3834.

About The Author

Nate Booth received his DDS degree from the University of Nebraska in 1991. He earned his master's degree in counseling from the same school in 1983. From 1987 through 1997, Nate worked closely with Anthony Robbins in the development and delivery of corporate training programs.

Nate is the author of the books, *The Diamond Touch: How to Get What You Want by Giving Others What They Uniquely Desire, Strategies for Fast-Changing Times*, and *Tiger Traits: 9 Success Secrets You Can Discover from Tiger Woods to Be a Business Champion*. He is the creator of the audio CD program, *DreamQuest: The Journey to the Life of Your Dreams.*

Nate Booth

Over the past twenty-five years, Nate has presented more than two thousand programs to audiences around the world. His high-energy and entertaining programs are packed with information that will improve your business and change your life. His programs include:

- TIGER TRAITS: 9 Success Secrets You Can Discover from Tiger Woods to Be a Business Champion
- THE DIAMOND TOUCH: How to Get What You Want by Giving Others What They Uniquely Desire
- Diamond Touch Influence
- Diamond Touch Service
- Diamond Touch Leadership
- THRIVING ON CHANGE: The Art of Using Change to Your Advantage
- LEGENDARY LEADERSHIP IN TIMES OF RAPID CHANGE
- DREAMQUEST: The Journey to the Life of Your Dreams

For more information on Nate's products or programs, visit his website at ***www.natebooth.com*** or call (800) 917-0008.

Appendix:
Game Results by Opponent

HARLAN CYCLONE FOOTBALL • SCORES
Through 2005 Season • All-Time Record: 665-261-48 (71.8 winning percentage)

ADAIR (1-1)
Home: 1-0 **Away:** 0-1
1916	Adair 19, Harlan 6
1917	Harlan 58, Adair 0

ADEL-DESOTO-MINBURN (1-0)
Home: 1-0 **Playoffs:** 1-0
1999	Harlan 24, A-D-M 7 ***

ALGONA (1-0)
Home: 1-0; **Play:** 1-0
1984	Harlan 33, Algona 14

AMES (0-0-1)
Away: 0-0-1
1909	(T) Harlan 0, Ames 0

ATLANTIC ALUMNI (0-1)
Home: 0-1
1896	Atlantic 14, Harlan 4

ATLANTIC (51-46)
Home: 27-20 **Away:** 24-26 **Playoffs:** 3-0
1901	Harlan 17, Atlantic 0
1901	Harlan 18, Atlantic 0
1902	Harlan 2, Atlantic 0
1902	Atlantic 6, Harlan 0
1905	Harlan 32, Atlantic 0
1906	Harlan 38, Atlantic 0
1914	Atlantic 13, Harlan 7
1915	Atlantic 13, Harlan 0
1916	Atlantic 3, Harlan 0
1917	Atlantic 25, Harlan 14
1919	Atlantic 6, Harlan 0
1920	Atlantic 41, Harlan 0
1922	Harlan 12, Atlantic 0
1923	Atlantic 3, Harlan 0
1924	Harlan 27, Atlantic 0
1925	Atlantic 6, Harlan 0
1926	Harlan 21, Atlantic 0
1927	Atlantic 25, Harlan 0
1929	Atlantic 29, Harlan 0
1930	Atlantic 7, Harlan 6
1931	Harlan 19, Atlantic 0
1932	Harlan 12, Atlantic 6
1933	Atlantic 19, Harlan 0
1934	Atlantic 7, Harlan 6
1935	Atlantic 40, Harlan 0
1936	Harlan 7, Atlantic 6
1937	Harlan 19, Atlantic 6
1938	Atlantic 6, Harlan 0
1939	Atlantic 6, Harlan 0
1940	Atlantic 38, Harlan 7
1941	Harlan 20, Atlantic 0
1942	Harlan 26, Atlantic 14
1943	Harlan 40, Atlantic 0
1944	Harlan 14, Atlantic 6
1945	Atlantic 12, Harlan 7
1946	Atlantic 19, Harlan 0
1947	Atlantic 13, Harlan 7
1948	Atlantic 7, Harlan 6
1949	Atlantic 34, Harlan 0

1950	Harlan 19, Atlantic 0
1951	Harlan 20, Atlantic 14
1952	Atlantic 19, Harlan 0
1953	Atlantic 12, Harlan 6
1954	Harlan 7, Atlantic 0
1955	Atlantic 34, Harlan 7
1956	Harlan 13, Atlantic 12
1957	Atlantic 13, Harlan 6
1958	Atlantic 13, Harlan 12
1959	Atlantic 6, Harlan 0
1960	Atlantic 14, Harlan 7
1961	Harlan 44, Atlantic 14
1962	Atlantic 7, Harlan 6
1963	Atlantic 47, Harlan 13
1964	Atlantic 41, Harlan 6
1965	Harlan 7, Atlantic 6
1966	Atlantic 21, Harlan 18
1967	Atlantic 21, Harlan 20
1968	Atlantic 41, Harlan 14
1969	Atlantic 34, Harlan 28
1971	Harlan 20, Atlantic 14
1972	Harlan 13, Atlantic 12
1973	Harlan 28, Atlantic 0
1974	Atlantic 26, Harlan 13
1975	Atlantic 6, Harlan 0
1976	Atlantic 21, Harlan 14
1977	Atlantic 30, Harlan 7
1978	Harlan 18, Atlantic 0
1979	Atlantic 6, Harlan 0
1980	Atlantic 20, Harlan 7
1981	Atlantic 28, Harlan 6
1981	Harlan 7, Atlantic 6 (ot)***
1982	Harlan 40, Atlantic 6
1983	Harlan 28, Atlantic 7
1984	Atlantic 20, Harlan 14
1984	Harlan 35, Atlantic 20***
1985	Harlan 14, Atlantic 0
1985	Harlan 33, Atlantic 21***
1986	Harlan 21, Atlantic 7
1987	Harlan 10, Atlantic 7
1988	Harlan 27, Atlantic 14
1989	Harlan 42, Atlantic 0
1990	Harlan 19, Atlantic 0
1991	Harlan 42, Atlantic 13
1992	Harlan 42, Atlantic 6
1993	Harlan 21, Atlantic 10
1994	Harlan 22, Atlantic 12
1995	Harlan 33, Atlantic 13
1996	Harlan 16, Atlantic 10
1997	Harlan 31, Atlantic 8
1998	Harlan 43, Atlantic 13
1999	Harlan 45, Atlantic 7
2000	Harlan 49, Atlantic 20
2001	Harlan 30, Atlantic 7
2002	Atlantic 24, Harlan 21 (ot)
2003	Harlan 48, Atlantic 21
2004	Harlan 49, Atlantic 13
2005	Harlan 48, Atlantic 34

AUDUBON (38-13-5)
Home: 21-5-2 **Away:** 17-8-3
1904	Harlan 26, Audubon 5

1905	Harlan 11, Audubon 0
1906	Harlan 11, Audubon 4
1908	(T) Harlan 0, Audubon 0
1908	Harlan 7, Audubon 5
1914	Audubon 14, Harlan 6
1914	Audubon 12, Harlan 7
1915	Harlan 18, Audubon 13
1915	Harlan 7, Audubon 6
1917	Harlan 19, Audubon 7
1917	(T) Harlan 12, Audubon 12
1918	Harlan 13, Audubon 0
1919	Audubon 6, Harlan 0
1919	Harlan 27, Audubon 6
1924	Harlan 35, Audubon 6
1925	Harlan 2, Audubon 0
1926	Harlan 7, Audubon 0
1927	Harlan 6, Audubon 0
1928	(T) Harlan 0, Audubon 0
1929	Harlan 20, Audubon 6
1930	Harlan 33, Audubon 0
1931	Audubon 7, Harlan 0
1932	Audubon 26, Harlan 0
1933	Harlan 19, Audubon 0
1934	Harlan 20, Audubon 0
1935	Harlan 12, Audubon 0
1936	Audubon 18, Harlan 14
1937	Harlan 28, Audubon 0
1938	Harlan 12, Audubon 0
1939	Harlan 13, Audubon 0
1940	Audubon 7, Harlan 0
1946	Harlan 13, Audubon 0
1947	Harlan 20, Audubon 0
1948	Harlan 39, Audubon 6
1949	(T) Harlan 12, Audubon 12
1950	Harlan 6, Audubon 0
1951	Audubon 28, Harlan 14
1952	Harlan 20, Audubon 6
1953	Audubon 26, Harlan 7
1954	Harlan 38, Audubon 0
1955	Harlan 14, Audubon 13
1956	Harlan 14, Audubon 13
1957	Harlan 7, Audubon 0
1958	Harlan 39, Audubon 13
1959	Harlan 22, Audubon 6
1960	Harlan 7, Audubon 0
1961	Harlan 13, Audubon 12
1962	Audubon 47, Harlan 6
1963	(T) Harlan 19, Audubon 19
1964	Audubon 20, Harlan 0
1965	Audubon 26, Harlan 7
1966	Audubon 14, Harlan 13
1967	Harlan 21, Audubon 7
1968	Harlan 34, Audubon 26
1969	Harlan 35, Audubon 8
1970	Harlan 49, Audubon 0

AVOCA (16-2-1)
Home: 8-2-0 **Away:** 8-0-1
1898	Avoca 23, Harlan 0
1900	Harlan 94, Avoca 0

1901	Harlan 63, Avoca 0
1927	Harlan 10, Avoca 6
1928	Harlan 14, Avoca 6
1929	Avoca 6, Harlan 0
1930	Harlan 22, Avoca 0
1931	Harlan 19, Avoca 0
1932	Harlan 14, Avoca 12
1933	Harlan 6, Avoca 0
1934	Harlan 20, Avoca 0
1935	Harlan 19, Avoca 0
1936	Harlan 20, Avoca 2
1937	Harlan 20, Avoca 12
1938	Harlan 13, Avoca 0
1939	Harlan 19, Avoca 0
1940	(T) Harlan 0, Avoca 0
1941	Harlan 33, Avoca 0
1942	Harlan 73, Avoca 0

BOONE (6-0)
Home: 4-0 **Away:** 2-0 **Playoffs:** 1-0

1903	Harlan 45, Boone 0
1993	Harlan 28, Boone 0 ***
1998	Harlan 33, Boone 12
1999	Harlan 25, Boone 7
2000	Harlan 21, Boone 7
2001	Harlan 28, Boone 7

BOYDEN-HULL/ROCK VALLEY (1-0)
Home: 0-0 **Away:** 1-0 **Playoffs:** 1-0

2000	Harlan 25, B-H/RV 0 ***

CARROLL (30-32-4)
Home: 15-16-3 **Away:** 15-16-1
Playoffs: 2-0

1900	Harlan 10, Carroll 6
1900	Harlan 22, Carroll 0
1901	Harlan 21, Carroll 0
1909	Harlan 18, Carroll 0
1909	Harlan 34, Carroll 6
1914	Carroll beat Harlan
1919	Harlan 27, Carroll 2
1920	Carroll 20, Harlan 0
1921	Carroll 34, Harlan 0
1922	Harlan 19, Carroll 13
1923	Carroll 20, Harlan 0
1924	Carroll 14, Harlan 0
1925	Carroll 27, Harlan 0
1926	Carroll 34, Harlan 0
1927	Harlan 15, Carroll 0
1928	(T) Harlan 12, Carroll 12
1929	Carroll 13, Harlan 0
1930	Carroll 6, Harlan 0
1931	Harlan 6, Carroll 2
1932	Carroll 18, Harlan 0
1933	Carroll 12, Harlan 6
1934	Carroll 18, Harlan 0
1935	Carroll 20, Harlan 7
1936	(T) Harlan 14, Carroll 14
1937	Carroll 6, Harlan 0
1938	Carroll 18, Harlan 13
1939	Harlan 6, Carroll 0
1940	Carroll 18, Harlan 12
1941	Carroll 13, Harlan 0
1942	Carroll 7, Harlan 6
1943	Carroll 14, Harlan 0
1944	(T) Harlan 0, Carroll 0
1945	Carroll 12, Harlan 0
1946	Harlan 12, Carroll 0

1947	Carroll 20, Harlan 0
1948	Carroll 7, Harlan 0
1949	Carroll 39, Harlan 0
1950	Carroll 28, Harlan 6
1951	Carroll 7, Harlan 0
1952	Carroll 21, Harlan 0
1953	Carroll 25, Harlan 7
1954	Carroll 27, Harlan 0
1955	Carroll 68, Harlan 0
1956	Harlan 10, Carroll 0
1957	Harlan 53, Carroll 6
1958	Harlan 33, Carroll 6
1959	Harlan 7, Carroll 6
1960	Harlan 20, Carroll 0
1961	Harlan 7, Carroll 0
1962	Carroll 18, Harlan 7
1963	(T) Harlan 18, Carroll 18
1964	Carroll 20, Harlan 14
1965	Harlan 21, Carroll 6
1966	Carroll 7, Harlan 6
1967	Harlan 26, Carroll 0
1968	Harlan 41, Carroll 7
1969	Harlan 21, Carroll 6
1970	Harlan 66, Carroll 0
1996	Harlan 48, Carroll 7 ***
1998	Harlan 48, Carroll 6***
2000	Harlan 39, Carroll 14
2001	Harlan 44, Carroll 14
2002	Harlan 31, Carroll 20
2003	Harlan 28, Carroll 21
2004	Harlan 41, Carroll 7
2005	Harlan 42, Carroll 20

CARROLL KUEMPER (30-1)
Home: 16-0 **Away:** 14-1. **Playoffs:** 1-0.

1971	Harlan 14, Carroll Kuemper 10
1975	Harlan 17, Carroll Kuemper 6
1976	Harlan 31, Carroll Kuemper 15
1977	Harlan 41, Carroll Kuemper 0
1978	Harlan 14, Carroll Kuemper 0
1979	Harlan 7, Carroll Kuemper 0
1980	Harlan 17, Carroll Kuemper 0
1981	Harlan 28, Carroll Kuemper 26
1982	Harlan 42, Carroll Kuemper 13
1983	Harlan 34, Carroll Kuemper 22
1984	Harlan 13, Carroll Kuemper 10
1985	Harlan 20, Carroll Kuemper 0
1986	Harlan 7, Carroll Kuemper 0
1987	Harlan 7, Carroll Kuemper 0
1988	Harlan 20, Carroll Kuemper 6
1989	Harlan 34, Carroll Kuemper 7
1990	Harlan 36, Carroll Kuemper 6
1991	Harlan 23, Carroll Kuemper 21
1992	Harlan 34, Carroll Kuemper 8
1993	Harlan 48, Carroll Kuemper 14
1994	Harlan 21, Carroll Kuemper 7
1995	Harlan 41, Carroll Kuemper 0
1996	Harlan 37, Carroll Kuemper 0
1997	Harlan 37, Carroll Kuemper 7
1998	Carroll Kuemper 21, Harlan 17
1998	Harlan 27, Kuemper 0 ***
1999	Harlan 26, Carroll Kuemper 0
2000	Harlan 16, Carroll Kuemper 13
2001	Harlan 45, Carroll Kuemper 15
2002	Harlan 48, Carroll Kuemper 0
2003	Harlan 42, Carroll Kuemper 14

CEDAR RAPIDS PRAIRIE (0-1)
Neutral: 0-1 **Play:** 0-1

1981	CR Prairie 13, Harlan 7***

(at UNI-Dome)

CEDAR RAPIDS REGIS (2-0)
Neutral: 2-0 **Play:** 2-0

1972	Harlan 14, CR Regis 12***
	(at Iowa City)
1982	Harlan 15, CR Regis 14***
	(at UNI-Dome)

CENTRAL LYON/G-LR (1-1)
Away: 0-1. **Playoffs:** 1-1. **Neutral:** 1-0.

1996	Central Lyon 20, Harlan 13***
1998	Harlan 21, Central Lyon 0***
	(at UNI-Dome)

CHARITON (1-0)
Home: 1-0 **Play:** 1-0

1989	Harlan 45, Chariton 13***

CHEROKEE (1-0)
Home: 1-0 **Play:** 1-0

1972	Harlan 22, Cherokee 14***

CLARINDA (28-1)
Home: 13-1 **Away:** 15-0

1971	Harlan 42, Clarinda 6
1972	Harlan 42, Clarinda 14
1973	Harlan 16, Clarinda 6
1974	Clarinda 20, Harlan 17
1975	Harlan 44, Clarinda 0
1976	Harlan 28, Clarinda 14
1977	Harlan 12, Clarinda 7
1978	Harlan 14, Clarinda 0
1979	Harlan 16, Clarinda 7
1980	Harlan 41, Clarinda 14
1981	Harlan 17, Clarinda 15
1982	Harlan 39, Clarinda 14
1983	Harlan 49, Clarinda 7
1984	Harlan 14, Clarinda 0
1985	Harlan 24, Clarinda 0
1986	Harlan 37, Clarinda 12
1987	Harlan 48, Clarinda 7
1988	Harlan 42, Clarinda 0
1989	Harlan 24, Clarinda 0
1990	Harlan 31, Clarinda 0
1991	Harlan 27, Clarinda 0
1992	Harlan 24, Clarinda 7
1993	Harlan 7, Clarinda 0
1994	Harlan 35, Clarinda 6
1995	Harlan 35, Clarinda 0
1996	Harlan 31, Clarinda 6
1997	Harlan 66, Clarinda 14
1998	Harlan 55, Clarinda 0
1999	Harlan 37, Clarinda 0

CLARKE (OSCEOLA) (1-0)
Home: 1-0 **Playoffs:** 1-0

1987	Harlan 17, Clarke 14 (ot)***

CLEAR LAKE (0-1)
Neutral: 0-1 **Playoffs:** 0-1
2000 Clear Lake 23, Harlan 20 (3ot) ***
(championship game; at UNI-Dome)

CB ABRAHAM LINCOLN (1-4)
Home: 0-2 **Away:** 1-2
1931   CB Abe Lincoln 19, Harlan 0
1932   CB Abe Lincoln 52, Harlan 0
1939   CB Abe Lincoln 20, Harlan 0
1940   CB Abe Lincoln 26, Harlan 0
1957   Harlan 12, CB Abe Lincoln 6

CB ABE LINCOLN 'B' (1-0)
Home: 1-0 **Away:** 0-0
1943   Harlan 45, CB Abe Lynx B
13

CB CENTRAL (6-7-3)
Home: 2-1-3 **Away:** 4-6
1897   Harlan 6, CB Central 0
1900   (T) Harlan 0, CB Central 0
1900   (T) Harlan 0, CB Central 0
1901   CB Central 17, Harlan 0
1901   Harlan 15, CB Central 0
1902   Harlan 8, CB Central 5
1902   CB Central 6, Harlan 5
1903   Harlan 15, CB Central 6
1903   Harlan 47, CB Central 0
1904   Harlan 14, CB Central 0
1904   CB Central 6, Harlan 0
1905   CB Central 10, Harlan 6
1905   (T) Harlan 0, CB Central 0
1915   CB Central 20, Harlan 0
1917   CB Central 24, Harlan 0
1918   CB Central 56, Harlan 0

CB LEWIS CENTRAL (37-2)
Home: 18-2 **Away:** 19-0 **Playoffs:** 3-0
1970   Harlan 62, Lewis Central 6
1971   Harlan 35, Lewis Central 6
1972   Harlan 28, Lewis Central 14
1973   Harlan 7, Lewis Central 6
1974   Harlan 18, Lewis Central 0
1975   Harlan 18, Lewis Central 13
1976   Harlan 58, Lewis Central 0
1977   Harlan 26, Lewis Central 8
1978   Harlan 10, Lewis Central 0
1979   Harlan 17, Lewis Central 15
1980   Lewis Central 10, Harlan 7
1981   Harlan 21, Lewis Central 7
1982   Harlan 28, Lewis Central 6
1983   Harlan 21, Lewis Central 0
1984   Harlan 26, Lewis Central 8
1985   Harlan 28, Lewis Central 7
1986   Harlan 17, Lewis Central 0
1986   Harlan 9, Lewis Cent. 6 (ot)***
1987   Harlan 20, Lewis Central 10
1988   Harlan 41, Lewis Central 6
1989   Harlan 42, Lewis Central 14
1990   Harlan 19, Lewis Central 0
1991   Harlan 21, Lewis Central 20
1991   Harlan 31, Lewis Cen. 27***
1992   Harlan 26, Lewis Central 16
1993   Harlan 37, Lewis Central 34
1994   Harlan 17, Lewis Central 6
1995   Harlan 20, Lewis Central 6
1996   Lewis Central 25, Harlan 24
1997   Harlan 14, Lewis Central 10
1997   Harlan 21, Lewis Cent. 16 ***
1998   Harlan 50, Lewis Central 24
1999   Harlan 35, Lewis Central 2
2000   Harlan 47, Lewis Central 14

2001   Harlan 44, Lewis Central 16
2002   Harlan 41, Lewis Central 7
2003   Harlan 49, Lewis Central 8
2004   Harlan 42, Lewis Central 2
2005   Harlan 43, Lewis Central 7

CB THOMAS JEFF. (0-0-1)
Home: 0-0 **Away:** 0-0-1
1962   (T) Harlan 12, CB Tee Jay 12

CREIGHTON PREP (1-1)
Home: 1-1 **Away:** 0-0
1906   Harlan 22, Creighton Prep 0
1919   Creighton Prep 75, Harlan 0

CRESTON (35-2)
Home: 17-1 **Away:** 18-1 **Playoffs:** 5-0
1971   Harlan 39, Creston 12
1972   Harlan 28, Creston 3
1973   Harlan 10, Creston 7
1974   Harlan 9, Creston 6
1975   Creston 19, Harlan 18
1976   Harlan 22, Creston 3
1977   Harlan 45, Creston 6
1978   Harlan 6, Creston 0 (ot)
1979   Harlan 35, Creston 15
1980   Harlan 7, Creston 0
1981   Harlan 35, Creston 7
1982   Harlan 35, Creston 0
1983   Harlan 47, Creston 6
1984   Harlan 26, Creston 0
1985   Harlan 38, Creston 14
1985   Harlan 21, Creston 11***
1986   Harlan 20, Creston 18
1987   Harlan 26, Creston 12
1988   Harlan 49, Creston 13
1988   Harlan 28, Creston 6***
1989   Harlan 35, Creston 14
1990   Harlan 40, Creston 7
1991   Harlan 13, Creston 12
1991   Harlan 34, Creston 0***
1992   Harlan 34, Creston 7
1993   Harlan 23, Creston 21
1995   Harlan 28, Creston 27 ***
1996   Harlan 44, Creston 7
1997   Creston 22, Harlan 17
1998   Harlan 41, Creston 13
1999   Harlan 48, Creston 13
2000   Harlan 48, Creston/O-M 35
2002   Harlan 31, Creston/O-M 7
2003   Harlan 54, Creston/O-M 0
2003   Harlan 63, Creston/O-M 22***
2004   Harlan 42, Creston/O-M 7
2005   Harlan 37, Creston/O-M 7

DALLAS CENTER-GRIMES (1-0)
Home: 1-0. **Playoffs:** 1-0.
2003   Harlan 35, DC-Grimes 14 ***

DECORAH (2-3)
Home: 0-1 **Neutral:** 2-2 **Playoffs:** 2-2
1974   Decorah 17, Harlan 7
1988   Decorah 21, Harlan 16***
        (at UNI-Dome)
1989   Decorah 21, Harlan 6***
        (at UNI-Dome)
1997   Harlan 14, Decorah 7***
        (at UNI-Dome)

2004   Harlan 42, Decorah 7 ***
(championship game; at UNI-Dome)

DENISON (46-32-4)
Home: 25-15-1 **Away:** 21-17-3
Playoffs: 7-0
1898   Harlan 24, Denison 0
1899   Denison 6, Harlan 5
1908   Denison 10, Harlan 0
1909   (T) Harlan 0, Denison 0
1916   Harlan 12, Denison 6
1917   Denison 68, Harlan 0
1918   Denison 31, Harlan 0
1920   (T) Harlan 6, Denison 6
1921   Denison 35, Harlan 0
1922   Denison 40, Harlan 0
1923   Denison 26, Harlan 0
1924   Denison 12, Harlan 0
1925   Denison 7, Harlan 0
1929   Denison 7, Harlan 2
1930   Harlan 14, Denison 13
1931   Denison 41, Harlan 6
1932   Denison 40, Harlan 13
1933   Denison 39, Harlan 0
1934   Harlan 20, Denison 6
1935   Denison 6, Harlan 0
1937   Denison 19, Harlan 6
1938   (T) Harlan 7, Denison 7
1939   Denison 18, Harlan 0
1940   Denison 14, Harlan 0
1941   Denison 20, Harlan 0
1942   Harlan 26, Denison 6
1943   Harlan 33, Denison 0
1944   Harlan 19, Denison 0
1945   Harlan 12, Denison 7
1946   Harlan 13, Denison 7
1947   Denison 6, Harlan 0
1948   (T) Harlan 6, Denison 6
1949   Denison 19, Harlan 0
1950   Denison 12, Harlan 6
1951   Denison 20, Harlan 0
1952   Denison 34, Harlan 14
1953   Harlan 26, Denison 7
1954   Harlan 40, Denison 0
1955   Denison 33, Harlan 6
1956   Denison 28, Harlan 6
1958   Harlan 32, Denison 6
1959   Harlan 14, Denison 0
1960   Harlan 6, Denison 0
1961   Harlan 18, Denison 6
1962   Harlan 19, Denison 6
1963   Denison 25, Harlan 6
1964   Harlan 19, Denison 18
1965   Harlan 20, Denison 6
1966   Harlan 24, Denison 20
1967   Harlan 21, Denison 7
1968   Denison 6, Harlan 0
1969   Harlan 35, Denison 28
1970   Harlan 62, Denison 0
1972   Harlan 42, Denison 0
1973   Harlan 50, Denison 0
1980   Harlan 33, Denison 19
1981   Harlan 32, Denison 6
1982   Harlan 42, Denison 0
1983   Harlan 49, Denison 7
1989   Harlan 34, Denison 14***
1990   Harlan 10, Denison 6
1990   Harlan 21, Denison 13***

1991	Harlan 25, Denison 18
1992	Denison 36, Harlan 33
1993	Denison 36, Harlan 10
1993	Harlan 14, Denison 0***
1994	Denison 18, Harlan 3
1995	Harlan 2, Denison 0
1995	Harlan 10, Denison 7 (ot) ***
1996	Harlan 42, Denison 17
1997	Harlan 31, Denison 13
1998	Harlan 22, Denison 7
1999	Harlan 35, Denison 34 (2ot)
2000	Denison 35, Harlan 9
2000	Harlan 30, Denison 24 (2ot)***
2001	Denison 26, Harlan 7
2001	Harlan 21, Denison 7 ***
2002	Harlan 31, Denison 14
2003	Harlan 31, Denison 6
2004	Harlan 28, Denison 0
2004	Harlan 35, Denison 0 ***
2005	Harlan 49, Denison 14

DENISON NORM. COLL. (2-2)
Home: 1-1 **Away:** 1-1

1896	Denison NC 10, Harlan 0
1896	Harlan 10, Denison NC 8
1896	Denison NC 28, Harlan 0
1897	Harlan 24, Denison NC 0

DES MOINES EAST (0-2)
Home: 0-2

1903	DM East 23, Harlan 6
1904	DM East 5, Harlan 0

DRAKE U FROSH (0-1)
Home: 0-1 **Away:** 0-0

1933	Drake U Frosh 34, Harlan 6

EMMETSBURG (1-1)
Home: 0-1 **Away:** 1-0 **Play:** 1-1

1978	E'Burg 6, Harlan 0***
1981	Harlan 10, E'Burg 7 (ot)***

ESTHERVILLE (0-1)
Away: 0-1 **Play:** 0-1

1987	Estherville 7, Harlan 6***

EXIRA (4-1)
Home: 4-0 **Away:** 0-1

1923	Harlan 14, Exira 7
1925	Harlan 7, Exira 0
1926	Exira 12, Harlan 6
1927	Harlan 31, Exira 6
1929	Harlan 7, Exira 0

FAIRFIELD (1-0)
Home: 1-0 **Play:** 1-0

1982	Harlan 41, Fairfield 21***

GLENWOOD (35-1)
Home: 17-1 **Away:** 18-0 **Playoffs:** 1-0

1971	Harlan 49, Glenwood 13
1972	Harlan 42, Glenwood 14
1973	Harlan 35, Glenwood 6
1974	Harlan 19, Glenwood 0
1975	Harlan 28, Glenwood 15
1976	Harlan 42, Glenwood 0
1977	Harlan 12, Glenwood 0
1978	Harlan 41, Glenwood 6

1979	Harlan 17, Glenwood 7
1980	Harlan 14, Glenwood 0
1981	Harlan 30, Glenwood 0
1982	Harlan 48, Glenwood 6
1983	Harlan 38, Glenwood 0
1984	Harlan 40, Glenwood 0
1985	Harlan 32, Glenwood 13
1986	Harlan 50, Glenwood 13
1987	Harlan 49, Glenwood 7
1988	Harlan 27, Glenwood 12
1988	Harlan 37, Glenwood 7***
1989	Harlan 24, Glenwood 7
1990	Harlan 7, Glenwood 0
1991	Harlan 40, Glenwood 16
1992	Harlan 41, Glenwood 12
1993	Harlan 16, Glenwood 7
1994	Glenwood 20, Harlan 17
1995	Harlan 19, Glenwood 0
1996	Harlan 35, Glenwood 7
1997	Harlan 43, Glenwood 0
1998	Harlan 50, Glenwood 0
1999	Harlan 40, Glenwood 0
2000	Harlan 46, Glenwood 21
2001	Harlan 35, Glenwood 25
2002	Harlan 55, Glenwood 0
2003	Harlan 46, Glenwood 7
2004	Harlan 48, Glenwood 7
2005	Harlan 38, Glenwood 7

GLIDDEN (1-0)
Away: 1-0

1944	Harlan 21, Glidden 0

GRINNELL (3-0)
Neutral: 3-0. **Playoffs:** 3-0.
1998: Harlan 49, Grinnell 7 ***
(UNI-Dome)
2000: Harlan 56, Grinnell 55 (4ot) ***
(UNI-Dome)
2001: Harlan 20, Grinnell 13 ***
(UNI-Dome)

HARLAN ALUMNI (3-5-1)
Home: 3-5-1

1901	Harlan 6, Harlan Alumni 0
1902	Harlan Alumni 10, Harlan 0
1902	Harlan Alumni 8, Harlan 6
1904	Harlan 6, Harlan Alumni 0
1905	(T) Harlan 0, Harlan Alumni 0
1906	Harlan Alumni 19, Harlan 0
1907	(T) Harlan 0, Harlan Alumni 0
1908	Harlan Alumni 11, Harlan 0
1914	Harlan 7, Harlan Alumni 0
1917	Harlan Alumni 18, Harlan 10

IDA GROVE (17-4-6)
Home: 9-2-2 **Away:** 8-2-4

1903	Ida Grove 35, Harlan 6
1903	(T) Harlan 0, Ida Grove 0
1937	(T) Harlan 7, Ida Grove 7
1938	(T) Harlan 13, Ida Grove 13
1939	Harlan 7, Ida Grove 0
1940	Ida Grove 12, Harlan 0
1941	Harlan 13, Ida Grove 0
1942	Harlan 14, Ida Grove 6
1943	(T) Harlan 0, Ida Grove 0

1944	Harlan 44, Ida Grove 6
1945	Harlan 52, Ida Grove 0
1946	Harlan 33, Ida Grove 7
1947	(T) Harlan 7, Ida Grove 7
1948	Harlan 27, Ida Grove 18
1949	Ida Grove 32, Harlan 19
1950	Harlan 13, Ida Grove 12
1951	Harlan 12, Ida Grove 0
1952	Ida Grove 14, Harlan 6
1953	(T) Harlan 6, Ida Grove 6
1954	Harlan 33, Ida Grove 0
1955	Harlan 13, Ida Grove 12
1956	Harlan 21, Ida Grove 0
1957	Harlan 20, Ida Grove 0
1958	Harlan 20, Ida Grove 6
1959	Harlan 19, Ida Grove 14
1960	Harlan 26, Ida Grove 0
1961	Harlan 27, Ida Grove 6

INDIANOLA (1-0)
Away: 1-0 **Play:** 1-0

1986	Harlan 26, Indianola 14***

JEFFERSON (21-22-2)
Home: 10-14 **Away:** 11-8-2 **Playoffs:** 0-1

1908	Jefferson 17, Harlan 0
1932	Jefferson 26, Harlan 6
1933	Jefferson 33, Harlan 0
1934	(T) Harlan 6, Jefferson 6
1935	Harlan 13, Jefferson 7
1936	Harlan 20, Jefferson 0
1937	Harlan 13, Jefferson 0
1938	Harlan 28, Jefferson 8
1939	Jefferson 6, Harlan 0
1940	Jefferson 44, Harlan 6
1941	Jefferson 21, Harlan 20
1942	Harlan 12, Jefferson 0
1943	Harlan 33, Jefferson 6
1944	Jefferson 6, Harlan 0
1945	Jefferson 7, Harlan 0
1946	Harlan 12, Jefferson 6
1947	Jefferson 13, Harlan 12
1948	Harlan 7, Jefferson 6
1949	Jefferson 27, Harlan 6
1950	Harlan 13, Jefferson 6
1951	Jefferson 26, Harlan 7
1952	Jefferson 18, Harlan 0
1953	Jefferson 26, Harlan 0
1954	Harlan 7, Jefferson 0
1955	Jefferson 31, Harlan 0
1956	Jefferson 18, Harlan 0
1957	Harlan 20, Jefferson 6
1958	Harlan 7, Jefferson 0
1959	Jefferson 14, Harlan 6
1960	(T) Harlan 7, Jefferson 7
1961	Harlan 24, Jefferson 0
1962	Harlan 13, Jefferson 6
1963	Jefferson 7, Harlan 0
1964	Jefferson 33, Harlan 0
1965	Jefferson 21, Harlan 6
1966	Harlan 27, Jefferson 13
1967	Harlan 13, Jefferson 0
1968	Jefferson 20, Harlan 14
1969	Jefferson 25, Harlan 19
1970	Harlan 53, Jefferson 0
1994	Harlan 7, JSPC 12
1995	Harlan 32, JSPC 7
1999	JSPC 6, Harlan 0 ***

2004	Harlan 42, JSPC 0
2005	Harlan 31, JSPC 0

JOHNSTON (2-0)
Home: 1-0 **Road:** 1-0 **Play:** 2-0

1992	Harlan 27, Johnston 9***
1996	Harlan 36, Johnston 7***

KNOXVILLE (2-0)
Away: 2-0 **Play:** 1-0

1971	Harlan 56, Knoxville 0
1990	Harlan 49, Knoxville 26***

LAKE CITY (10-4)
Home: 6-2 **Away:** 4-2

1915	Harlan 6, Lake City 0
1958	Harlan 39, Lake City 13
1959	Harlan 13, Lake City 0
1960	Harlan 14, Lake City 0
1961	Harlan 31, Lake City 20
1962	Harlan 19, Lake City 6
1963	Lake City 19, Harlan 13
1964	Lake City 38, Harlan 6
1965	Lake City 26, Harlan 14
1966	Harlan 26, Lake City 7
1967	Harlan 32, Lake City 0
1968	Harlan 14, Lake City 12
1969	Harlan 21, Lake City 7
1970	Lake City 19, Harlan 7

LEMARS (14-1)
Home: 5-0 **Away:** 7-1 **Neutral:** 2-0
Playoffs: 3-1

1977	Harlan 29, LeMars 7
1978	Harlan 34, LeMars 0
1979	Harlan 8, LeMars 0
1992	Harlan 31, LeMars 21
1993	Harlan 28, LeMars 0
1994	Harlan 29, LeMars 0
1995	Harlan 42, LeMars 14
1996	Harlan 54, LeMars 13
1997	Harlan 21, LeMars 7
1997	Harlan 35, LeMars 14***
1998	Harlan 47, LeMars 7
1999	Harlan 30, LeMars 21
2002	Le Mars 24, Harlan 21 ***
2003	Harlan 62, Le Mars 21 ***
	(at UNI-Dome)
2005	Harlan 35, Le Mars 21 ***
	(at UNI-Dome)

LINCOLN, NE (0-3)
Away: 0-3

1904	Lincoln 18, Harlan 0
1905	Lincoln 16, Harlan 0
1907	Lincoln 38, Harlan 0

LOGAN (16-8-3)
Home: 6-5-2 **Away:** 10-3-1

1910	Logan 46, Harlan 0
1914	Logan 28, Harlan 0
1914	Logan beat Harlan
1915	Logan 7, Harlan 0
1917	Logan 12, Harlan 0
1919	(T) Harlan 0, Logan 0
1920	Harlan 2, Logan 0
1921	(T) Harlan 0, Logan 0
1922	Harlan 19, Logan 13

1923	Harlan 12, Logan 0
1924	Harlan 20, Logan 0
1934	Logan 25, Harlan 0
1935	Logan 13, Harlan 0
1943	Harlan 33, Logan 6
1944	Harlan 14, Logan 0
1945	Logan 13, Harlan 7
1946	Harlan 7, Logan 0
1947	Harlan 19, Logan 0
1948	Harlan 26, Logan 0
1949	Harlan 14, Logan 13
1950	Harlan 7, Logan 0
1951	(T) Harlan 14, Logan 14
1952	Harlan 46, Logan 0
1953	Harlan 26, Logan 6
1954	Harlan 33, Logan 6
1955	Harlan 26, Logan 21
1956	Harlan 18, Logan 12

MANILLA (5-0)
Home: 2-0 **Away:** 3-0

1921	Harlan 27, Manilla 0
1922	Harlan 1, Manilla 0
1923	Harlan 20, Manilla 0
1930	Harlan 39, Manilla 0
1931	Harlan 13, Manilla 0

MANNING (10-3-1)
Home: 5-1 **Away:** 5-2-1

1900	(T) Harlan 0, Manning 0
1919	Harlan 71, Manning 0
1924	Harlan 36, Manning 0
1925	Manning 20, Harlan 0
1926	Manning 23, Harlan 0
1927	Manning 25, Harlan 6
1928	Manning 15, Harlan 6
1932	Harlan 13, Manning 6
1933	Harlan 26, Manning 0
1934	Harlan 27, Manning 13
1935	Harlan 14, Manning 7
1936	Harlan 12, Manning 6
1937	Harlan 41, Manning 0
1938	Harlan 34, Manning 0

MISSOURI VALLEY (11-8-4)
Home: 6-3-2 **Away:** 5-5-2

1906	Harlan 28, Mo Valley 6
1920	Harlan 13, Mo Valley 6
1921	Mo Valley 17, Harlan 7
1922	Harlan 25, Mo Valley 0
1923	Mo Valley 19, Harlan 0
1924	Harlan 7, Mo Valley 0
1925	Harlan 7, Mo Valley 0
1926	Mo Valley 20, Harlan 0
1927	(T) Harlan 0, Mo Valley 0
1928	Mo Valley 19, Harlan 6
1929	Mo Valley 6, Harlan 0
1930	Harlan 6, Mo Valley 0
1931	Harlan 35, Mo Valley 6
1932	Harlan 26, Mo Valley 0
1933	Mo Valley 7, Harlan 6
1934	Harlan 20, Mo Valley 13
1935	Harlan 20, Mo Valley 6
1936	(T) Harlan 0, Mo Valley 0
1937	Harlan 7, Mo Valley 7
1938	Mo Valley 13, Harlan 0
1939	Harlan 7, Mo Valley 6
1941	Mo Valley 14, Harlan 7

1949	(T) Harlan 13, Mo Valley 13

MOC-FLOYD VALLEY (3-0)
Home: 1-0. **Away:** 2-0. **Playoffs:** 3-0.

2001	Harlan 42, MOC-FV 13 ***
2002	Harlan 24, MOC-FV 17 ***
2004	Harlan 52, MOC-FV 43 ***

MOUNT PLEASANT (4-0)
Home: 1-0. **Away:** 1-0. **Neutral:** 2-0.

1996:	Harlan 17, Mt. Pleasant 14
	(at Indianola)
1997	Harlan 38, Mt. Pleasant 3
	(at SE Polk)
2002	Harlan 55, Mt. Pleasant 6
2003	Harlan 29, Mt. Pleasant 0

MOUNT VERNON (1-0)
Neutral: 1-0. **Playoffs:** 1-0.

2003	Harlan 38, Mt. Vernon 35 ***

(championship game; at UNI-Dome)

NORWALK (4-0)
Home: 2-0 **Away:** 2-0 **Playoffs:** 2-0

1983	Harlan 49, Norwalk 0***
1992	Harlan 26, Norwalk 21***
2004	Harlan 52, Norwalk 17
2005	Harlan 37, Norwalk 7

OAKLAND (2-0-1)
Home: 1-0-1 **Away:** 1-0-0

1905	Harlan 18, Oakland 5
1929	(T) Harlan 0, Oakland 0
1930	Harlan 7, Oakland 0

OMAHA CENTRAL (3-4)
Home: 1-3 **Away:** 2-1

1903	Harlan 23, Omaha Central 0
1906	Harlan 6, Omaha Central 0
1907	Omaha Central 42, Harlan 0
1908	Omaha Central 16, Harlan 0
1909	Omaha Central 12, Harlan 6
1915	Harlan 12, Omaha Central 6
1916	Omaha Central 7, Harlan 6

OMAHA COMM. COLL. (2-0-1)
Home: 2-0-1

1904	Harlan 21, Omaha CC 12
1916	(T) Harlan 0, Omaha CC 0
1916	Harlan 7, Omaha CC 0

OMAHA NORTH (1-0)
Home: 1-0

1945	Harlan 25, Omaha North 0

OMAHA SOUTH (1-1)
Home: 1-0 **Away:** 0-1

1909	Harlan 28, Omaha South 6
1910	Omaha South beat Harlan

ONAWA (2-0)
Home: 1-0 **Away:** 1-0

1941	Harlan 35, Onawa 0
1942	Harlan 33, Onawa 6

OSKALOOSA (1-0)
Neutral: 1-0 **Play:** 1-0

1983	Harlan 26, Oskaloosa 0***
	(at UNI-Dome)

PELLA (2-0)
Home: 1-0. Away: 1-0 Play: 2-0
1987   Harlan 30, Pella 0***
1997   Harlan 24, Pella 18 ***

PERRY (4-3-1)
Home: 3-1 Away: 1-2-1
1963   Perry 19, Harlan 13
1964   Perry 20, Harlan 7
1965   Perry 8, Harlan 6
1966   Harlan 41, Perry 14
1967   (T) Harlan 12, Perry 12
1968   Harlan 32, Perry 0
1969   Harlan 33, Perry 14
1970   Harlan 55, Perry 8

PLEASANT VALLEY (0-1)
Neutral: 0-1 Play: 0-1
1985   Pleasant Vly 10, Harlan 7***
  (at UNI-Dome)

RED OAK (44-7-2)
Home: 22-3-2 Away: 22-4-0
1902   (T) Harlan 0, Red Oak 0
1903   Harlan 6, Red Oak 0
1904   Harlan 34, Red Oak 0
1950   (T) Harlan 13, Red Oak 13
1951   Harlan 20, Red Oak 13
1952   Red Oak 27, Harlan 0
1953   Red Oak 27, Harlan 0
1954   Harlan 18, Red Oak 0
1955   Red Oak 6, Harlan 0
1956   Red Oak 6, Harlan 0
1957   Harlan 14, Red Oak 0
1958   Harlan 12, Red Oak 7
1959   Harlan 18, Red Oak 0
1960   Harlan 7, Red Oak 6
1961   Harlan 27, Red Oak 6
1962   Harlan 13, Red Oak 0
1963   Harlan 12, Red Oak 0
1964   Red Oak 19, Harlan 0
1965   Red Oak 39, Harlan 0
1966   Harlan 13, Red Oak 6
1967   Harlan 25, Red Oak 0
1968   Harlan 26, Red Oak 0
1969   Red Oak 21, Harlan 15
1970   Harlan 49, Red Oak 0
1971   Harlan 49, Red Oak 7
1972   Harlan 14, Red Oak 6
1973   Harlan 34, Red Oak 14
1974   Harlan 29, Red Oak 0
1975   Harlan 34, Red Oak 7
1976   Harlan 12, Red Oak 7
1977   Harlan 33, Red Oak 0
1978   Harlan 14, Red Oak 3
1979   Harlan 15, Red Oak 14
1980   Harlan 20, Red Oak 0
1981   Harlan 28, Red Oak 0
1982   Harlan 62, Red Oak 6
1983   Harlan 40, Red Oak 0
1984   Harlan 34, Red Oak 0
1985   Harlan 33, Red Oak 6
1986   Harlan 48, Red Oak 0
1987   Harlan 13, Red Oak 6
1988   Harlan 39, Red Oak 6
1989   Harlan 54, Red Oak 6
1990   Harlan 19, Red Oak 6
1991   Harlan 51, Red Oak 6
1992   Harlan 51, Red Oak 17
1993   Harlan 56, Red Oak 12
1994   Harlan 21, Red Oak 0
1995   Harlan 48, Red Oak 14
2000   Harlan 62, Red Oak 8
2001   Harlan 2, Red Oak 0 (forfeit)
2002   Harlan 55, Red Oak 0
2003   Harlan 61, Red Oak 6

SAC CITY (24-11-3)
Home: 14-4-1 Away: 10-7-2
1933   Sac City 13, Harlan 6
1934   Harlan 12, Sac City 6
1935   Sac City 7, Harlan 0
1936   Sac City 18, Harlan 0
1937   (T) Harlan 7, Sac City 7
1938   Harlan 13, Sac City 6
1939   Sac City 12, Harlan 6
1940   Harlan 12, Sac City 6
1941   Harlan 33, Sac City 0
1942   Harlan 33, Sac City 6
1943   Harlan 41, Sac City 0
1944   Harlan 18, Sac City 0
1945   Sac City 13, Harlan 0
1946   Harlan 12, Sac City 0
1947   Harlan 13, Sac City 12
1948   (T) Harlan 12, Sac City 12
1949   Sac City 41, Harlan 0
1950   Harlan 24, Sac City 13
1951   Sac City 13, Harlan 7
1952   Sac City 34, Harlan 0
1953   Sac City 20, Harlan 13
1954   Harlan 6, Sac City 0
1955   Sac City 21, Harlan 7
1956   Harlan 28, Sac City 0
1957   Harlan 7, Sac City 0
1958   Harlan 37, Sac City 6
1959   Harlan 47, Sac City 0
1960   Harlan 33, Sac City 14
1961   Harlan 46, Sac City 24
1962   (T) Harlan 0, Sac City 0
1963   Harlan 19, Sac City 13
1964   Harlan 6, Sac City 0
1965   Sac City 19, Harlan 7
1966   Harlan 21, Sac City 7
1967   Harlan 26, Sac City 0
1968   Harlan 26, Sac City 13
1969   Harlan 48, Sac City 16
1970   Harlan 41, Sac City 14

SHELBY (6-0-1)
Home: 2-0-0 Away: 4-0-1
1897   Harlan 22, Shelby 0
1899   Harlan 16, Shelby 0
1904   Harlan 26, Shelby 0
1906   Harlan 9, Shelby 6
1906   Harlan 11, Shelby 0
1925   Harlan 13, Shelby 0
1926   (T) Harlan 0, Shelby 0

SHENANDOAH (20-2)
Home: 9-2 Away: 11-0
1969   Harlan 25, Shenandoah 20
1971   Harlan 56, Shenandoah 6
1972   Harlan 48, Shenandoah 6
1973   Harlan 30, Shenandoah 6
1974   Harlan 17, Shenandoah 6

6 - Harlan Scores

1975   Harlan 29, Shenandoah 7
1976   Harlan 10, Shenandoah 7
1977   Shenandoah 28, Harlan 7
1978   Harlan 14, Shenandoah 7
1979   Shenandoah 14, Harlan 12
1980   Harlan 13, Shenandoah 0
1981   Harlan 20, Shenandoah 6
1982   Harlan 34, Shenandoah 6
1983   Harlan 53, Shenandoah 0
1984   Harlan 15, Shenandoah 6
1985   Harlan 36, Shenandoah 0
1986   Harlan 14, Shenandoah 0
1987   Harlan 17, Shen 14 (ot)
1988   Harlan 20, Shenandoah 0
1989   Harlan 39, Shenandoah 6
1990   Harlan 35, Shenandoah 6
1991   Harlan 51, Shenandoah 0

SIOUX CITY EAST (0-2)
Home: 0-1 Away: 0-1
1975   Sioux City East 42, Harlan 12
1976   Sioux City East 30, Harlan 12

SIOUX CITY LEEDS (0-1-1)
Home: 0-0-1 Away: 0-1-0
1945   (T) Harlan 0, SC Leeds 0
1946   SC Leeds 27, Harlan 0

SPENCER (4-2)
Home: 2-0 Away: 2-1
Neutral: 0-1 Play: 4-2
1988   Harlan 19, Spencer 10***
1989   Harlan 21, Spencer 14***
1990   Spencer 31, Harlan 6***
1991   Spencer 41, Harlan 7***
  (at UNI-Dome)
1992   Harlan 21, Spencer 7***
1995   Harlan 10, Spencer 7 (playoffs)

STORM LAKE (2-0)
Home: 1-0 Away: 1-0
1947   Harlan 6, Storm Lake 0
1948   Harlan 18, Storm Lake 0

URBANDALE (1-0)
Away: 1-0 Play: 1-0
1978   Harlan 23, Urbandale 22***

WALNUT (7-0)
Home: 4-0 Away: 3-0
1903   Harlan 29, Walnut 0
1921   Harlan 7, Walnut 6
1922   Harlan 47, Walnut 0
1927   Harlan 25, Walnut 0
1928   Harlan 4, Walnut 0
1935   Harlan 13, Walnut 0
1936   Harlan 34, Walnut 6

WATERLOO COLUMBUS (1-1)
Neutral: 1-1 Play: 1-1
1984   Harlan 14, Columbus 13***
  (at UNI-Dome)
1986   Columbus 24, Harlan 7***
  (at UNI-Dome)

WAUKEE (2-0)
Home: 1-0. **Neutral:** 1-0. **Playoffs:** 2-0.
1925   Harlan 51, Waukee 17 ***
           (at UNI-Dome)
2005   Harlan 48, Waukee 17 ***

WAVERLY-SHELL ROCK (0-1)
Neutral: 0-1 **Playoffs:** 0-1
1992   Waverly-SR 14, Harlan 6***
           (at UNI-Dome)

WEBSTER CITY (6-0)
Home: 2-0 **Away:** 4-0 **Playoffs:** 4-0
1982   Harlan 28, Webster City 6***
1983   Harlan 28, Webster City 0***
1985   Harlan 3, Web City 0 (ot)***
1986   Harlan 21, Webster City 10***
2004   Harlan 48, Webster City 6
2005   Harlan 60, Webster City 0

WEST DELAWARE (3-0)
Neutral: 3-0 **Playoffs:** 3-0
1993   Harlan 34, W. Delaware 20***
(championship game at UNI-Dome)
1995   Harlan 27, W. Delaware 7***
(championship game; at UNI-Dome)
2005   Harlan 34, W. Delaware 13***
(championship game; at UNI-Dome)

WESTERN DUBUQUE, EPWORTH (0-1)
Neutral: 0-1. **Playoffs:** 0-1.
2001   W. Dubuque 12, Harlan 9***
(championship game; at UNI-Dome)

WDM VALLEY (1-2)
Home: 1-1 **Away:** 0-1
1972   Harlan 20, WDM Valley 0
1973   WDM Valley 14, Harlan 3
1974   WDM Valley 26, Harlan 9

WINTERSET (3-0)
Home: 2-0 **Away:** 1-0 **Playoffs:** 3-0
1984   Harlan 28, Winterset 0***
1993   Harlan 31, Winterset 0***
2005   Harlan 23, Winterset 13 ***

WOODBINE (11-3-2)
Home: 5-2-1 **Away:** 6-1-1
1920   Harlan 7, Woodbine 6
1921   Harlan 27, Woodbine 6
1922   Harlan 25, Woodbine 0
1923   (T) Harlan 13, Woodbine 13
1924   Woodbine 31, Harlan 7
1925   Woodbine 25, Harlan 0
1926   Harlan 7, Woodbine 6
1927   Woodbine 13, Harlan 0
1928   (T) Harlan 6, Woodbine 6
1929   Harlan 6, Woodbine 0
1930   Harlan 20, Woodbine 0
1931   Harlan 7, Woodbine 0
1932   Harlan 19, Woodbine 0
1936   Harlan 14, Woodbine 7
1942   Harlan 32, Woodbine 0
1943   Harlan 7, Woodbine 0

WOODBINE NORM. COLL. (2-1)
Home: 1-1 **Away:** 1-0
1897   Woodbine NC 24, Harlan 6
1904   Harlan 13, Woodbine NC 0
1905   Harlan 42, Woodbine NC 0

The Iowa Hall of Pride is the first and only one of its kind in the nation. The $13 million, 26,000 square foot project is located in the Iowa Events Center in Des Moines. The Hall of Pride is the vision of Bernie Saggau, long-time Executive Director of the Iowa High School Athletic Association.

The Hall honors past and present Iowa high school students involved in extracurricular activities, including athletics, academics, and the arts. With countless touch screens and interactive games, the Hall's twenty-six exhibits tell stories of Iowa's rich traditions in education and extracurricular activities.

Eight interactive kiosks showcase outstanding alumni, individual, and school accomplishments and outstanding attractions in each of the towns and cities that make up the 403 school districts in Iowa.

The Iowa Hall of Pride

To learn more about the Hall of Pride, visit its website at *www.iowahallofpride.com.*

The Iowa Hall of Pride
330 Park Street
Des Moines, IA 50309
(515) 280-8969

The following All-State Teams were selected by the Iowa Newspaper Association and the *Des Moines Register*. Before 1978, it appears that players were selected from one class of teams. After that date they were selected from multiple classes— 1A, 2A, 3A, and 4A. Since 1936, HCHS has a total of 260 all-state players. During his career at HCHS, Curt Bladt has coached 197 all-state players.

* HM stands for honorable mention.

1936:
1st team ... Phil Phelps

1942:
1st team ... Clay Pauley

1943:
1st team ... Don Camery
HM .... Robert Petersen, Richard Carl, and Richard Pauley

1945:
1st team ... Gene Gettys
HM .... Rex Sorenson, Miles Camery, and Don Larimore

1946:
5th team ... Miles Camery
HM .... Don Larimore, Russ Block, Rand Petersen, and Paul A. Pauley

1953:
HM .... Skip Louis and Kenny Christensen

1954:
7th team ... Charles Therkildsen
HM .... Franklin Sisson, Gary Larsen, Kenny Jacobs, Gaylord Rasmussen, and Jerry Rold

1957:
2nd team .. John Laube
6th team ... Gary Wilcox
HM .... John Dornon, Dean Pedersen, Derrill McConnell, and Gary Larsen

1958:
2nd team .. Darrell McConnell;
HM .... Gary Larsen, Ron Hansen, Charles Graves, Bill Lewis, and David Nielsen

1959:
6th team ... Bill Lewis and Gary Jorgensen
HM .... John Hemminger, George Graves, Larry McDermott, Jerry Lytle, and Don McDermott

1960:
6th team ... Max Brodersen
HM .... Don McDermott, Lee Moran, Chuck Stanley, and Bill Beauchamp

1961:
5th team ... Allen Burchett and Kenny Hoogensen
HM .... Randy Conrad, Jerry Myrtue, Keith Svendsen, and Gary Klindt

1962:
3rd team ... Allen Burchett
HM .... Bryce Hansen

1963:
HM .... Rick Burchett

1965:
HM .... Marshall Burchett

1967:
2nd team .. Steve Jacobsen and Jim Larsen
HM .... Bill Larsen, Keith Burchett, Joe
Turnbach, and Bill Findlay

1968:
5th team ... Roger Boeck
HM .... Phil Larsen

1969:
5th team ... Gary Lansman

1970:
1st team ... Todd Nelson
4th team ... Craig Petersen
7th team ... Verne Nelson

1971:
1st team ... Jeff Branstetter
6th team ... Steve Daeges
HM .... Roger Jacobsen, Bob Norgaard,
and Farrell Zimmerman

1972:
3rd team ... Jeff Allen
4th team ... Doug Deskin
HM .... Farrell Zimmerman, Robin
Jacobsen, Tim Conrad, and
Mike Larsen

1973:
1st team ... Mike Larsen
4th team ... Terry Barton
HM .... Mark Sorenson and Randy
Nowatzke

1974:
HM .... Brian Petersen

1975:
1st team ... Dean Thielen
HM .... Tom Leinen, Mark Martin,
Dan Frazier, and Sam Allen

1976:
HM .... Ross Jacobsen, Gary Schneider,
Ron Doran, and Sam Allen

1978:
1st team ... Bill Murtaugh, Galen Schnack,
Mike Byrnes, Dean Wilke, Dan
Donlin, John Murtaugh, and
Kerry Boltinghouse
2nd team .. Scott Sojka, Mark Stamp, and
Randy Snyder

1979:
1st team ... Pete Fromm
2nd team .. John Murtaugh

1980:
1st team ... Pete Leinen
2nd team .. Dan Jones

1981:
2nd team .. Mike Jensen
HM .... Tom Koos

1982:
1st team ... Steve Peake
2nd team .. Gene Schmitz

1983:
1st team ... Perry Sibenaller, Alan Patten,
Todd Koos, and Mike Kloewer
2nd team .. John Barton and Pete Finken
HM .... Jim Lehan, John Bogler, Scott
Mahlberg, and Rick Noble

1984:
1st team ... Dave Kline and Mike O'Bryan
2nd team .. Dave Larson

1985:
1st team ... Mike Wilwerding
2nd team .. Rick Blum

1986:
1st team ... Ken Schechinger, Kurt Jensen, and Robby Kloewer
HM .... Pat Connor, Chad Ellsworth, and Dave Wilwerding

1987:
1st team ... J.P. Hemminger, Dave Schechinger, and Shawn Gessert
3rd team ... Gary Petersen
HM .... Dale Fink, Todd Hansen, and Curt Schulte

1988:
1st team ... Curt Schulte and Todd Hansen
2nd team .. Tony Burger
HM .... Scott Baker, Chris Johannsen, Alan Hall, Jason Moore, Tyler Jacobsen, and Duane Brus

1989:
1st team ... Scott Schiltz, Jeff Bladt, and Scott Arkfeld
2nd team .. Cohen Johnson and Troy Schulte
3rd team ... Lance Grummert

1990:
1st team ... Steve Wilwerding
2nd team .. Kevin Musich and Chris Hogzett
HM .... Scott Heese

1991:
2nd team .. Dallas Schwery, Chris Hogzett, and Scott Heese
HM .... Kiron Andersen, Troy Kloewer, and Kelly Gaer

1992:
1st team ... Dallas Schwery and Michael Burger
2nd team .. Troy Kloewer
HM .... Jamie Buckholdt, Chad Schechinger, and Josh Leinen

1993:
1st team ... Michael Burger (honorary captain); Chris Cundiff and Allen Leinen
2nd team .. Jim Chamberlain

1994:
HM .... Chad Hansen

1995:
1st team ... Jared Blum, Steve Schechinger, Rob Klinkefus, and Matt Leinen
2nd team .. Justin Cox and Billy Cundiff
HM .... Jeremy Fiscus and Jeff Bruck

1996:
1st team ... Justin Cox, Dax Doran, Bill Erlbacher, and Billy Cundiff
2nd team .. Chris Cue and Jeff Bruck
HM .... Matt Studer, Doug Chamberlain, and Mark Schmitz

1997:
1st team ... Chris Cue, Ryan Fagan, Billy Cundiff, Shawn Wegner (honorary captain), and Nick Christensen
HM .... Nick Carter and Tim Hemminger

1998:

1st team ... Ryan Fagan, Todd Bladt, and Tim Hemminger

2nd team .. Adam Pash and Adam Studer

HM .... Ben Hall, Chad Plumb, and Tony Studer

1999:

1st team ... Matt Schechinger and Steve Wegner

2nd team .. Ryan Lawler and Bryan Schwartz

HM .... Jamie Martin and David Bruck

2000:

1st team ... Matt Lauterbach, Kyle Murtaugh, Jamie Martin, Steve Wegner, and Bryan Schwartz

HM .... Dominic Leinen, Kyle Gross, and Monty Boltinghouse

2001:

1st team ... Matt Lauterbach, Brent Schmumacher, John Petsche, and Karl Freml

HM .... Jason Leinen, Andy Petersen, Kyle Martin, Rick Ohlinger, and Heath Schechinger

2002:

1st team ... Andy Petersen

2nd team .. Mike Schneider, Spencer Wegner, Dan Assman, and Kyle Martin

HM .... Joel Osborn and Tyler Muller

2003:

1st team ... Greg Applegate, Aaron McCutcheon, Joel Osborn, Kyle Martin, Ben Arentson, and Randy Kaufman

2nd team .. Kevin Kruse

3rd team ... Tobey Jacobsen

2004:

1st team ... Greg Applegate, Ross Hastert, Kevin Kruse, and Eric Lauterbach

2nd team .. Matt Bartelson and Andy Schneider

3rd team ... Trent Svendsen

2005:

1st team ... Dan Smith, Todd Schwartz, and Jared Boysen

2nd team .. Adam Leinen, Mark Blum, and Zach Kaufman

RAGTIME Productions and Ruthanne Grimsley have been serving Southwest Iowa and Eastern Nebraska since 1998. Born and raised in Harlan, Iowa, Ruthanne has been an instructor at Metropolitan Community College (MCC) for the past eight years. At MCC, Ruthanne teaches various certificate programs for Community and Workforce Education. They include classes in Database Management, Excel, Web Design, and QuickBooks. In addition, Ruthanne also teaches computer courses at Offutt Air Force Base in Bellevue, Nebraska, for civilian personnel.

Ruthanne has been a Certified QuickBooks Pro Advisor specializing in QuickBooks Small Business Accounting programs since the Pro Advisor program began in 1999. Ruthanne consults with individuals and businesses on QuickBooks and Web Design. She has created over one hundred websites and is the webmaster for the City of Harlan and the Harlan Municipal Utilities.

Ruthanne Grimsley, RAGTIME Productions

Leah Spieker

Moxie Photo and Design
Former Harlan resident Leah Spieker
is a freelance designer and
photographer who designed
the book cover. Visit
www.moxiephotoanddesign.com
to view her collection of print
and web materials.